THE RELIGION
of the
LANDLESS

THE RELIGION
of the
LANDLESS

The Social Context of the Babylonian Exile

DANIEL L. SMITH

MEYER
STONE
BOOKS

Published in the United States by Meyer-Stone Books,
a division of Meyer, Stone, and Company, Inc.,
2014 South Yost Avenue, Bloomington, IN 47403
Tel.: 812-333-0313

All biblical quotations, unless otherwise noted, are from the Jerusalem Bible in English and the Biblia Hebraica Stuttgartensia in Hebrew.

Cover design: Terry Dugan Design

Typesetting output: TEXSource, Houston

Manufactured in the United States of America
93 92 91 90 89   5 4 3 2 1

Library of Congress Cataloging in Publication Data

Smith, Daniel L., 1955-
    The religion of the landless : the social context of the Babylonian exile
/ Daniel L. Smith.
        p.   c.m.
    Revision of the author's thesis (Ph.D.) — Oxford University.
    Bibliography: p.
    Includes indexes.
    ISBN 0-940989-54-9 — ISBN 0-940989-50-6 (pbk.)
    1. Jews — History — Babylonian captivity, 598-515 B.C.   2. Jews —
Politics and government — To 70 A.D.   3. Bible. O.T. — Theology.
4. Exiles — Biblical teaching.   I. Title
DS121.65.S64   1989
221.6'7 — dc20   89-9211
                                                            CIP

FOR MICHELE

What the world most needs is not a new Caesar, but a new style. A style that is created, updated, projected not by a nation or a government, but by a people. This is what moral minorities can do — what they have done time and again. Liberation is not a new King. ... Liberation is the presence of a new option, and only a non-conformed, covenanted people of God can offer that. Liberation is the pressure of the presence of a new alternative so valid, so coherent, that it can live without the props of power and against the stream of statesmanship. To be that option is to be free indeed. ...

Over against the paradigm of leaving Egypt and destroying the Pharaoh on the way, we find in the Old Testament, more often, another model of how to live under a pagan oppressor. It is the way of Diaspora. ...

JOHN HOWARD YODER

Contents

Part II   Selected Texts

Foreword

It is strange that students of ancient Israel have been so slow to undertake a comprehensive sociological analysis of the Babylonian Exile. The vast majority of exilic studies grapple with the political history or the development of religious institutions, practices, and ideas. Daniel L. Smith, by contrast, has taken the first steps toward a genuinely social critical understanding of this watershed in Jewish experience.

The salient contribution of the present work is a simple methodological maneuver, so obvious that one wonders why it had not been done long before. Smith has examined well-documented cases of modern communities that have been subjected to forced migration and minority status in order to see what comparative light they throw on the plausibility of various hypotheses about the Jewish exiles. The author arrives at strategies of survival that he explicates as social mechanisms demonstrable in biblical exilic literature. In addition, he identifies stress lines along which tension and conflict developed both within the exilic communities and between them and their host populations, on the one hand, and the Palestinian Jews among whom they sought to resettle, on the other hand.

Smith argues persuasively that social structural adaptation among the exiles led to large, factitiously named "fathers' houses" intended to preserve identity, facilitate self-management, and cope with the economic and political demands of the Babylonian conquerors. In this connection, he makes astute use of Weinberg's hypothesis of a "citizen-temple-community" composed of the "fathers' houses" from at least the time of Ezra. Rituals of survival in the Priestly Code are interpreted as measures to insure social "boundary maintenance," along the lines of Mary Douglas's work on purity and social threat. The latest redactional levels in P are shown to maximize this process of boundary maintenance. Diaspora stories, whose literary patterns have been much treated in recent biblical scholarship, are conceived as serving a definite social purpose: the folkloric hero is set forth as a communal model to be emulated. The author is also illuminating on the topic of "imprisonment" as a dominant descriptor of exilic life, seen not as penalty for crime but as political detention and disenfranchisement.

Employing the comparative method, Smith alerts us to expectations of social conflict along several predictable fronts. We should expect to see struggles over leadership correlated to conflicting policies of accommodation and resistance. We should also expect that the shocks and disruptions of the initial deportations would pose problems socially different from the shocks and disruptions of a return of the exiles to their homeland. Likewise, we should expect that the attempt of the returning exiles to reintegrate themselves with their former compatriots would be charged with conflict over property, status, leadership, and ideology. By recognizing the twists and turns typical of exilic adaptations, Smith properly cautions us against prevailing simplistic judgments about the "easy" conditions of Jewish exilic life and about the reduction of conflicts in the restored community to face-offs between Aaronid and Levitical priests or between returned exiles and Samaritans. In sum, the comparative approach of Smith opens up a more refined social calculus for evaluating options in the interpretation of difficult texts in Chronicles, Ezra-Nehemiah, and the later prophetic writings.

The limits of Smith's project have their premise in his choice of a structural-functional paradigm rather than a historical-material paradigm. He develops typologies of exilic behavior and ideology that are lifted out of their social systemic settings. As a result, not enough is said about how the recent deported communities were located in a larger social system, both the system from which they were dislodged and the system into which they were inserted. The same oversight appears in the absence of base-line profiles of Judahite society before and after 586 B.C.E., of Babylonian and Persian societies in which the exiles lived, and of the restored Jewish Palestinian society after 538 B.C.E.

These omissions are perfectly defensible on the terms of a structural-functional paradigm that arbitrarily chooses the size of the social unit to examine. But the consequence is a sociological exegesis of selected biblical texts rather than a reconstruction of the social history of the Jewish Exile. An analysis of the political economy of the time, in its native tributary mode of production (in independent Judah) and in its foreign tributary mode of production (in Babylon, Persia, and the restored Palestinian community) would have provided a framing unity to begin social reconstruction. As it is, Smith is unable adequately to attend to important aspects of the situation, such as the originally upper-class status of the Judahite exiles and the impact of Babylonian and Persian political economies both as constraints and initiators that shaped Jewish survival and return in particular ways. Nevertheless, we are indebted to Smith for providing social data and comparative insights that contribute materials toward a reconstruction of the political economy and social history of the Exile.

The postscript on a contemporary theology of exile, written from the hermeneutical stance of a radical Reformation Protestant, challenges the appropriateness of Exodus and liberation as master themes for Christian communities today. In so doing, Smith plunges into the never-finished age-long debate over the interface between church and society/culture. The dialogue between adherents of liberation theology and heirs of the radical Reformation should be an increasingly lively one (cf., for example, Daniel S. Schipani, ed., *Freedom and Discipleship: Liberation Theology in an Anabaptist Perspective*, Orbis, 1989), if only because both believe that the Bible centrally addresses issues of peace and justice, while they differ in hermeneutical paradigms and strategic conclusions.

In my judgment, Smith's attempt to catch up the differences in paradigms and strategies by posing "Exodus" and "Exile" as polar opposites does not work sociologically or theologically. The exodus was not the direct precursor of Israelite statehood but of the Israelite tribes, and the Exile did not renounce the exercise of political power but only enforced limits on its exercise in the forms of self-management and circumscribed home rule. Exodus and Exile alike share in the social reality and moral ambiguity of the human exercise of corporate power.

The issues that Smith opens up theologically remind me of H. Richard Niebuhr's cogent typology in *Christ and Culture*. In that classic work, Niebuhr delineated five "typical answers" that Christians have given about how Christ and Christian identity are related to culture: (1) Christ against Culture; (2) the Christ of Culture; (3) Christ above Culture; (4) Christ and Culture in Paradox; and (5) Christ the Transformer of Culture. Recently I was engaged in an intense discussion of Niebuhr's models involving people of many theological persuasions. Surprisingly, we began to develop a rough consensus that exclusive adherence to any single paradigm is less faithful to our experience than a dialectical hermeneutic that moves continuously through all the paradigms as inescapable dimensions or "moments" of every practical Christian involvement in the world. Nevertheless, we agreed that the paradigms must be interconnected and prioritized, and that most of us have a preferred one. For liberation theology the "preferential option" is clearly Christ the Transformer of Culture, while for Daniel Smith the "preferential option" is as clearly Christ against Culture. Still, the two orientations can converse and learn from one another, since each preferred option contains some elements of the other — just as there is a touch of exile in every Exodus and a dash of exodus in every Exile.

Norman K. Gottwald
W. W. White Professor of Biblical Studies
New York Theological Seminary

Acknowledgments

There have been a number of people who have been helpful in this project. This book began as a doctoral dissertation for the Faculty of Theology, Oxford University. I have revised it — I hope making it more readable — and have included the "Postscript" on a theology of exile. As most scholars of the Bible readily admit, there is something inevitably autobiographical about biblical studies, despite one's best efforts for "objectivity." For those who seek the "relevance" of this topic of biblical studies, this Postscript is an attempt to address that concern.

I would like to express my appreciation to a number of people who have been involved in this work. First of all, I feel a large debt of gratitude to both my doctoral supervisors at Oxford, Dr. John Barton of the Faculty of Theology and Dr. Bryan Wilson of the Faculty of Social Science, for their advice and guidance in helping me to complete the study that this book is based on. I would also like to acknowledge my debt to the ideas and provocative analysis that is typical of the scholars I have been privileged to work with: Arthur O. Roberts, John Howard Yoder, Steven Schwarzschild, Millard Lind, Clarence Bauman, and Jacob Enz. They will recognize their influence, and will be the first to know that their light on my path is diminished by my own shortcomings.

I must also thank those involved with the scholarship program of the World Council of Churches, which made my study in England possible, especially my friends Lis, Alex, and Bernard at Christian Aid in London. The Memorial Foundation for Jewish Culture helped me with an invaluable grant for my last year of study and for writing my dissertation. Of course, they are not in any way responsible for the perspectives that I have with regard to issues that they have an interest in. Finally, I express my appreciation to John Eagleson and Meyer-Stone Books for their interest in this project and their help in completing it. I thank my parents, R. Dean and Virginia Smith, for loving encouragement.

But most important, I must thank Michele, my wife, who had to live with my eccentricities and my frustrations, as well as my joys in working on this project.

Introduction

Sociological Exegesis and Its Critics

This work is an experiment in the sociological interpretation of the Bible. While sociological and anthropological study of biblical texts is not new, it has yet to reach a state where methods (much less results) are generally agreed upon. The "experimental" nature of the enterprise is clear from a reading of the two short summaries of social and anthropological studies of the Old Testament: Robert Wilson's *Sociological Approaches to the Old Testament* and John Rogerson's *Anthropology and the Old Testament.*[1]

At the outset, it is helpful to differentiate between two emerging "movements" or "trends" within sociological exegesis of biblical texts. Wilson and Rogerson document many facets of one of these trends, but very little of the other. The trend within which Wilson and Rogerson work, which certainly includes the work of Paul Hanson, George Mendenhall, and Thomas Overholt, consists of scholars who are attempting to make use of anthropological data in a scientific and "objective" manner.[2]

The other trend is illustrated in the United States by the work of Norman Gottwald, whose book *The Tribes of Yahweh* electrified American Old Testament scholarship with a perspective much closer in spirit to the European "materialist" exegetical school to which Michel Clevenot's *Materialist Approaches to the Bible,* and Fernando Belo's New Testament study certainly belong.[3]

The first trend has a somewhat longer heritage. As Rogerson has noted, Stade was making use of anthropological speculations about the evolutionary development of society from primitive organization to cities as early as 1881. The most significant works of this time that contributed to the discussion of social-anthropological insights were those of W. Robertson Smith and Julius Wellhausen. Both Smith and Wellhausen believed that the study of pre-Islamic Arabic sources, as well as careful observation of contemporary Near Eastern life and culture,

1

could give clues about many of the customs and beliefs of Old Testament material.[4]

Much of the data used for this older program of research included European travel accounts, as well as more systematic case studies. An example of the latter (but including elements of a travelogue) is S. I. Curtiss, *Primitive Semitic Religion Today* (1902). Curtiss, like others, believed in the concept of "survivals." A "survival" was an observed behavior pattern, the use of a term, or a ritual that was thought to have endured over centuries, and thus serves as a link to biblical history. A similar use of data is seen in Alt's essay, "The God of the Fathers," which includes epigraphic material that comes from Arabic sources dated from 50 B.C.E. to 350 C.E., yet Alt used this material to draw conclusions about patriarchal narratives.[5]

Infamous are the number of observations in "scholarly" journals and monographs based upon the travelogues and observations of visitors to the "Orient." The Quaker John Wilhelm Rowntree wrote of his visit in 1895 to the "Apostles' Well":

> Round this is gathered a concourse of Bedanese, donkeys, women, children, horses, and fine-looking men, in black and yellow striped cloaks and black kuffiyehs, armed with a short knife and gun. They are of particular interest when one remembers that they give us a picture of what those wandering Hebrew tribes, under their great powerful sheikh Moses must have looked like, when they came as invaders to the land of the Canaanite.[6]

Certainly not all the observations from travels were as apparently innocent as John Rowntree's. S. I. Curtiss incorporated disparaging remarks about contemporary Arabic culture, which leads to serious questions about his research method. A case in point is his observation that:

> ... it is easy to see that the modern Semite has no ethical conception of God as holy, or as just, hence we shall find that his views of sin are entirely deficient, and do not possess a moral quality.... We may be sure that in the conceptions of God, which the ignorant Arab or Fellahin entertains today, we have men at the same stage as when God began to reveal himself in terms which the childhood of the ancient Semites could understand.[7]

Recently, anthropologists have raised serious doubts about older assumptions regarding "nomadism" and "Bedouins" largely as a result of questions about the date of the domestication of the camel.[8] Today we realize that nineteenth- and early twentieth-century observations of Arabic cultures must be carefully scrutinized. Edward Said's work

Orientalism delivers a devastating critique of the often questionable assumptions of "value free" Orientalist scholarship and should provide the basis of a critical re-evaluation of twentieth-century models of Near Eastern society often implicit in Old Testament scholarship — assumptions that persist to the present.[9]

Anthropological material continued to be of interest to biblical scholars in the early twentieth century, up until 1939, when (for example) the subcategory of the *Elenchus* biblical studies index (Rome) called "Anthropology and the Old Testament" was dropped until its revival in another form in 1979. It is, furthermore, instructive to note that this interest has taken decidedly different forms, according to the theoretical orientation of the commentator in question.

R. Wilson has given the most attention to method among the writers of the "objectivist" trend in sociological analysis of the Bible. Indeed, he has even enumerated "guidelines" for the use of sociological and anthropological data in biblical studies. Prominent among these guidelines is the persistent call to avoid cultural bias, anachronistic examples, and ideological formulations of the sociologists/anthropologists whose work is being cited. Wilson's impressive book, *Prophecy and Society in Ancient Israel,* attempts to illustrate these guidelines at work.[10] However, Wilson's use of a functionalist model of sociological analysis determines the manner in which he compares prophets to seers, shamans, witches, etc. We are not given any socio-economic analysis of the society out of which prophets speak (or the societies out of which the shamans, seers and witches speak, either). We see individuals more clearly than societies. Materialist critics would prefer a more "diachronic" analysis that considers individuals as manifestations of the communities in which they arise. That such an analysis is typical of Marxist-influenced exegetes seems to raise suspicions for Wilson. The question remains, however, whether one simply substitutes one "bias" for another.

False objectivity may result in unintended bias, such as a functionalist model that does not provide a wider analysis. Recent criticism about Evans-Pritchard's work on Nuer Religion in Africa, for example, suggests that Evans-Pritchard's theoretical model totally neglected the dynamic of European colonialism and its possible influences or pressures on the culture of the Nuer.[11] Debate over just such an issue represents an important divergence between the two trends of sociological exegesis of the Bible.

Sociological exegesis of a text adds no new data; it simply attempts a reinterpretation on the basis of the social construction of reality. Sociological exegesis approaches many of the conclusions of contemporary literary and textual criticism with the acid question, "Do people really act that way?" Attention must therefore be given to the social reality of the reader as well as the text itself, and this point provides the most trenchant critique of the "objectivist" trend of sociological exegesis of the Bible.

Attention to the reader, of course, raises the problem of bias with a vengeance. The importance of these issues of the "sociology of knowledge" is illustrated by Cahnman and Boskoff when they point out that "the selection of facts for descriptive purposes always presupposes some criteria of relevance which in turn are grounded in an explanatory system."[12] Yet it is at the crossroads of the sociology of knowledge and textual analysis that we find the potential for revolution in biblical analysis. To return to our discussion of trends, the first trend, including the work of Wilson and Hanson (and most of the American New Testament contributions) tends to emphasize careful, but static comparison with little attention to the "pre-knowledge" and "prejudices" of the contemporary reader, except in the negative attempt to maintain "objectivity," i.e., "not allowing one's own prejudices to influence the conclusions." While it may be claimed that a science progresses when facts contradict theory, totally apart from "ideological" considerations, it is precisely this notion that is called into question by scholars working in the "materialist" exegetical trend of sociological analysis of the Bible. Furthermore, the materialist case is strengthened by recent work in the history of scientific theory. Feyerabend, for example, points out that many of the most significant theoretical advances, e.g., the Copernican Revolution, quantum theory, the wave theory of light, occurred only because certain scientific theorists "decided not to be bound by certain 'obvious' methodological rules, or because they unwittingly broke them."[13]

But if biblical studies works within a scientific tradition (as most textual interpreters would claim), from what source can these challenges come other than factual discrepancy (including the addition of texts previously unknown)? The point is that factual discrepancies alone do not always force a change in a theoretical "paradigm" or worldview (to use Thomas Kuhn's terminology[14]). In the somewhat puckish view of Feyerabend, it is the persistence of alternative worldviews that provides new insights and methodologies in order to challenge our assumptions even when existing theories appear to account for much of the data before us. In such cases, suggests Feyerabend, "it is clear that allegiance to the new ideas will have to be brought about by means *other than arguments*. ... To express it differently: Copernicanism and other 'rational' views exist today only because reason was overruled at some time in their past" [emphasis added].[15]

This is because the competing theories themselves dictated what facts were considered relevant, and indeed, in terms of a pattern of investigation, determined what "facts" would be looked for.[16]

But what is revolutionary in the suggestions of Feyerabend is the need for persistent alternative worldviews. Feyerabend himself calls for an "anarchist theory of knowledge" (that is, one that is not dictated by a theoretical orthodoxy). In the language of biblical studies, this is tantamount to a call for textual critics to abandon their nonideological, "ecumenical" pretenses and nurture the diversity of perspective that informs varieties of methodological and theological approaches to the study of the Bible. This requires a focussed attention to these theological and ideological assumptions, rather than attempting to avoid them by means of "objective" guidelines.

Some materialist exegetes demand a further step. Füssel, for example, is concerned that an exegete not only have an awareness of the reader's own "fore-meanings" and "prejudices," but that the reader have the *correct fore-meanings and prejudices*:

> Attempts at a non-idealist approach to the Bible do not originate in the academic world of the university theologian, but rather in the commitment of the leftist Christians who opt for the oppressed in the class struggles of our time and join them in the fight for liberation.[17]

One need not agree whole-heartedly with the Marxist assumptions of Füssel in order to see that the wider challenge is that there may be *appropriate* "biases" to bring to a text. The work that follows is a test of precisely this notion. It is the argument of this book that a good beginning point for the study of the Babylonian Exile is the construction of such an exegetically "alternative" worldview, in this case a worldview constructed from the perspective of those who have *known* exile. The importance of a new view of the Babylonian Exile is obvious, if we consider that the Exile is arguably the most significant biblical event that challenges the place of the Exodus event as the "foundational event of biblical history."

Biblical Scholarship of the Exile:
Theological and Sociological Exegesis and Its Ideological Foundations

How a different worldview would revise our ideas about the Exile is a question that assumes some familiarity with the current consensus. It is not difficult to generalize about the significance of the Exile in Old Testament scholarship. It is usually considered a watershed event, but often (since Wellhausen, at least) is seen to herald a steady decline from the pristine greatness of Prophetic-Deuteronomic religion to "priest-dominated, legalistic religiosity."

As recently as 1945, for example, G. R. Berry could write of the otherworldly desperation of the post-exilic Jewish community.[18] The creativity of this era, if any is recognized, is typically focused on the

exilic expectation of possible restoration. An obvious example of this
is the study of messianism as a "personified restoration." However,
emphasis on the exilic hope for restoration, by the very nature of this
term, tends to highlight what once was, and the depth of the loss. The
implicit "norm" becomes the power of the Josianic (revived Davidic)
state. This can be briefly illustrated by considering the evaluation of the
Exile from a more traditional literary-critical perspective (Ackroyd) and
a behavioral, sociological perspective (Max Weber).

One of the most important historical-theological surveys of the period is P. R. Ackroyd's *Exile and Restoration*.[19] Ackroyd consciously
dealt with this tendency to view the Exile negatively, and against this
saw his task as an attempt to "see all sides of the picture."[20] In his conclusions, Ackroyd tried to see the theological interpretation of the Exile
(especially in Jeremiah) as essential to understanding the restoration.
The context for understanding the nature of the restored community is
that the Exile taught theological lessons. This is essentially the view of
the major recent works on the exilic period.[21]

An exclusive focus on theological responses to the Exile, however,
creates problems. Emphasis on the restoration community's theology
can easily be dictated by contemporary concerns to see the most "relevant" and "interesting" aspects of that theology. Ackroyd's comments
show that he is acutely aware of this problem. But Ackroyd did not
challenge the basic judgment between the "positive" and the "negative"
aspects in contemporary exegesis and commentary, but called for "balance," e.g.: "The handling of the law which is so important an aspect
of post-exilic religion... is expressed both in the delight in the works of
God which is always an element of true worship... but may issue in the
casuistry of the worst forms of Pharisaism."[22] The modern notion of
what is positive or negative is not significantly altered in such a view.
Merely changing from a theologically-oriented analysis of the Exile to
a behavioral analysis of the community involved does not immediately
deal with the problem. This is obvious when one considers Max Weber's
classic work, *Ancient Judaism*. These essays, originally published in the
Archiv für Sozialwissenschaft und Sozialforschung in 1917–1919, represent an original overview of many of the sociological and exegetical
problems of recent study.

In the very first few paragraphs, Weber provided a programmatic
statement:

> Sociologically speaking Jews were a pariah people, which means...
> that they were a guest people who were ritually separated, formally
> or de facto, from their social surroundings. All the essential traits
> of Jewry's attitude toward the environment can be deduced from
> this pariah existence — especially its voluntary ghetto, long an-

teceding compulsory internment, and the dualistic nature of its in-group and out-group morality.[23]

The concept of the "pariah people" formed the goal toward which Weber's analysis of ancient Judaism progressed. The event of the Exile was only the *completion* of a religio-ethical development that led to this religion of a "pariah people."

Weber traced the evolution of Yahweh from "war-god" (with a possible henotheistic relation to other gods) toward the monotheism (or "monolatry") of late classical prophecy.[24] This evolution of the war-god to universalism was an important aspect of his view of the later "pariah people," because it is only when the One God is conceived that the problem of this god's relation to foreigners is resolved through the concept of the "chosen people." Monotheism, in short, creates a theodicy of particularism.[25]

The prophets developed this religious ideology not only by romanticizing the exploited as "God's chosen" and romanticizing stranger status in the Exodus, but also by justifying suffering and defeat as logical outcomes of a sojourning people whose God can teach them through defeat as well as victory, suffering as well as joy. The hammering of the prophets against fatalistic religion — expressed either as God's own defeat or as God's abandonment of God's own people — prepares the way for the Priestly creation of a "pariah people" who can adjust to exile or defeat and still see in it the hand of their God. Prophecy appeals to the only form of warfare still available to the powerless, e.g., miracle as an ethic of premonarchical "utopianism" (and of no use to practical politics). The peace promoted by prophetic utterance was a peace without elites; even the idea of a "Messiah" (an exilic innovation, according to Weber) was an inarticulate synthesis of the Davidic monarchy, incorporating nonmonarchical themes like the suffering servant.[26]

Despite his many insightful comments, Weber's discussion of the Exile from a sociological perspective (albeit a dated one) included no challenge to the prevailing trend in scholarly assessment of the exilic era in generally negative terms. For Weber, the development of Judaism is rooted in the evolution of a basically archaic religion (the peasant ecstatic tribal warrior religion of premonarchical Israel) as it faced urbanization and bureaucratic power. Yahwism, and then Judaism, came from the struggle of the ancient spirit of the people's religion (Yahweh as war-god) against technological power. One hears echoes, yet again, of German nineteenth-century romanticism, and thus it comes as no surprise that Weber considered the prophetic spirit to have "saved" exilic religious thought from falling into a meaningless ritualism dominated by priests.

Weber, as many others since, failed to appreciate the development of Priestly codes and concerns, not so much as internal power-struggles, but as *alternative strategies of resistance* to very real outside dangers presented by the horror of Mesopotamian imperialism and the social realities of Exile itself. This is nowhere more evident than in Weber's brief consideration of the Exile. The Exile was simply the culmination of internal theological struggles in ancient Israel; Weber gave merely two or three pages to consideration of the possible social conditions of the Exile itself. This is a direct result of his attempt to explicate a "pariah" religion from the raw materials of earlier pre-crisis elements of Israelite traditions. These conclusions would be radically altered from another perspective, and it is to the elaboration of such an alternative perspective that we now turn, in an attempt to understand the dynamics of exile as a unique challenge to religious and social structure.

Biblical Studies in the Fourth World

The alternative worldview presented in this study could be called a "Fourth World" perspective. In modern sociological literature, exiled peoples have come to be included among those otherwise collectively known as "the Fourth World." Graburn's definition of the Fourth World provides a helpful beginning:

> all aboriginal or native peoples whose lands fall within the na-
> tional boundaries and techno-bureaucratic administrations of the
> countries of the first, second, and third worlds. As such, they are
> peoples without countries of their own, peoples who are usually in
> the minority, and without the power to direct the course of their
> collective lives.[27]

Weber's analysis, like theological analyses that focus on restoration of former national glory, shares a basic socio-political assumption with Marxist-oriented studies, namely, the idea that the most significant social determinant for exilic theology and structure was *what was missing from it* — its statelessness as well as landlessness. Consequently, the goal of restoration theology in a good deal of Christian (and Jewish) analysis of exile is understood to be the return to power, the struggle to regain landed, national status, most clearly expressed in the norm of the Davidic state. The theological/ideological assumptions behind such a reading of the biblical text could hardly be more transparent. In Christian terms, we would consider this a clear manifestation of what Yoder has called "Constantinianism,"[28] and its Jewish equivalent in many forms of "Zionism" (particularly evident in early Zionist debates between A. D. Gordon and Lilienblum on whether the prophet Jeremiah was a patriot or not[29]). Furthermore Marxist conflict models also share this

concept of restoration, which typically informs the meaning of "liberation." The significance of the Exile is, in all three theological/ideological
orientations, focused on the theological and sociological "adjustment to
deprivation," preparation for political restoration, or backdrop for a
"return to history" (Fackenheim) defined as a return to "statehood."

Would a different alignment of "positive" and "negative," the "de-
pravity" or "creativity" of the exilic era result if the interpreter had a
different hermeneutical orientation? If progress in textual understanding of the Bible reveals itself to be dependent on values and theories
partially derived from "outside" the mere accumulation of new texts
or manipulation of existing data (as I have argued) then it becomes
clear that a "Fourth World" hermeneutic would radically reassess the
meaning of the exilic era of biblical faith.

Such an alternative worldview has its precedents in both Jewish and
Christian historiography. An entirely different sociological approach had
been argued already in the late nineteenth century by the noted Jewish
historian Simon Dubnow:

> It is becoming clear that the Jewish people during the millennia
> have not only "thought and suffered" but have in all possible cir-
> cumstances proceeded to build their life as a separate social unit;
> and, accordingly, that to reveal this process of the building of its
> life as a separate social unit is the primary task of historiography.[30]

Dubnow's view suggests a different perspective from which to approach
the problems of exile: *the perspective of the exiled themselves.* Dubnow's
own challenge to rethink Jewish history was clearly rooted in his diver-
gent notions about nationalism: "the decisive factor for the destiny of
a nation is not its external power but its spiritual force, the quality of
its culture, and the inner cohesion of its members."[31]

Therefore, there exists also a "Fourth World" theology. It is the theology of those "migrants" and "refugees" who choose to live without
power, yet as a people. The paradigms for Fourth World theology contrast sharply with theologies of liberation (with their focus on the biblical
events of Exodus) that have either made their peace with power or seek
to restore power. With typical clarity, John Howard Yoder has suggested
that such a "Constantinian" theological fascination with Exodus theology obscures the fact that Exodus is not the only biblical paradigm for
a biblical people:

> Instead of following the only pattern of going out into the wilder-
> ness — which the Exodus taken alone really was ... and instead of
> dreaming of a theocratic takeover of the land of bondage by the
> brickmakers — which ideological exegesis has sought to do with

the Exodus imagery — we [can] work more creatively to describe what can best by done by creative minorities in a society they don't control.[32]

What is the meaning of liberation theology or theologies of restoration for permanent refugees? What is the meaning of Exodus for exiled peoples — exiled because of total physical defeat or theological choice? The analysis of Exile will be the beginning of a biblical paradigm that speaks with equal power to, for example, American Indians and Japanese-Americans, Russian Molokans and Italian Waldensians, Egyptian Copts and Arab and Asian Christians, and Christians in Communist countries. Exodus has no paradigmatic meaning for exiles. For the Fourth World (as well as earliest Christianity) *Babylon* is the most meaningful image for a contemporary theology.

This book will argue that the most accurate "bias" from which to understand the Exile is a worldview informed by the Fourth World, that is, the view of social events and values that become operative for a minority in a conditions of forced removal and settlement under imperial control and power.

By identifying the sociological mechanisms of minorities who are confronted with the culture of power, the behavior and theology of the Babylonian Exile can be illuminated as a *creative response* to social realities, and not merely the desperate struggle of a culture in decline. This forms the major methodological shift and the contribution of this study of the Judean response to Exile. A consideration of the creative responses of minorities to forced removal and minority existence will, I hope, suggest new perspectives for biblical analysis.

By surveying the experience of exile, deportation, forced migration, refugee camps, and ethnic identity preservation among minorities, four social and socio-psychological behavior patterns that recur in these situations are identified. Although I have chosen four, there are many other patterns that we could work with. The four that I chose, however, were those that suggested striking biblical analogies:

1. Structural adaptation, including changes in the leadership and authority patterns, or changes in the basic social units of the society in question, often as a conscious strategy of survival and resistance.

2. The split in leadership between new leaders who arise to replace the old, defeated leaders who are usually unable to rule the minority group directly. The split in the leadership is invariably between those who advise a strong strategy of resistance, often violent, to the ruling group or population, and those that advise a strategy of *social* resistance.

3. The creation or elaboration of patterns of ritual practice that emphasize ritual weapons or ritual resistance against foreign influence, often expressed in concern over purity and pollution from foreign elements.

4. The creation of new folk literature or folklore patterns, especially seen in the prominence of the "hero story," with the hero as a new role model for the group.

I have called these behavior patterns "mechanisms for survival." These mechanisms are employed by social groups in order to maintain their identity, social structure, and religious/cultural life under stress. Many of these mechanisms have been documented in careful studies of communities that have experienced disaster, forced migration, and minority existence. I have surveyed a large amount of this secondary literature consciously citing examples from a variety of national, ethnic, historical, and socio-economic circumstances. I have focused on four case studies for special examination to illustrate the mechanisms: (1) Japanese-American internment during World War II in the western United States, (2) South African movement of black Africans to Bantustans and the religious responses of the "Zionist" churches, (3) slave societies and religious responses in pre–Civil War United States, and (4) the movement of the population of the Bikini Islands by the United States in the 1950s in order to conduct atomic tests. The point of this book is not to suggest a direct analogy between any of the cases that are considered and the Babylonian Exile (an overly simplistic generalization), but rather to use the collective sociological and anthropological data to suggest themes and questions to inform exegesis. We are interested in how groups respond, especially in religious patterns, to the specific kind of crisis that mass deportation represents.

After identifying these mechanisms and illustrating them from the cases, the mechanisms are illustrated in biblical material from the Babylonian Exile period.

First, I have examined the role of elders in the Exile, and the changing nature of the *Bēt 'Āb/Bēt 'Ābôt* (basic social structures of Judean/Israelite society) as indicators of social adaptation under the conditions of exile. The presence of elders in the context of prophets, and in the context of gatherings, suggests maintenance of elder meetings as an indigenous form of leadership and organization. This suggests self-government and large groups of exiled communities. Second, however, there is a significant change in the nomenclature of the basic social units of Israelite society. The *Bēt 'Āb* in the pre-exilic period was an extended family of two or three generations living under the leadership of the eldest male. But the post-exilic *Bēt 'Ābôt* is much larger and repre-

sents a basic change in the size of the social unit, which was then a
large group (often as many as 3,000) unified by a familial fiction. The
theories of Joel Weinberg, who suggests a social configuration called a
"Bürger-Tempel-Gemeinde" are considered and, with some reservation,
accepted.

Second, I consider the conflict between Jeremiah and Hananiah as
an example of the conflict between new leaders in crisis who advise
conflicting strategies of resistance and/or cooperation with the ruling
dominant group. This rise of new leaders is inevitable from both the
fall of the leadership structure in military defeat and the encouragement
of a "cooperative" elite by dominant groups. The "Letter of Jeremiah"
in Jeremiah 29 is considered in the light of Deuteronomic "Holy War"
exemptions. I argue that Jeremiah's letter represents a direct challenge
to the exiles to abandon the strategy of force, exemplified in Hananiah's
expectation of God's violent and quick end to the Exile by "breaking
the yoke of Babylon" and returning the king to the throne.

Third, the exilic redaction of the "P" legislation of purity is typified
by ritual concerns for purity and separation of the community of faith
from the impurity and dangers that surround a minority group. Citing
the theory of Mary Douglas, I explain the meaning and importance of
ritual among minority groups undergoing stress. According to recent
work on the legislation of P, the laws have undergone extensive redactional activity that develops older (sometimes premonarchical!) laws for
new situations. I have shown that the final redactional layer of P, represented, for example, in Leviticus 11, has purity and separation as
its major concern. A consideration of the root *BDL* (*bādal*) reveals
that separation was a concern also of the post-exilic community in the
"separation" of foreign wives from the "holy seed" of the "Sons of the
Golah" (post-exilic community).

Fourth, I review scholarship on folk literature as an expression of social circumstances, especially noting the significance of the "hero story"
and its emergence as a fictitious role model for survival in new conditions. I have examined the "diaspora novella," especially the stories
of Daniel and Joseph as examples of new heroes, and compared the
social symbols of these stories to the messianic expectations of the exilic period, especially the image of the Suffering Servant. Messianism
is also an expression of a "diaspora hero." Each of the diaspora stories emphasizes the low-status beginnings of the hero before a rise to
prominence in the eyes of the non-Jewish population. The hero is then
faced with a challenge by members of the majority population, who are
always seen as the real threat, and not the leader/king, often portrayed
as a kindly or bumbling ruler easily swayed by his evil advisors. The
success of the hero is always with the "weapons" available to the diaspora Jews among whom these stories were preserved and cherished —

the weapons of cleverness and especially piety. Finally, imprisonment as an institution, and as a motif of the diaspora hero story, is examined as the *major symbol of exile,* particularly important since it is absent as a judicial institution of Israel. All diaspora heroes face imprisonment, as does the Suffering Servant.

Finally, as a measure of the separate development of the faith and practice of the exile community, I review evidence for conflict between the exile community and those left in the land at the time of the restoration. I conclude that the religious values of the exiles, including the religious development of the mechanisms for survival, were at the root of the conflicts of the restoration, which were only further exacerbated by the conflicts over property and religious intolerance.

In summary, the task of a sociological analysis of the Exile is a formidable one. Not only does the practice of sociological exegesis have to deal with the threat of distortion from inappropriate assumptions on the part of the reader of a text; it also must maintain the caution against drawing conclusions from insufficiently analyzed assumptions about how human groups behave. It is futile to try to remove assumptions, prejudices, and "fore-meanings," since historical understanding is arguably impossible without them. But it is also futile to insist "in the end" that the reader must "allow the text" to dictate when sociological analysis can reveal the defects in our comprehension of what the text is actually saying. It therefore follows that familiarity with cases of human behavior in forced removal and minority existence will allow a reader of a text to comprehend a text more fully when that text comes from similar social circumstances. In the following chapters, I will illustrate why this is particularly true in reference to the Babylonian Exile. Finally, by way of tentative conclusions, I will suggest the outlines of a Fourth World theology for contemporary debate.

NOTES

1. Robert Wilson, *Sociological Approaches to the Old Testament* (Philadelphia, 1984); John Rogerson, *Anthropology and the Old Testament* (Oxford, 1978).

2. Paul Hanson, *The Dawn of Apocalyptic,* 2nd ed. (Philadelphia, 1975); T. W. Overholt, "The Ghost Dance of 1890 and the Nature of the Prophetic Process, *Ethnohistory,* 21 (1974), pp. 37–63, and "Jeremiah and the Nature of the Prophetic Process," in *Scripture in History and Theology: Essays in Honour of J. Coert Rylaarsdam* (Pittsburgh, 1977); George Mendenhall, *The Tenth Generation* (Baltimore, 1973).

3. Norman Gottwald, *The Tribes of Yahweh* (Maryknoll, N.Y., 1979); Michel Clevenot, *Materialist Approaches to the Bible* (Maryknoll, N.Y., 1985); Fernando Belo, *A Materialist Reading of the Gospel of Mark* (Maryknoll, N.Y., 1975); Georges Casalis, *Correct Ideas Don't Fall from the Skies* (Maryknoll, N.Y., 1984).

4. Rogerson, *Anthropology and the Old Testament,* p. 27.

5. A. Alt, "Der Gott der Väter," in *Kleine Schriften* (Munich, 1953).

6. J. Wilhelm Rowntree, *Palestine Notes and other Papers* (London, 1906), p. 31.

7. S. I. Curtiss, *Primitive Semitic Religion Today* (New York, 1902), p. 66.

8. Discussion of this issue is found in Clinton Bailey, "Dating the Arrival of the Bedouin Tribes in Sinai and the Negev," *Journal of Economic and Social History of the Orient* (Leiden), 28, part 1 (February 1985), pp. 15f.; R. D. Barnett, "Lachish, Ashkelon and the Camel: A Discussion of Its Use in Southern Palestine, *Institute of Archaeology Occasional Papers*, no. 11 (London, 1988); R. W. Bulliet, *The Camel and the Wheel* (Cambridge, 1975); and John Van Seters, *Abraham in History and Tradition* (New Haven, 1975), pp. 13ff.

9. Edward Said, *Orientalism* (London, 1978).

10. Robert Wilson, *Prophecy and Society in Ancient Israel* (Philadelphia, 1980).

11. See "The New Left Critique of Anthropology," in Talal Adad, *Anthropology and the Colonial Encounter* (London, 1973), p. 25.

12. W. Cahnman and A. Boskoff, *Sociology and History* (New York, 1964), p. 3. Further interesting discussions can be found in M. Somers and T. Skocpal, "The Uses of Comparative History in Macro-Social Inquiry," *Comparative Studies in Society and History,* 22 (1980), and V. Bonnell, "The Uses of Theory, Concepts, and Comparison in Historical Sociology," *Comparative Studies in Society and History,* 22 (1980).

13. Paul Feyerabend, *Against Method: Outline of an Anarchistic Theory of Knowledge* (Atlantic Highlands, N.J., 1975), p. 23.

14. See Thomas Kuhn, *The Structure of Scientific Revolutions* (Chicago, 1962).

15. Feyerabend, *Against Method*, pp. 152–155.

16. "What the fluid theory of electricity did for the subgroup that held it, the Franklinian paradigm later did for the entire group of electricians. It suggested which experiments would be worth performing, and which because directed to secondary or to overly complex manifestations of electricity, would not" (Thomas Kuhn, *The Structure of Scientific Revolutions*, p. 18).

17. Kuno Füssel, "The Materialist Reading of the Bible," in Norman Gottwald, ed. *The Bible and Liberation* (Maryknoll, N.Y., 1983), p. 138.

18. G. R. Berry, "The Unrealistic Attitude of Post-Exilic Judaism," *Journal of Biblical Literature,* 64 (1945).

19. Peter Ackroyd, *Exile and Restoration*, Old Testament Library (London, 1968).

20. Ibid., p. 7.

21. See, e.g., R. S. Foster, *The Restoration of Israel* (London, 1970); T. M. Raitt, *A Theology of Exile* (Philadelphia, 1977); J. D. Newsome, *By the Waters of Babylon* (Edinburgh, 1979); Ralph Klein, *Israel in Exile: A Theological Interpretation* (Philadelphia, 1979).

22. Ackroyd, *Exile and Restoration*, pp. 6–7.

23. Max Weber, *Ancient Judaism,* trans. H. Gerth and D. Martindale (New York, 1967; originally published in 1921), p. 11.

24. Ibid., p. 138.

25. Ibid., p. 135.

26. Ibid., p. 331.

27. Introduction, Nelson Graburn, *Ethnic and Tourist Arts: Cultural Expressions from the Fourth World* (Los Angeles, 1976).

28. John Howard Yoder, *The Priestly Kingdom* (Notre Dame, 1986), esp. chap. 7.

29. I owe this interesting reference to Dr. Marcus Moseley, currently working at YIVO in New York. The debate was initiated by Gordon's poem, "Hezekiah in Prison," to which Lilienblum replied. S. Brayman has edited Lilienblum's letters to Gordon (Hebrew); see also Jonathan Frankel, *Prophecy and Politics: Socialism, Nationalism and the Russian Jews, 1862–1917* (Cambridge, Eng., 1981).

30. Simon M. Dubnow, *History of the Jews: From the Beginning to Early Christianity,* trans. Moshe Spiegal (South Brunswick, N.Y., 1967), p. 27.

31. Ibid., p. 79.

32. See John Howard Yoder, "Exodus and Exile: The Two Faces of Liberation," *Cross Currents,* 23 (1973).

Part I

The Experience of Exile

Chapter 1

The Context of Empire: Historical/Sociological Questions

The Historical Background

The Assyrian Rise to Power

In the standard recent histories of Israel available in English (especially Herrmann, Bright, and Soggin[1]) the historical data of the Exile are considered through a comparison between the available cuneiform records of the Neo-Babylonian and Persian Empires, and the biblical history provided mainly in 2 Kings, Jeremiah (especially the "prose" sections), Isaiah, and Ezra-Nehemiah, along with the relevant material from the P stratum of the Pentateuch, the prophets Ezekiel, Haggai, Zechariah, and Malachi, and selected portions of the Psalms that may be considered exilic or post-exilic.[2] Ackroyd's survey provides a solid starting point for any historical review of the "Exile and Restoration."[3] Therefore, the purpose of this section is not merely to reconsider details of history. Instead, it will be politically and socially focused, dealing with those issues that have more than strictly theological significance, in order to more fully understand the Exile.[4]

As Noth suggested, the Exile is correctly seen as the last event in a series that can be thought of as "the fall" of Israelite power in the Ancient Near East.[5] The crisis faced by Judah really began, therefore, with the threat of the Neo-Assyrians even before the Neo-Babylonian Empire. This threat becomes sociologically, as well as historically, important, as we shall see. Otzen has pointed out that the rise of the Davidic-Solomonic empire was largely possible because of the vacuum left by a declining Egyptian hegemony and the emergent empire of the Assyrians in the North and East.[6] A major change in Assyria arrived with the kingship of Tiglath-Pileser III (745–727). Tiglath-Pileser III is considered the true inaugurator of Assyrian power on an "empire scale."

He is credited with a major reform of the Assyrian administration and the Assyrian war-machine. Larsen summarizes the major elements of this reform:

> (1) the old provincial system was reorganized so that previously existing very large provinces were divided into smaller units to lessen the danger of revolts from "over-vigorous" governors.... (2) the central bureaucracy of the king was strengthened by way of a reform of the army and administrative system, and (3) the area under direct, provincial rule was expanded so that a number of new provinces were created in lands situated beyond the traditional borders of the empire.[7]

In 729, Tiglath-Pileser III secured the throne of Babylon from the troublesome Chaldean tribes, whose historical moment would not arrive for another century. In 738 Tiglath-Pileser had received tribute from most of the states in the Syrian vicinity (Hamath, Tyre, Byblos, Damascus), and in Israel (Judah was at that point not directly involved). Upon the death of Jeroboam II (786–746) a series of court intrigues resulted in the brief rule of Zechariah and "Shallum" (745), both of whom preceded Menachem. The Deuteronomic Historian says of Menachem, in his stereotypical fashion, that he "did evil in the sight of the Lord; he did not depart all his days from the sins of Jeroboam." But more specifically, the text recalls a sizeable tribute paid to Tiglath-Pileser III under his Babylonian throne name *Pûl.* In return for this payment of tribute, Israel was spared direct interference (if one does not consider paying such protection money "interference," 2 Kings 15:20) and with that, the Deuteronomic Historian once again refers the reader to the regrettably unavailable "Chronicles of the Kings of Israel" (v. 21). This payment of tribute, however, indicates that Israel was treated as a vassal state, and not ruled as a province of the Empire under the direct rule of Nineveh.

After Menachem's son Pekahiah was killed in a coup led by Pekah ben Ramaliah, Pekah attempted to lead a more independent Israel from Assyrian domination. 2 Kings 15:29 recounts a campaign of Tiglath-Pileser at that time in the West, but despite the show of force, Pekah attempted an anti-Assyrian coalition, in league with Edom and Rezin of Damascus. When Ahaz in Judah would not join this coalition, Pekah and Rezin inaugurated the "Syro-Ephraimite War" against Judah. Trapped on his North and South flanks, Ahaz appealed to Tiglath-Pileser, who crushed the power of the coalition. The account of the altar in 2 Kings 16:10–20, which Ahaz commissioned after meeting with *Pûl,* has given rise to considerable debate. McKay notes that Uriah the priest made no protest about this new altar and thus assumes that the altar was simply a new design that pleased Ahaz and was not a form of worship imposed by Ahaz at the behest of Tiglath-Pileser.[8] The Assyrians, according to McKay, had no form of burnt offering cult.[9] But surely the literary context of the Deuteronomic Historian's *condemnation* of Ahaz leads one to suspect that, while a specifically Assyrian cult is not mentioned, the removal of the old altar and the replacement with a new one certainly had something to do with Ahaz's contact with Tiglath-Pileser and somehow reflected his new political status in relation to the Assyrian. Otherwise this story of the altar, mentioned where it is, strikes one as superfluous. McKay focuses on the final phrase of 16:18, which concludes a description of the changes that Ahaz made in the temple with the phrase "in deference to the King of Assyria" (Jerusalem Bible). The RSV states that this is "because of" rather than Olmstead's more literal reading of "before the face of,"[10] which he then associates with an *actual* representation (statue, stele) of Tiglath-Pileser III in the temple itself.[11] In any case, Ahaz's actions were taken in the context of his loss of independence. This is significant irrespective of the imposition of specific cultic practices.

Eventually, Hoshea killed Pekah, whereupon Hoshea tried again to withhold tribute and sent to Egypt for aid in an attempt to break free from Assyrian rule. It was to be the last political decision of an independent northern king. There is dispute between the biblical claim that it was Shalmaneser who succeeded in the conquest of Samaria in 722, and the claim of Sargon II to have deported 27,290 people in his punishing war against Samaria. 2 Kings 17 recounts the bringing of many peoples from various parts of the Assyrian empire in exchange for the deported Israelites. What became of the Northern exiles continues to be a point of interesting speculation.[12]

The fall of Samaria led to the deportation, or more correctly, the *exchange,* of populations in keeping with the Assyrian martial policy inaugurated by Tiglath-Pileser.[13] This exchange of population resulted, according to 2 Kings 17, in a massive religious upheaval with a spread of foreign cults and religious practices. Immediately following the texts that recount the pagan practices of the fallen Northern kingdom, we are introduced in 2 Kings 18 to King Hezekiah. The account of his reign begins with a positive evaluation, comparing him to David, "his father." Hezekiah did not immediately withhold tribute from Assyria, but during the political instability that occurred with Sennacherib's rise to power (704–681), it appears Sennacherib was totally occupied with serious rebellions in the Mediterranean districts and in Babylonia.[14]

It is likely that Egyptian propaganda had stirred the rebellious desire of Lule, king of Sidon; Sidka, king of Ascalon; Hezekiah himself; and the inhabitants of Ekron, to sever links with Nineveh.[15] The response of Sennacherib in 701–700 resulted in the siege of Jerusalem, which Hezekiah attempted to end by massive payments of tribute (2 Kings

18:14–15). However, Sennacherib sent his officers, including the "Rab-šāqē," the "tartān," and the "Rab-sārîs" to demand the surrender of the city. Although some have seen the content of the "Rab-šāqē's" speech as a Deuteronomic polemic against Egypt,[16] we do have cuneiform evidence of Assyrian army officers who made speeches before the walls of besieged cities,[17] and it would be in keeping with the significance of propaganda in Assyrian war policy to see this as a means of promoting terror among the general population. Note the appeal by Hezekiah's officials to the Rab-šāqē not to speak in the language of Judah, "within the hearing of the people who are on the wall...." The reply is an example of a most calculated propaganda: "Do you think my lord sent me here to say these things to your master or to you? On the contrary, it was to the people sitting on the ramparts who, like you, are doomed to eat their dung and drink their urine...." A polemical speech follows which echoes a previous speech (2 Kings 18:19–26), even claiming that the god of the Jews cannot defeat the Assyrian monarch, as the gods of "Hamath and Arpad" were also powerless to stop them.

Despite the Deuteronomic Historian's tributes to the reforms of Hezekiah and Josiah, the text continues to document a steady decline. The description of Josiah's reforms occupies considerable detail, but 2 Kings 23:26ff. concludes the reform narrative by stating that the reforms were not enough to overcome the evil of Manasseh.

The description of Josiah's abortive campaign at Megiddo, has given rise to speculation over the exact circumstances of his death.[18] Josiah's action becomes more significant in the context of empire. The earliest mention of Assyria and Egypt as *allies* is found in the so-called Gadd Chronicle,[19] which is dated 616 B.C.E. Seeing the threat of a growing Babylonian-Median alliance, Egypt undoubtedly saw an opportunity to secure the coveted Palestinian trade routes and land by shoring up the failing strength of the Assyrians at Harran under Ashur-uballit II. No doubt this was intended to preserve a small Assyrian power as a buffer against the advancing Median-Babylonian alliance.[20] Malamat goes even further in suggesting that Josiah's action was a sign that there was a broad strategic plan or military alliance between Judah and Babylon.[21] This action by Josiah, when combined with earlier Jewish contact between Merodach-Baladan II and Hezekiah, may be a significant factor in the exilic social alignments and conflicts evident in the book of Jeremiah and in the behavior of the prophet himself. Was Jeremiah part of a pro-Babylonian "fifth column" (see Jer. 39:11f.)? The fall of Josiah led to a four-year Egyptian presence in Palestine in 609–605, despite their failure to save the last of the Assyrian Empire. On his retreat from the North (it appears, according to Josephus, that he never made it to the Euphrates) Necho placed Eliakim on the throne, renaming him Jehoiakim. Jehoiakim's fame comes mainly from his encounters with Jeremiah, including his "fiery" reaction to the scroll of the prophet.

The Chaldean Conquest of the West

In 605, the Egyptians once again encountered the Chaldean army at Carchemish. At this battle, the crown prince Nebuchadrezzar was given control of the Chaldean forces, and the Wiseman Chronicles record a resounding defeat for the Egyptians, which is graphically portrayed in the oracles of Jeremiah 46ff.

Jehoiakim died in 598, and Jehoiachin, eighteen years old (2 Kings 24:8), had reigned for only three months when the Chaldeans struck. In 597, Jehoiachin surrendered to Nebuchadnezzar, and the Chaldeans took their first group of exiles. While this initial group was small, it is important to note that it was the king and aristocracy who were removed, in an attempt to remove leadership and the potential for revolt.[22]

Mattaniah-Zedekiah was made "king" by Nebuchadnezzar, but the prophet Ezekiel continued to date his oracles according to the years of the exile of "king" Jehoiachin (Ezek. 1:1). In time, Zedekiah also sought to rebel against Babylon (against Jeremiah's warning). 2 Kings 25:1-2 recounts the resulting siege, which ended with a breach in the wall. Jerusalem itself was occupied. This time, Jerusalem suffered severe destruction. Zedekiah, Nebuchadnezzar's chosen ruler, tried to escape but was captured and suffered brutal punishment (25:7). This exile, as recounted in 2 Kings 25:11ff. and Jer. 52:15ff., was more general than the surrender of Jehoiachin. Only some of the "poorest of the land" were left to be "vinedressers'" and "plowmen" according to the text.[23] Included in the events were executions of some of Zedekiah's co-conspirators (2 Kings 25:18-21). Nebuchadnezzar then appointed Gedaliah the governor, who moved his capital to Mizpah, a move possibly indicating the extent of the destruction of Jerusalem. It appears that Jeremiah was also among those who joined Gedaliah.

The Chronicler in 2 Chron. 36:21-22 rather briefly summarizes the entire Exile experience by telescoping it into the words "the land enjoyed its Sabbaths," and attention is then promptly turned to Cyrus at the end of the events of Exile.

The Conquests of Cyrus

It is inconceivable that the victories of Cyrus of Anshan would have passed unnoticed by the Jews in exile. Deutero-Isaiah's famous hymn to Cyrus (Isa. 44–45) and the oracles against Babylon (Isa. 43, 47, 48) seem to indicate a knowledge that the Persian victory was coming, and there is no reason to suppose that they were all written after the fact.

The historical sequence of events in Babylon itself, however, suggests that the final ruler, Nabonidus, helped to bring the end on himself.

Nebuchadnezzar's last years appear to have ended in some disorder.[24] Awel-Marduk (biblical "Evil-Merodach') ruled two years (561–560) and was replaced by a general, Neriglissar. Neriglissar's son was murdered, and eventually an Aramean of high rank was raised to the throne. Nabonidus was in his sixties (or older!) when he became king and was the son of a priestess of Sin, the moon god. One of our most important sources of information about Nabonidus, the so-called "Verse Account of Nabonidus," is clearly Babylonian propaganda to vilify this king who alienated the priests of Marduk by giving so much attention to the moon god and its temples. We now have accounts of Nabonidus telling of his dreams,[25] and this, in combination with the less-than-flattering picture of the "Verse Account" and other information, has led modern exegetes to wonder if the fragment from the Dead Sea Scrolls that associates Daniel with Nabonidus, rather than Nebuchadnezzar, is a more accurate tradition than the current book of Daniel, given Daniel's portrayal of the Babylonian ruler.

In the Cuneiform Chronicles, Nabonidus is depicted as spending a great deal of time in the Arabian desert oasis of Tema. In the meantime, during Nabonidus' ten-year absence, his son Belshazzar was on the throne in Babylon. Again, we have evidence that Daniel may report accurate information about Nabonidus. Galling has suggested that Belshazzar's "irresponsibility" reported in Daniel may also be based on traditions of Nabonidus' religious "heresies."[26] Belshazzar died in the battle of Opis, and Nabonidus was probably killed at the fall of Babylon in 539.

The growing power of Cyrus was undoubtedy the stuff of legend long before the final capture of Babylon. There are a number of fascinating accounts of the childhood of Cyrus, many of which come to us in Herodotus and Xenophon. One of these legends tells of the saving of the child by switching him with a still-born baby to fool the King who wanted his death. The stories are reminiscent of those about Sargon of Akkad[27] and Moses. The Greek historians knew of the tradition that Cyrus was an enlightened ruler, but Herodotus tempers his enthusiasm with reports of the levelling of whole cities at the defeat of Croesus the Lydian and the sack of Akkad after the victory at Opis.[28]

The fall of Babylon is described in the Nabonidus Chronicle.[29] The Battle of Opis was in late September of 539. By October 10, the holy city of Sippar fell without a struggle. The Babylonian governor of Giutium, one "Ugbarau" (whom Xenophon called Gobryas), defected to Cyrus, and he led the assault on Babylon. By October 29, Cyrus was able to march into Babylon as a herald of peace, and the Chronicle describes the laying of branches before him.[30] In the "Cyrus Cylinder,"[31] and also the Chronicles of Nabonidus, the Persian conqueror relates his great piety toward the conquered city. Cyrus boasted that his soldiers did not draw their swords near the Temple,[32] but Herodotus records that the Persian soldiers diverted the Euphrates and then marched in through the floodgates and into the city, thus presenting the Babylonians with a *fait accompli.* In any case, Babylon was not destroyed, as the biblical prophets had expected. But the event obviously created excitement in Jewish circles. We know that messianic language was used of Cyrus in Isaiah, where Cyrus is called God's "shepherd" (Isa. 44:28) and even God's "anointed" (45:1).

The Restoration: Problems of Dating the Return of the Jews

When Cyrus was in control of Babylon in 539, he began his policy of returning cult statues to their rightful places.[33] Consistent with this is the edict allowing the rebuilding of the Temple of Jerusalem under the mission of Sheshbazzar.

The Persian Edicts of Ezra-Nehemiah have given rise to speculation. Wilhelm Smitten considers the Cyrus Edict of Ezra 1 to be modelled after the more general edict of Darius in Ezra 6. Among his reasons are (1) there is less of a Yahwistic stamp to the content of Ezra 6, i.e., phrases like "the Lord, the God of Heaven" (1:2) and "He is the god who is in Jerusalem" (1:3), (2) the factual description of the financial and material provisions stand out as added later, and (3) the use of the word "Jerusalem" by itself, rather than pairing it with Judah, is more to be expected in Ezra 6 than the pairing in Ezra 1, which is found very often in the Book of Chronicles.[34] Galling, too, has doubts about the authenticity of Ezra 1, but his scepticism must be balanced by the views of Bickerman.[35] The main doubts about Ezra 1 center on the actual time of the return of the Jews to Palestine.

The traditional view, as supported by our only biblical source, Ezra, is that the "prince of Judah" was given a large sum of money and an entourage to return to Jerusalem in the first year of Cyrus's reign as the conqueror of Babylon. But Sheshbazzar disappears when the first "Golah List" is given. There, the prominent figure is Zerubbabel, and it is Zerubbabel and Jeshua who are the leaders of the community in chapter 3 of Ezra. Sheshbazzar in Ezra 5:10ff. is described as if he were in the distant past, although it could be argued that the compiler of Ezra-Nehemiah assumed that Zerubbabel, Jeshua, and everyone in the Golah List *were* with Sheshbazzar. The evidence of Haggai, however, suggests that Zerubbabel is to be associated with a later time.

The most prolific writer on the problems of the restoration is certainly Galling.[36] Galling believes that Sheshbazzar, while able to return with some of the wealth and a small entourage, was not successful in rebuilding the Temple. Haggai (2:3), referring to the Temple, wondered if it was "as nothing to you"? This "as nothing" is taken to suggest that the Temple was lying in ruins at the time of Haggai, i.e., 520. Indeed, Galling reads Haggai 2:10–14 and 20–23 as proclamations made on the day of dedication of the foundation stone of the Temple. The measuring line of Zech. 1:16ff. also indicates that work was being done on the Temple itself. If one is willing to see some historical validity in the work of Ezra-Nehemiah, then the conclusion is that Sheshbazzar failed in the attempt to rebuild the Temple in 539 under Cyrus, and Zerubbabel was not in the entourage that accompanied Sheshbazzar.

Alt had already suggested that the main return of the exiles probably came about as a result of Cambyses' campaigns in Egypt, when the Syrian lands were first firmly under the control of the Persians.[37] While Galling wants to date the return later yet, he nevertheless agrees that a return under Cyrus was highly unlikely, given the uncertainties of his authority in Syria at the time. Sheshbazzar must have found the same opposition in Palestine that the later returning exiles found under Zerubbabel (Ezra 4).[38]

Galling believes that Haggai's message about the drought was addressed to those who had only recently arrived back in the land, about 522 or 521. Otherwise, if the Jews had had many fertile years before that, with only one or two bad years, the warning of Haggai would have fallen on deaf ears.[39] Also, one must assume that Haggai is scolding Jews who have been concerned with their "panelled houses" for the last few years, but surely not for the last eighteen years! Finally, Zech. 5:1–4 is taken to refer to land disputes with those who stayed behind, indicating recent arguments. Alt wanted to date the main return to the time of Cambyses (Cambyses was in firm control of the upper and lower kingdoms in 525). Galling suggested most recently that a logical moment would be at Darius's successful quelling of the revolt of Nidintu Bel, or the self-proclaimed "Nebuchadnezzar III." At this point, reasoned Galling, Zerubbabel could have appealed to Darius on the basis of Jewish loyalty to the Persians during the troubles.

It is certainly the case that Haggai and Zechariah make much more sense when read in the context of recent returning exiles, and this also seems to make sense of the shadowy figure of Sheshbazzar and his eclipse by Zerubbabel. Finally, however, the Golah List itself gives us clues. The picture of the return under Sheshbazzar is a small entourage that required a donated expense account from the provincial coffers in order to succeed. This attempt to rebuild, as we see from Haggai, was considered as good as no start at all. In contrast, the Golah List indicates wealthy Jews, able to pay large donations to the work of the Temple.[40] The general upheaval of the beginning of the reign of Darius may also have been the occasion of Haggai's triumphant proclamation about Zerubbabel in messianic terms. Haggai's messianic proclamation may have been in conscious opposition to the denial of further Davidic kings implicit in Jeremiah's earlier prophecy, and also in opposition to Deutero-Isaiah's image of a peaceful Messiah who suffers.[41] The latter pacifist image is more in line with Zechariah's image of Zerubbabel as one who will rule not by might or by power, but by the spirit of God. Thus, if a politically opportune moment was to occur for the new David, it may have been during the struggles of Darius. The text of Ezra 6 is occupied with the completion of the Temple, and then the celebration of the Passover. In this way we are brought to the end of Zerubbabel's career in the Bible.

The text of Ezra jumps in 7:1 to the reign of Artaxerxes. We are thus left with a gap in the historical accounts of some seventy years before the story of Ezra's mission to Jerusalem. A possible source for this period may be the book called Malachi. The two major concerns of Malachi are improper cult observance and the problems of mixed marriage. If Malachi does indeed come from the period before Ezra-Nehemiah, then we have evidence of a concern that will reach crisis proportions in the work of Ezra. What is of particular interest in these events is how the exile community reacts to the return, and how this reflects the experience of the Exile itself.

The final date of our period is also debated, i.e., 458, or the seventh year of Artaxerxes.[42] The story of Ezra's mission to restore the normative law of the "God of Heaven" is contained in Ezra 7–10 and then resumes with the dramatic reading of the law in Neh. 8–9. Nehemiah, on the other hand, begins his mission in 445. Thus, the text suggests that Ezra came with a small group, and his attempts at reform appear to fail. Nehemiah appears much more authoritatively some time later and takes major architectural, administrative, and military steps at reorganization. It would appear that Nehemiah was able to succeed where Ezra failed. But does Ezra's reappearance in Neh. 8–9 suggest that, in reality, they worked together, or that this section should have appeared in the book of Ezra and their work has been artificially mixed together? Noth, for example, believed that Nehemiah came first, and his "political" reform prepared the way for Ezra's "spiritual reform."

Finally, there are those who doubt that an "Ezra" existed at all! Noting how often the Ezra narrative mirrors that of Nehemiah, In der Smitten believes that Ezra the Priest may well have been a pious fiction created to contrast with Nehemiah, once again contrasting Priestly (and largely nonviolent) ethics to those of a Persian official.[43]

Historical Questions

From this historical overview, there are a number of issues that are of particular significance for sociological analysis, most specifically:

1. Did the Assyrians and/or Neo-Babylonians impose their religion on conquered people?

2. What was the nature of deportation as a martial tactic?

3. How many Judeans were deported to the Babylonian heartland?

4. What happened to the Judeans left behind?

5. What do we know about the life of the exiles from literary or archaeological sources?

Did the Assyrians or Neo-Babylonians impose their religion on conquered people?

We have noted that Assyrian propaganda was aimed at the demoralization of the enemy by claiming that their own god(s) had abandoned them. This was the claim against Jerusalem as well. But how far did the Assyrians (or, after them, the Neo-Babylonians) carry this? Were the subject populations of these two empires subject to the imposition of foreign religious cults by the conquerors? This has been the subject of a lively debate. It is important to consider this as an aspect of the context of empire before and during the Exile. A "crisis" in the life of a social group is compounded, and made all the more unsettling, if it is a crisis composed of a *series of events* rather than just one event (see discussion of this point in the following chapter). In the light of this, it is important to see how the contact with empire and military power began even with the Neo-Assyrian conquests in Palestine and its resemblance, indeed inspiration, to Neo-Babylonian tactics.

There was a Neo-Assyrian ideology of the superior power of Ashur because of Ashur's ability actually to defeat the other gods: "Boastfully, the claim is put forward that the enemy's gods had abandoned their faithful in submission to Assyria's Ashur."[44] The martial spirit is clear in the policies of Assyrian treatment of conquered people's cults. Often, the foreign gods were captured so that guarantees of loyalty could accompany their return, symbolizing superior Assyrian might.[45]

Although the cult of conquered gods was known to continue in the statues' absence, nevertheless, in the instance of Ashurbanipal's return of an older Marduk statue, the return of the old and revered image was greeted with great enthusiasm.[46]

But Assyrian symbols of power were expressed in more tangible ways, too, including the placing of military symbols in the realm of the conquered nations and areas, often marking the path of Assyrian armies of conquest and the limits of Assyrian domination.[47] What modern scholars debate, despite all the explicit political symbols of domination (which was obviously a major concern of the Assyrians, attested in both biblical and cuneiform sources), is that the Assyrians "coerced" Judah or Israel into the adoption of specifically Assyrian cult practices. The problem is the absence of any reference in the biblical material to any specific Assyrian deity.

Cogan and McKay do not believe that Assyrians imposed worship, but Hermann Spieckermann's research has led him to significantly different conclusions.[48] In the chapter of his work entitled, "Religionspolitische Massnahmen der Assyrer gegenüber Juda und anderen besiegten Völkern" ("Religious and Political Measures of the Assyrians against Judah and other Besieged Peoples"), Spieckermann paints a picture of the martial tactics of Assyrian practice in dark colors.

According to cuneiform sources like ABL 736, the Assyrian garrisons were "hated."[49] Furthermore, the garrisons ensured the payment of the heavy tribute and there were specifically religious associations with the collection of this tribute payment.[50] Thus, it can be suggested that the altar set up by Ahaz was "in addition" to the Yahwistic altar. The additional altar was to make sacrifices for the Assyrian rulers, while the other remained a Yahwistic altar. Indeed, Spieckermann believes that a consideration of the Assyrian materials means that one must *assume* that the Assyrian gods replaced the local gods in conquered territories. Therefore, by the end of the Assyrian presence in Palestine, Assyria was engaged in an economic "strangulation" through tribute payments, and the religiously based symbolization of occupation and conquest.[51]

The salient factor is that after an extended discussion of the Assyrian "language of oppression," the punishing tribute that required robbing the very temple walls (2 Kings 16:8, 16:17ff., 2 Kings 18:15), taxing the people heavily (2 Kings 15:20, 2 Kings 18:14ff.), and finally the physical removal of significant numbers of the population itself, it seems hardly reasonable to insist, as if it were a matter of great importance, on the notion that the Assyrians or Babylonians did not *also* impose the specific worship of Assur or Marduk.

Spieckermann's view is far more alive to the actual conditions of being a conquered people. "Freedom of religion" has a rather hollow meaning if it means freedom to worship in a Temple stripped of its luxury and beauty and possibly containing documents or images of the conquering power boasting of their mighty victories over gods and people. Thus, the idea that such freedom of religion would at least "strengthen the resolve of the people to resist"[52] seems a rather anemic argument and tends to exaggerate the leniency of Assyria. Finally, the important point is that, from the time when Tiglath-Pileser III asserted the power of Neo-Assyrian armies in Mesopotamia, the power of the dominating empire was clearly a part of everyday life, and it would have had religious significance if any symbol of foreign domination were found in Judah, whether it was worshipped or not.

We do better, therefore, to understand the social context of empire and begin to see how the Jews were already becoming acquainted with the taste of limited freedom and the propaganda of defeat even before the Exile of the southern kingdom became a reality.

Empire suggests certain socio-political realities, and Larsen sums this up graphically as "a huge military and administrative apparatus designed to secure a constant flow of goods from the periphery to the center."[53]

A significant aspect of the Assyrian war-machine that has left a lasting legacy both in extant texts and also in biblical history is the use of propaganda, as already indicated. The "calculated frightfulness" of the Assyrian war tactics may be seen in practices such as the following, cited in a cuneiform text:

> [Against Suru of Bit-Halupe] I built a pillar over against the city-gate and I flayed all the chief men who had revolted, and I covered the pillar with their skins.... Ahiababa I took to Nineveh.... I spread his skin upon the wall of Nineveh.[54]

It is interesting to note that the last grisly "example" was taken back to Nineveh itself. Mario Liverani, in his analysis "The Ideology of Assyrian Empire," has commented on the fact that the aims of propaganda in relation to empire were directed not only toward the enemy:

> Without any doubt the main receivers of the ideological propaganda were the whole of the Assyrian population, in so far as they provide the human material for the war machine and for the production machine. The propaganda must achieve the arduous aim of prompting them to perform an active role, not a passive one; that of the ruler, not of the ruled, without reaping the annexed benefits. It is essential to avoid, or at least to check the tendency of, the lower classes to rise in the inner core of the empire; it is also essential to avoid a union between the lower classes and the conquered peoples. It is essential to get the instruments of imperialism to be efficient, self-convinced and enthusiastic, as if they were working in their own interest against the foreigners, whilst in fact they are working with the foreigners to the advantage of the ruling class.[55]

These kinds of analyses give the modern reader the critical orientation so as not to confuse propagandist history with "annalistic" or "objective" history. If there was concern to direct propaganda toward the Assyrian heartland itself, then one can conclude that the dominated populations in the outlying areas were only too familiar with this propagandist effort as well, whether in texts, or in pictorial stelae.[56]

Liverani suggests that empires, and specifically the Assyrian empire, attempted to explain and justify the imbalance presupposed in empire building, the need to see the tasks as right and just in conquering land and people, the latter reflected in the common Neo-Assyrian refrain in inscriptions about the conquered race, "I counted them among the Assyrians...."[57]

In sum, it is in the context of Assyrian practices that we more fully understand the events that led to the Neo-Babylonian conquest of Judah, the placing of chosen rulers on the throne, and the significance of deportation.

What was the nature of deportation as a martial tactic?

Deportation *was an act of empire,* or "propaganda by the deed." As it was a policy largely perfected by the Neo-Assyrians before the Neo-Babylonians, it is important to consider the Assyrian practice.

Analysis of the policy of deportation is dependent on six major sources including (1) royal inscriptions, (2) chronicles, (3) administrative and legal texts, (4) reliefs, (5) the Hebrew Bible, and (6) the ancient historians. These materials, however, often raise problems. The problem with the royal inscriptions is that they use stereotypical phrasing to describe different historical events, and one must contend with royal exaggeration in numbers and scale of conquests.[58] Among the administrative and legal texts, the fragmentary condition combines with the "terse contents" to make conclusions difficult.

Oded has estimated that over three centuries in which Assyrian deportation was practiced, 4,500,000 people were forcibly uprooted and exiled.

The largest single deportation was 208,000 taken from Babylonia in the south into Assyrian territory in the north. *These numbers dwarf even the highest estimates for the Babylonian Exile of the Jews from Judah.*

Significantly, it is clear that whole families were deported by both the Neo-Assyrians and the Neo-Babylonians. This is concluded from (1) the typical phrase "people, great and small, male and female...."[59] (2) the reliefs, and (3) administrative lists of deportees (including the so-called Weidner Texts,[60] which were ration lists that referred specifically to young King Jehoiachin and sons, sons whom he did not have when he was deported, according to 2 Kings. Finally, (4) Jeremiah's letter to the exiles, advising them to "take wives and have sons, and take wives for your sons and give daughters in marriage..." (Jer. 29). Citing 2 Kings 15:29, 17:6, 24:14–16, and Jer. 52:28–30, the Neo-Babylonian system appears to have been more selective, rather than simply deporting large portions of the populations. It is clear that the purpose of taking whole families is to remove the major incentive to return to the homeland and thus to encourage settlement. In the case of those Judeans who stayed after the restoration, this policy appears to have succeeded.

The condition of the earlier Assyrian exiles appears to reflect their economic importance. Chains were rare, and animals and supplies are depicted in the reliefs. In cuneiform texts one finds commands of rulers to take care of prisoners and prevent the soldiers from taking advantage of them.[61]

Josephus, however, in his review of the history of the "prisoners of war" taken to Babylon, spoke of binding, and possibly chains. How far this can be taken to be historically reliable, and how far it is reconstruction on the basis of his time period is unclear. Note also the language about "fetters" in Jer. 40:1 (cf. Nahum 3:10).[62]

It is furthermore interesting to note that deportees' communities had a typical "minority" role, supported by a cuneiform letter (ABL 915), a letter by "exiles" requesting protection from the local population.[63] In sum, the aims of deportation were decidedly imperialist.

While deportees were sometimes presented to the Temple or to officials of the royal army, they appear not to have been considered a special or separate class, although one does find the stereotypical phrase about "counting them [conquered peoples] among the Assyrians, together with the citizens/subjects of Assyria."[64] However, this phrase is not consistently used, and the reliefs from a later period depict hard physical labor. Finally, information increases about distribution of the spoils of war among Assyrians.

With regard to the general practice of deportation, we have no reason to doubt, from the less plentiful evidence that is available from the Neo-Babylonian era, that the Chaldeans were effective students of the martial tactics of the Neo-Assyrians. While specific details of practice differ (note, for example, the centralization policy of the Chaldeans whereby exiles were brought into the Babylonian heartland, in contrast to the Assyrian practice of exchanging populations) the imperial power exhibited in these actions is more starkly presented in the Neo-Assyrian materials only because of the wealth of extant archaeological data from that period.

Biblical traditions of proclamation against Babylon lead one to believe that Babylonian policies were severe. The words of the oracles in Jer. 50:1–51:58 threaten punishment of Babylon for its severity (50:15–16, 29, 51:20–22) and idolatry (50:2, 36, "a sword for her diviners,"

51:44, etc.). A tradition of religious temptation is associated with Babylon in Ezekiel, Daniel A and B, and long into the Intertestamental and Common era.[65] The imagery of "prison" and "prisoners" is a significant metaphor from the exilic period (see discussion below). All of these observations support the contention that the details of the Neo-Assyrian practice serve to illuminate the tactics and policies of the Neo-Babylonian Empire. In sum, Exile was a punishing experience, more effective than any symbol left in the homeland, which unavoidably reminded the Jews that they were conquered.

How many Judeans were deported to the Babylonian heartland?

Given these general remarks about the policy of deportation, we can see the debate about the numbers involved in the Babylonian Exile of the Jews in a better perspective. Unfortunately, there are factors that make any conclusions on this question highly doubtful. First, we do not know if only men are counted in the text, although many scholars have assumed this to be the case. The text of Kings uses only *'am* ("people"), as do Jeremiah and Chronicles. The Golah List of Ezra 2 ‖ Neh. 7, which lists families, apparently counts only men, so this seems a fair assumption, given the predominantly patriarchal structure of the time. Second, if families are to be estimated (and we have established that they were definitely included among the exiles) by what number does one multiply? A wife and two children sounds too modern. Three children? Six? Estimates will obviously vary widely, depending on one's decision on this matter. Certainly, the ancient Hebrews considered large families to be a blessing.[66] Thirdly, we must contend with the problems of determining the population of Jerusalem and Judah, so as not to "allow" too high a figure for the number of exiles — assuming (as most scholars now do) that the majority of the population was left in the land. Finally, there are the problems of the total figures in the text themselves, and of how many different events of "exile" there were.

First, let us consider the numbers themselves. 2 Kings 24:14 says that there were 10,000 captives, but then in v. 16, it lists 7,000 "men of valor," and 1,000 craftsmen. Jer. 52:28ff. lists the following: in Nebuchadnezzar's seventh year, 3023 Jews, in his eighteenth year, 832, and in the twenty-third year, 745, yielding a total of 4,600. On the other hand, the Golah List of the return suggests the number of those who returned (if that is what this list really is) as 42,360.

In a very interesting suggestion, Wurz has noted the frequency of citations in the Bible that separate Jerusalem from the surrounding "cities of Judah."[67] On this basis, Wurz wonders whether Jeremiah 52:28 records an earlier deportation from the countryside ("cities of Judah") of roughly 3,000 before the larger deportation from Jerusalem itself, which would accord with the second figure of 2 Kings 25, roughly 7,000. Thus, the first figure in 2 Kings 25 is the total of the two, or roughly 10,000 for the total of this exile. Wurz himself believes that the total number may be between 70,000 and 80,000 for all the exiles, from all "four" exile events (the earliest he considers is reported in Daniel 1:1, and hinted at in Josephus, *Ant.,* 10.6.1 87, i.e., Nebuchadnezzar's "fourth year").[68]

The usual figure is taken to be "a typical family" times the 4,600 who are assumed to be only men, and thus the result is in the vicinity of 20–25,000 (four or five members of an immediate family).[69] However, if only "important" men were counted, e.g., heads of households, then the total figure could easily be much higher, and without too much imagination could approach the higher figures suggested by Wurz. If Albright once argued, on the basis of archaeological remains, that the population of Judah in the eighth century was approximately 250,000 and fell to roughly half that number between 597 and 586, then surely we can find a reasonable middle ground.[70] But once it is granted that a body of people were exiled large enough to form large "communities" of disaster and exile victims, then the specific numbers become less relevant. The more important question is whether the number left in the land was so small that the continued life of Judaism was necessarily with the exilic community. Therefore, the next issue for consideration must be the state of the land of Palestine during the Exile.

What happened to the Judeans left behind?

The books of Chronicles, with their emphasis on the land "enjoying its sabbaths" (2 Chron. 36:21), suggest that the land was completely desolate. In some measure, this is supported by archaeological evidence. The damage reflected in Jerusalem itself is extensive, although Stern has found examples of Babylonian/exilic era pottery to suggest that some culture and life continued in this period.[71] Lakhish received terrible punishment, with no signs of renewed activity until 450. 'En Gedi in the south shows further signs of destruction, although not as total as in Jerusalem itself.

Do we also have literary evidence for ascribing continued importance to the community that remained in Judah? Archaeological evidence can be cited for either side of the issue, and opinion has shifted toward the community that remained as a source of the major history book of the Bible, the Deuteronomic Historian. Noth originally suggested that the exiles were a "mere outpost," and the "real nucleus" of Israel remained in Palestine.[72]

The most definitive recent defense of the view that Judah remained the center of activity has come from Enno Janssen. Janssen suggested four reasons in addition to Noth's arguments in support of a Palestinian authorship for the Deuteronomic history. Considered together, these are

1. Noth thought that the sources of the Deuteronomic Historian were in the land, especially when the author deals with the local traditions from the area of Bethel and Mizpah.

2. Noth believed that the Deuteronomic Historian did not speak of a renewal of hope, but spoke in very dark tones in the depth of the crisis. To this, Janssen adds

3. the "paranetic" concern of the Deuteronomic Historian to preach against "Canaanization" of the cult would be sensible only where such pagan practices were a threat, namely, back in Palestine.

4. Solomon's speech (1 Kings 8:33f.) refers to the Temple as a place of prayer rather than offering, which may imply that offerings had ceased when it was destroyed.

5. The vivid descriptions of the destruction of the land suggest a people who saw this destruction, and the terms used are similar to those used for the destruction of Canaanites in the land.

6. Terms such as "Golah" and "Shevah" are hardly found in the Deuteronomic Historian.[73]

Jeremiah is clearly concerned with events in the land and remains the most important source for the political information about Gedaliah and the apparently "pro-Babylonian" factions. But some have suggested that the book of Jeremiah was redacted in Egypt.[74] Lamentations, on the other hand, is clearly from "the land."

If Janssen is correct, there is good ground for considering that there was, among those who remained behind, a prolific group of writers and, more importantly, a zealous group of faithful worshipers of God. This is particularly important in the light of the fact that there were others among the remaining population who interpreted the exile as punishment for Josiah's anti-syncretistic actions. Therefore those who remained in the land and remained faithful Yahwists confronted a resurgence of syncretistic practices (perhaps also noted in Ezekiel's vision of his return to the Temple in Ezek. 8).

The discussion regarding the cultic practice of those orthodox Yahwists left behind tends to focus on two key passages, i.e., Solomon's speech that refers to prayer instead of sacrifice, and Jer. 41:4–5, where a pilgrimage to the Temple site is apparently mentioned. Since Ezra 3:2–5 does not mention an old altar, the standard conclusion was that all sacrifice, all ritual, had ceased. This was certainly the intention of the Babylonians who destroyed the Temple. Welch, however, had suggested otherwise.[75] He was mainly concerned with the re-establishment of the Temple community, but his most interesting contribution is his suggestion that Nehemiah 10:1bff. and 29ff. refer to a covenant made by those Jews who still lived in Palestine between the fall of Jerusalem and the return (in 522–520) of a substantial number of the exiles under the leadership of Zerubbabel and Jeshua.

Welch reasons that Nehemiah legislated *after* the practices mentioned in v. 10, and thus one cannot reason that these passages deal with Israelites acting in *obedience* to Nehemiah's legal enactions. The problem is that Ezra 3:3ff. indicates a new altar, implying that no other altar was there in its place before. Ezra 6:3 is taken to be a reference to altar practices before the Exile, not immediately before the rebuilding of the Temple. Ezra 4:2 certainly does appear to suggest that a group of people were offering some form of sacrifice until the restoration — but the implication of "since Esarhaddon brought us here" would call this passage into question, since this refers to a time preceding even the beginning of the Exile by almost a century (the fall of Samaria, 722). Furthermore, the classic passage in Jeremiah that mentions celebrants from the North uses terms that can refer to cereal and incense offerings in the absence of animal sacrifice, and we may note with Jones that the Elephantine sanctuary was permitted these forms of sacrifice even after their inquiry to the Palestinian officials.[76] Thus, whatever forms of ritual practice these are, they are not necessarily indications of full animal sacrifice, but may indicate some use of the Temple ruins.

Jones further argues on the basis of what he sees as an emerging Deuteronomic "anti-Temple" or "non-Temple" piety that was "outside of sacrifice." This can be illustrated in Psalms, such as 40:6–8, 51, 69, and 102, as well as the Solomonic prayer mentioned in 2 Kings 8:46ff. All this results in Jones's conclusions, against Welch, that sacrifice must have ceased in order for this kind of piety to arise.

A key point is whether the theology of "non-Temple piety" was formulated in Palestine or during the Exile. Naturally, the exiles would formulate some kind of non-Temple piety — since for them there was no Temple, even if some kind of cult continued in the ruins of the Temple back in Palestine. A source of conflict may well have been those who returned from Exile finding another group with a separately developed cultic tradition that used the Temple ruins, or developing a non-Temple theology when the exiles have looked forward to the rebuilding of the Temple. The fact that a community in Palestine continued to exist with its own ritual traditions as well as the likelihood that there was a resurgence of pagan ritual and worship supports a view of social conflict in the post-exilic community, by drawing many possible lines that such a conflict might follow, e.g., exiles vs. pagan Palestinians or exiles vs.

Yahwistic cult of the Temple ruins. This will be pursued in more detail below.

Finally, Graham has gathered the textual and archaeological evidence available in an attempt to see how economic activity may have continued in Palestine under Babylonian rule. Taking the references to "vintners" in 2 Chron. 26:10, 2 Kings 25:12, Jer. 52:16, and Isa. 61:5 (but not Joel 1:11), Graham points to workers *in service of authority.* Evidence of jar handles from Mozah and possibly Gibeon also suggests continued agricultural activity in Palestine after the Exile. But whether this was independent or in the service of Babylonian rule is unstated. Graham believes that the use of terminology suggests service of the king rather than independent work.[77]

The work on Palestine during the Exile, however, does not justify Noth's belief that the exiles were "merely an outpost." As will be shown their unique social and religious attitudes became major determinants in the post-exilic reconstruction. Scholarly work on the continued religious and cultural life back in Palestine, however, creates even more support for religious and social conflict at the return. This will be developed at some length in the last chapter below.

What do we know about the life of the exiles
from literary or archaeological sources?

As we have stated, we have no direct evidence of Neo-Babylonian treatment of deportees generally, with the interesting exception of the so-called Weidner texts.

These texts are lists of oil and grain rations given to the specifically mentioned Jehoiachin, the "prince" of Judah (a title to be expected, since the Babylonians had placed Zedekiah on the throne of Judah in his place.) The problem with this "ration list" is that we have no way of determining for certain the number in Jehoiachin's entourage, and thus we are not able to decide whether the portions are generous or not. Weidner himself assumes that the tablets reveal stringent security, but not physical mistreatment.[78] But with such slim and uncertain evidence I cannot go along with Weidner's confident view.

There has been work with "name" (onomastica) texts from Mesopotamian sources, but strained assumptions have also been defended solely on the basis of ethnic names, e.g., theophorous names in the case of the Jews. The use of onomastica in determining social factors strikes me as perilous, but worthy of consideration. The discovery in 1893 of a number of documents in Nippur that turned out to be "business records" from a "company" known today as the "Murashu family"[79] stirred a great deal of interest, particularly because of the presence of clearly Hebrew names among the some 2,500 names cited therein. Already in

1910, Samuel Daiches attempted to glean demographic/historical information from these names. Daiches identified thirty-eight Hebrew names, of which eleven did not occur in the Old Testament at all, and sixteen only in post-exilic books. The other eleven occurred through the Old Testament with varied frequency.[80]

The majority of the theophorous elements are based on *Yah* rather than *el.* Daiches believed that this was intended to make a clear theological distinction from *el,* which was a widely used Semitic term for a divinity. Daiches perhaps strained the evidence when he concluded: "We thus see that the Babylonian Jews were firm in their belief in God and were greatly attached to their land and brethren."[81] A more interesting suggestion, however, was Daiches's view that the name "Sabbtai" reflected the growing importance and popularity of the Sabbath as a diaspora "mark" of the Hebrews. This same point is picked up more recently in onomastic studies.[82]

More extensive is M. D. Coogan's monograph, which cautiously agrees with Daiches, seeing the popularity of this name as indicative of an attitude toward a social "marker" such as observance of the Sabbath.

Coogan believes that the exile had major influences on the names used by the Jews. The first is the use of loan names, i.e., *šešbassar,* Zerababel, and, interestingly, *mordekay* (mar-duk-a), formed from the name of Babylon's patron god, Marduk. Most of the names, with the notable exception of Mordecai, are neutral and non-theophorous (Ezra 2:11, 8:11, 10:28; Neh. 7:16, 10:16). Such an apparent reticence to use theophorous names *may* show "a religious sensitivity, an unwillingness on the part of at least some to adopt Mesopotamian deities as theophorous elements."[83] Secondly, Coogan cites "lexical" influences. Roots that were rare in previous biblical material turn up with more frequency in exile. Some of these may be due to homonyms, that is, names that are Hebraic, but sound sufficiently like Akkadian names to attract little attention, like *'el* and Jacob, which sounds like the Akkadian *qabu.*

Onomastic evidence is not very solid ground for philosophical arguments. Taking Zerubbabel as an example, here is a Davidic son in whom messianic hopes were placed, yet bearing a distinctly Babylonian name. Furthermore, Nebuchadnezzar and Pharaoh Necho both *changed* names in the act of dominance over a vassal (Daniel, 2 Kings 23:34, 2 Kings 24:17), and in the case of Jehoiakim, it was a change to a good Hebrew Yahwist name! Indeed, in the book of Daniel, emphasis is placed on the fact that *despite* the change of the name of the Jews, they were still loyal and observant Jews. One therefore cannot be certain about using onomastic evidence to draw sociological or theological, much less demographic, conclusions. A "pagan" name does not necessarily mean a rejection of Yahwistic practice or faith.

The argument for the increasing popularity of certain names seems to be on more logical ground. The increasing use of the names with the root *ŠLM* is possibly significant, in the light of the desire for peace among those who have enjoyed so little peace.[84]

Furthermore, studies of the Elephantine documents reveal that the Egyptian Jewish community, while not exiles in the same sense as the deportees of Assyria and Babylonia, also had an increasing use of the names such as Haggai and Sabtai,[85] making clear reference to the social "markers" of the Jews in reference to Sabbath and festivals.

Zadok concludes from his onomastic and economic survey of the Murashu documents that in the Persian period the majority of the Jews were small farmers and agriculturalists. This conclusion is based on the kind of contracts in which their names appear. He furthermore concludes that by the time of the mid-Persian period, the social circumstances did not differ significantly between Jews in Mesopotamia and Jews in Palestine.[86] Do the names of Jews reflect social conditions under the Babylonian rulers? Zadok believes that conditions must not have been much different from the later Achaeminid period, but one must keep in mind that the onomastic evidence of the Marashu tablets come from a *much* later period. What about Babylonian society itself?

The noted Soviet scholar M. A. Dandamayev suggests a four-part division of Chaldean society. At the top is the person with full civil rights. This social standing, however, included a wide variety of occupations, both rich and poor together. The significant aspect of this seems to be the political power of this class in terms of participation in political life. Those that did not own land within the city's lands had no part in civil government. This landless class would include free-born persons, but foreign officials and aliens (merchants, craftsman) were included in this category as well. This category then merges into the third class that included those who were assigned to officials or to royal and Temple lands. They were not slaves that could be bought and sold, but were without civil rights. Fourth was slavery proper. Dandamayev, however, has found no evidence for a large slave class. As opposed to Rome and Greece, the economy was not suited to absorb large numbers of slaves.[87] Slavery requires supervision, free labor less so. This would appear to add further weight to Zadok's conclusions about the socio-economic "location" of foreign exiles — at least in terms of questioning a form of chattel slavery as foreign to the Neo-Babylonian social structure. However, J. M. Wilkie believes that the social state of the exiles was not uniform during the period of Exile. This is a significant departure from the typical scholarly view about the Exile, which suggests that life could not have been too bad.[88] Do we really understand what we mean, however, when we speak of slavery in different historical periods? This is a complicated question.

Slavery and the Symbols of Power

Slavery is the most explicit example of dominated minorities. It is often suggested in studies of the Babylonian Exile that the exiles were not slaves. This argument is usually accompanied by references to late biblical texts that mention economically prosperous Jews who either stayed in Mesopotamia because of their success, or contributed heavily to the return from Exile (Ezra 2 ‖ Neh. 7). It is important to point out, however, that there appeared to be a difference in the economic contributions as recorded in Ezra 1 for Sheshbazzar's return, and the more affluent contributions of Ezra 2, under Zerubbabel's return. Galling reasoned that the "success" of the Babylonian Jews was in the time between the fall of Babylon to Cyrus and the return under Zerubbabel.[89] Further, reference is made to the Murashu documents, which mention the names of Jews in the contexts of land contracts (see above). Other than the texts themselves, which are considered in detail below, it is important to clarify the meaning and possible complications of using the term "slavery" in the context of the Babylonian Exile.

Until 1920, almost all slavery studies were limited to classical sources for Greek and Roman slavery and to antebellum American slavery. This exclusive scholarly attention led to many false assumptions. Although all writers were aware that slavery was widespread:

1. Slavery was seen as a stage of development.

2. Progressive development was seen in slavery: it was "better than" mass killings, for example.

3. There was a connection seen between slavery and economic development.

4. All scholars saw gradations and differences in the phenomenon of slavery itself.

5. Labor was only one of the uses to which slaves were put.

6. Thus slavery did not always mean that slaves were defined as "property."

7. As slavery was seen as a point in progress, it was not analyzed as a thing in itself.

8. Co-existing features that would lead to a more functionalist analysis were not noted because of the evolutionary view of economic systems.[90]

Marxism provided a convincing explanation for slavery, and therefore attention was focused on the level of economic development of the society in question. But economics was clearly not the only, or even the predominating, factor in the cases where slavery was far from a financially viable institution. Furthermore, it was found that slavery did not exist in every instance where economic conditions were favorable to slavery.

With the decline of classical education, American slavery became the prime example of the institution so that some other slave systems were not even recognized. In some systems former slaves were made pseudo-relatives as a matter of public myth that benefited all concerned, and no informant in such a circumstance was going to rock the boat by explaining this to anthropologists or other outsiders who inquired about their status. In other cases, slaves were often addressed with kinship names, but in some places these names convey authority and subordination, not nurture or closeness.[91] This, too, was not fully understood by anthropologists whose image of slavery was dominated by the Afro-American system.

Among Africanists, slavery once again became a subject of interest after 1960, and since that time, the problem of definition has become critical. Afro-American slavery was no longer accepted as the paradigm, because there were so many unique features about it, among them:

1. Slavery was exclusively for production labor.

2. Slavery was linked to an international market.

3. Masters did not marry slaves.

4. Slavery and racism were inter-mixed.

5. Therefore, there was an inhibition about using slaves in a variety of contexts.[92]

Clarifying the definition of slavery mitigates against over-confident assertions that the Jews in Babylon were, or were not, slaves, without giving prior consideration to assumptions. Some of the problems include (1) the meaning of "property" — a meaning that is not the same in different social contexts, (2) the assumption in post-Enlightenment society of the "un-naturalness" of slave relationships, (3) questions arising in situations where labor is not a clear aspect of that relationship, and, finally, (4) the place of coercion and the meaning of freedom.[93]

The way around the problems of definition, according to Kopytoff, is a social analysis of slavery:

> The slave begins as a social outsider and undergoes a process of becoming some kind of insider. A person, stripped of his previous social identity, is put at the margins of a new social group and is

given a new social identity in it.... The sociological issue in slavery is thus not the dehumanization of the person, but rather his or her re-humanization in a new setting and the problems that this poses for the acquisitors.[94]

This symbolic analysis is preeminently represented by Patterson in his book *Slavery and Social Death.*[95] Patterson reviewed the structure of the slave relationship using data from over forty different slave systems from all over the world and in different time periods. Common to all is the significance of symbolic institutions:

> The symbolic instruments may be seen as the cultural counterpart to the physical instruments used to control the slave's body. In much the same way that...whips were fashioned from different materials, the symbolic whips of slavery were woven from many areas of culture. Masters all over the world used the special rituals of enslavement upon first acquiring slaves: the symbolism of naming, of clothing, of hairstyle, of language, and of body markers. And they used, especially in the more advanced slave systems, the sacred symbols of religion.[96]

Patterson's symbolic analysis overcomes the problem of a purely economic view (Nieboer/Marx) that cannot account for purely symbolic slavery. In some slave-holding societies, slaves do not "produce" any profit and are dependent on slave-holders economically. A better definition would thus be "the permanent violent domination of natally alienated and generally dishonored persons."[97] Patterson notes the frequency of linguistic systems that use the same word for "foreigner" as "slave,"[98] which accords with the idea of alienation. "Natal alienation," a term often used by Patterson, refers to the ritual social death of the slave. The achievement of this state of natal alienation can be accomplished through many different ritualized ceremonies. The slave may, for example, "eat" his old identity, through a food ceremony, or have his name changed.[99]

Hence, according to Patterson's analysis, slavery is, in essence, removal of identity and "social death." Therefore, the reconstruction and resistance of an ethnic group can be seen as a potential response to just such a threat of social death. Van den Berghe's statement that slavery must be an individual phenomenon if it is to be considered slavery is born out by Patterson's analysis.[100] However, once we consider many of the techniques of slavery, and particularly the significance of the symbolization of domination that makes up the symbols of social death, then the modern reader of the Bible is prepared for the significance of the symbols of alienation that were associated with Neo-Babylonian rule.

For example, even though the stories of Daniel and his friends come from a late era in their final form, the symbol of name-changing is an important fact of their association with the Babylonian court and may not be an incidental detail. Furthermore, Nebuchadnezzar also changed the name of Zedekiah when he placed him on the throne of Judah in Jehoiachin's absence (2 Kings 24:17).

In this book, I do not argue that the Jews were "slaves" in Babylonia according to all the definitions of Patterson. But the dismissive statement that the Jews were not slaves can be a hasty generalization, depending on the "type," or characteristics, of slavery that are suggested by the term "slave." Indeed, we have important hints that the exiles did face symbolic *aspects* of slavery in Patterson's sense, and this insight must inform our view of the social conditions of the Exile. It is the symbols of power and conquest that form the main emphasis of Patterson's analysis, and we must be aware of the possible consciousness of these symbols in the exilic literature of the Old Testament. Seen in this light, both the policy of name changing and constant reassurances by the prophets that it was Yahweh who willed the Exile, and not the power of foreign gods, seem to reflect an awareness of the symbols of power that the exiles had to live with and struggle against. Slavery is a point on a "continuum of domination." The Babylonian exiles may not have been slaves, but evidence suggests they were most assuredly on this continuum.

In sum, we are unable to make definite conclusions about exilic existence apart from the biblical text itself. What these texts can reveal about the life of the exiles is the task for the chapters that follow.

NOTES

1. S. Herrmann, *A History of Israel in Old Testament Times,* trans. J. Bowden, rev. ed. (Philadelphia, 1981); J. Bright, *A History of Israel,* 3rd ed. (Philadelphia, 1981); J. Soggin, *A History of Israel* (London, 1984); B. Oded, "Judah and the Exile," in *Israelite and Judean History,* ed. J. H. Hayes and J. M. Miller (London, 1977); G. R. Berry, "The Unrealistic Attitude of Post-Exilic Judaism," *Journal of Biblical Literature,* 64 (1945); "The Old Testament Historiography of the Exilic Period," *Studia Theologica* 33 (1979), pp. 45–67; W. G. Lambert, "The Reign of Nebuchadnezzar I: A Turning Point in the History of Ancient Mesopotamian Religion," *The Seed of Wisdom* (Toronto, 1964); D. Winton Thomas, "The Sixth Century B.C.: A Creative Epoch in the History of Israel," *Journal of Semitic Studies,* 6 (1961); S. B. Frost, "The Death of Josiah," *Journal of Biblical Literature,* 87 (1968); C. F. Whitley, "Carchemish and Jeremiah," *Zeitschrift für die Alttestamentliche Wissenschaft* (Berlin), 80 (N.F. 39), 1968, pp. 38ff.; Simon Dubnov, *History of the Jews: From the Beginning to Early Christianity,* trans. Moshe Spiegal, vols. 1–3 (New York, 1967); D. N. Freedman, "Son of Man, Can These Bones Live?" *Interpretation,* 29 (1975); George Fohrer, *The History of Israelite Religion,* trans. D. Green (London, 1973); W.O.E. Oesterley and W. Robinson, *Hebrew Religion* (London, 1930); R. Braun, "Chronicles, Ezra and Nehemiah: Theology and Literary History," Studies in the Historical Books of

the Old Testament, *Supple. Vetus Testamentum*, 30 (1979); J. M. Myers, "Edom and Judah in the 6th-5th Centuries BC," H. Goedicke, ed. *Ancient Near Eastern Studies in Honor of W. F. Albright* (Baltimore, 1971); R. E. Clements, "The Prophecies of Isaiah and the Fall of Jerusalem in 587 BCE," *Vetus Testamentum*, 30, no. 4; Johannes Nikel, *Die Wiederherstellung des Jüdischen Gemeinwesens nach dem Babylonischen Exil* (Freibourg, 1900); Adolf Rozenzweig, *Das Jahrhundert nach dem Babylonischen Exil mit besonderer Rücksicht auf die religiöse Entwicklung des Judentums* (Berlin, 1885); Abraham Kuenen, "Die Chronologie des persischen Zeitalters der Jüdischen Geschichte," *Gesammelte Abhandlungen zur Biblischen Wissenschaft*, trans. K. Budde (Leipzig, 1894); E. Meyer, *Die Entstehung des Judentums* (Halle, 1896); J. Wellhausen, "Die Rückkehr der Juden aus dem babylonischen Exil," *Nachrichten von der Königlichen Gesellschaft der Wissenschaften zu Göttingen* (Göttingen, 1895); K. Balzter, "Das Ende des Staates Juda und die Messias-Frage," *Studien zur Theologie der Alttestamentlichen Überlieferungen*, Rendtorff and Koch (Berlin, 1961); C. H. Gordon, *The World of the Old Testament* (London, 1935); H.C.M. Vogt, *Studie zur Nachexilischen Gemeinde in Esra-Nehemia* (Werl, 1966); W. D. Davies and L. Finkelstein, eds., *The Cambridge History of Judaism, 1, The Persian Period* (Cambridge, 1984); K. Galling, *Studien zur Geschichte Israels im persischen Zeitalter* (Tübingen, 1964).

2. Recent theories suggest that the "J" source is exilic. The first work to appear on this theme is perhaps the most formidable in scope and depth: Thomas Thompson's *The Historicity of the Patriarchal Narratives* (Berlin and New York, 1974).

It has often been suggested, especially by the Albright school, that the patriarchal narratives reflect aspects of the second millennium that we can recognize from archaeological data, especially from texts such as the Nuzi tablets. But Thompson charges that those scholars who have placed the patriarchs in the first half of the second millennium have considered *only* the material from that time period, and not the material from later eras.

After an analysis of migration and settlement patterns in the second millennium, Thompson rejects the common assumption that these patterns resemble the patriarchal milieu: "We cannot be justified, no matter what the linguistic affiliations are, in speaking of the Early West Semites in Ur 3 and the OB period as a single unified group.... If migrations and movements can be seen, it is from the peripheral regions into the settled areas. No movement whatever is discernible which resembles a movement from Ur towards the NW to Harran. If a trend is to be noticed, it is in the opposite direction!... In no way does this resemble the traditions about the patriarchs in Genesis.... We do not have what might be described as a general wandering of nomadic groups (among whom we can somehow imagine the family of Abraham); we have rather a picture of West Semitic immigrants" (Thompson, *The Historicity of the Patriarchal Narratives*, p. 87).

In 1975, Van Seters argued in *Abraham in History and Tradition* (New Haven and London, 1975) that nomadic existence was possible only in the *first* millennium, since that is the earliest record we have of the domesticated use of the camel as a beast of burden; and not until the eighth and seventh centuries, notes Van Seters, did this caravaning use become common. Furthermore, the familial structure of the patriarchal stories suggest households augmented by subordinates, slaves, etc., in contrast to Ishmaelites, who were considered truly nomadic.

In a related article, "Confessional Reformulation in the Exilic Period"(*Vetus Testamentum*, 22 [1972]), Van Seters cites the statement in the exilic prophet Ezekiel (20:5-6) and points out that the promises of God are made to those in *Egypt*, but not to earlier figures. Indeed, in Ezek. 33:24, Abraham does turn up, but in a context where the conditionless promise given to him for a nation as his progeny in J is contradicted. The exilic prophets know only of an Exodus tradition. Finally, Van Seters argues that Deuteronomy knows of patriarchs in the context of the *conditional* giving of the land, while J sees the promises given to the patriarchs as *unconditional.*

Finally, in 1976, H. H. Schmids's work, *Der sogenannte Jahwist* (Zurich, 1976) appeared (with a title that rather reveals the iconoclastic perception that Schmid had of the implications of his work). Schmid works with the *Moses* material. Beginning with the generally recognized feature that the image of Moses in the E-Hosea-Deuteronomy matrix appears to be influenced by the view of the prophets that these documents reveal, Schmid considers the call of the prophets and compares these elements with the call of *Moses* (pp. 19–21). The fact that J follows this pattern for the call of Moses proves for Schmid that J must have known the prophetic materials. Otherwise, we are left with the clear difficulty that patterns such as those found in materials like Exod. 3, Judg. 6, and 1 Sam. 9 (which suggest a common literary pattern) do not appear again until the written prophets. Schmid asks whether we are supposed to believe that this was simply "forgotten" in the supposed meantime.

Even by literary standards going back to Gunkel, long speeches between man and God suggest a Deuteronomistically influenced speech style. Schmid concludes that the "Yahwist" exhibits stylistic techniques (in the presentation of Moses as a prophet) that could not be any older than the monarchy and the written prophets. Even further, Schmid believes that Exod. 3f. has its *engsten Parallelen*, its closest parallels, in Deuteronomic theology — and thus post-Josianic Judah.

It is not appropriate to argue these points in detail here (that would be a separate book). It is certain that the exilic dating of elements of J material would have added a few interesting source materials for this study, but would not provide us with substantially contradictory materials that would seriously modify our conclusions from analysis of exilic material. Nevertheless, one could imagine how analysis of the familial structure of the patriarchal materials, for example, may substantiate our theories about the impact of the Exile on social structure. Interestingly, the suspicion of Van Seters and Thompson that the "ger-like" existence of Abraham may have exilic overtones would confirm fairly impressively the sociological insights of Weber's *Ancient Judaism* when he pointed out precisely this aspect of the "landless" patriarchs as significant for the exilic-post-exilic nature of Judaism. In reaction to Schmids's work on Moses, and in relation to our own work on elders, one is impressed with the potential light that could come from explaining the story of the appointment of "elders" to "ease Moses' burden" as related not only to the exilic role of the elders, but also to the significant number of elders, the important number seventy.

Finally, the often noted "pacifistic ethos" of the patriarchs in J (Von Rad) would combine with the "demilitarized" nature of the P narratives and the additions to Isaiah (chaps. 2, 4, 9, 11, 19, etc.), as well as Jeremiah's attitudes, to confirm the interesting theories of Lind on precisely this issue; it would, however, shift this attitude to the exilic, rather than the premonarchical period indicated in Lind's thesis (*Yahweh Is a Warrior* [Scottdale, Pa., 1982]).

A detailed study of the sociological conditions suggested by J material should *follow* the successful debate begun by a sociological analysis of *known* exilic materials and therefore will not be considered as primary materials in this study.

3. Peter Ackroyd, *Exile and Restoration* (London, 1968).

4. See the notes on the theological work on Exile.

5. See Martin Noth, *The History of Israel,* 2nd ed. (London, 1960), p. 289, and H. L.,Ginsberg, "Judah and the Transjordan States from 734 to 582 BCE," *Alexander Marx Jubilee Volume* (New York, 1950).

6. Benedict Otzen, "Israel Under the Assyrians," *Mesopotamia,* no. 7, ed. M. T. Larsen, "Power and Propaganda" (Copenhagen, 1979).

7. Mogens Trolle Larsen, "The Tradition of Empire in Mesopotamia," *Mesopotamia* no. 8, p. 86.

8. John McKay, *Religion in Judah under the Assyrians,* Studies in Biblical Theology, no. 26 (London, 1973); see chap. 2, "The Reign of Ahaz..." for this discussion. Also, Morton Cogan, *Imperialism and Religion,* SBL Monograph Series, 19 (Chicago, 1974).

9. McKay, ibid., p. 78.

10. Olmstead, *History of Palestine and Syria to the Macedonian Conquest* (New York, 1931), quoted in McKay, ibid. This is surely an exaggeration on Olmstead's part. This phrase is used over and over again in the chapter, and in wider context, and in no case is the meaning what Olmstead is suggesting. As Brown, Driver, and Briggs suggest in their

Hebrew Lexicon, this phrase can have a causative meaning, which McKay does not seem to make much of; this is surely a reaction too far in the opposite direction.

11. On this issue, see A. Alt, "Die Rolle Samarias bei der Entstehung des Judentums," *Kleine Schriften zur Geschichte des Volkes Israel,* 2 (Munich, 1953), pp. 316ff., and E.C.B. McLaurin, "The Beginnings of the Israelite Diaspora," *Australian Journal of Biblical Archaeology,* 1, no. 4 (1971), for another view, specifically with regard to the Northern exiles; see also C. Gordon, "Colonies and Enclaves," *Pubblicazioni Dell'Instituto Per L'Oriente,* no. 52, Studi Orientalistici in onore di Giorgio Levi Della Vida (Rome), 1, no. 2 (1956), and the article by Stephanie Dalley, which the author was kind enough to let me read before publication, "Foreign Chariotry and Cavalry in the Army of Tiglath-Pileser III and Sargon II."

12. It is interesting to note that the Rab-šāqē describes the deportation itself in terms meant to make it sound almost inviting!

13. Georges Roux, *Ancient Iraq* (London, 1964), p. 295.

14. Ibid.

15. On this issue, see M. Weinfeld, "Cult Centralization in Israel in the Light of a Neo-Babylonian Analogy," *Journal of Near Eastern Studies,* 23 (1964).

16. See H.W.F. Saggs, "The Nimrud Letters," *Iraq,* 17 (1955), pp. 21ff.

17. For a discussion of the various views, see A. Malamat, "The Last Wars of the Kingdom of Judah," *Journal of Near Eastern Studies,* 9, no. 13 (1950), pp. 220 ff. See also M.D. Rowton, "Jeremiah and the Death of Josiah," *Journal of Near Eastern Studies,* 10 (1951).

18. Malamat, ibid., p. 223.

19. Rowton, "Jeremiah and the Death of Josiah," p. 129.

20. Malamat, "The Last Wars of the Kingdom of Judah," pp. 218–219.

21. Ibid., p. 223.

22. Ernst Kutsch, "Das Jahr der Katastrophe: 587 v. Chr.; Kritische Erwägungen zu neueren chronologischen Versuchen" *Biblica,* 55 (1974), p. 529.

23. See J.N. Graham, "Vinedressers and Plowmen: 2 Kings 25:12 and Jeremiah 52:16," *Biblical Archaeologist,* March 1984.

24. Roux, *Ancient Iraq,* p. 351.

25. C.J. Gadd, "The Harran Inscriptions of Nabonidus," *Anatolian Studies,* 8 (1958), pp. 35ff.

26. K. Galling, *Studien zur Geschichte Israels im Persischen Zeitalter,* p. 11.

27. See Brian Lewis, *The Sargon Legend,* American Schools of Oriental Research Dissertation Series, no. 4 (Cambridge, Mass, 1980).

28. See J.M. Cook, *The Persian Empire* (London, 1983).

29. The Nabonidus Chronicle is among the texts found in James Pritchard, *Ancient Near Eastern Texts,* 3rd ed. (Princeton, N.J., 1969).

30. See ibid., pp. 306ff.

31. The Cyrus Cylinder is found in ibid., p. 315.

32. Ibid., p. 306.

33. See D.L. Weisberg, *Guild Structure and Political Allegiance in Early Achaeminid Mesopotamia* (New Haven, 1967).

34. Wilhelm Th. in der Smitten, "Historische Problem zum Kyrosedikt und zum Jerusalemer Tempelbau von 515," *Persica,* 6 (1972–1974), pp. 167ff.

35. Elias Bickerman, "The Edict of Cyrus," *Journal of Biblical Literature,* 65 (1946). See also J. Harmatta, "The Literary Patterns of the Babylonian Edict of Cyrus," *Acta Antiqua* (Budapest), 19 (1971).

36. Galling, *Studien zur Geschichte Israels im Persischen Zeitalter.*

37. Alt, "Die Rolle Samarias bei der Entstehung des Judentums."

38. Galling, *Studien zur Geschichte Israels im Persischen Zeitalter,* p. 40.

39. Ibid., p. 57.

40. Ibid., p. 105.

41. George Sauer, "Serubbabel in der Sicht Haggais und Sacharjas," *Das Ferne und Nahe Wort*, Beihefte zur Zeitschrift für die Alttestamentliche Wissenschaft, 105 (Berlin, 1967).

42. The problem of "Artaxerxes" becomes clear (or unclear!) by skimming over the list of the Achaeminid kings:

Cyrus
Cambyses
Bardiya [Smerdis]
Darius
Xerxes 1 (486–465)
Artaxerxes 1 [Arshu?] (465–424)
Xerxes II (424)
Sogdianos (424–423)
Darius II [Ochos] (423–405/404)
Artaxerxes II [Arsakes] (405/404)–359/358
Artaxerxes III [Ochos] 359/337–336
Artaxerxes IV [Arses] 338/337–336
Darius III [Kodomannos] 336–330

(Cook, *The Persian Empire*, p. 266).

43. See W. T. in de Smitten, *Ezra*, Studia Semitica Neerlandica 15 (Assen, 1973).

44. M. Cogan, *Imperialism and Religion* (Chico, Calif., 1974), pp. 20–22; John McKay, *Religion in Judah under the Assyrians*.

45. Cogan, ibid., p. 22; see also ibid., p. 36 note 1.

46. Ibid., pp. 34 and 40.

47. Ibid., pp. 53 and 56.

48. Hermann Spieckermann, *Juda unter Assur in der Sargonidenzeit* (Göttingen, 1982).

49. Ibid., p. 309.

50. Ibid., p. 362.

51. Ibid., pp. 369–374.

52. E. W. Nicholson, "The Centralization of the Cult in Deuteronomy," *Vetus Testamentum*, 13 (1963), pp. 380ff.

53. Larsen, "The Tradition of Empire in Mesopotamia," p. 100.

54. See H.W.F. Saggs, "Assyrian Warfare in the Sargonid Period," *Iraq*, 25 (1963), esp. pp. 149ff.

55. See Mario Liverani, "The Ideology of the Assyrian Empire," *Mesopotamia*, no. 7.

56. See the interesting article on the art of propaganda by the placement of stelae in the palace, Julian Reade, "Ideology and Propaganda in Assyrian Art," *Mesopotamia*, no. 7; other articles in the same issue include work on Achaeminid art.

57. Liverani, "The Ideology of the Assyrian Empire," p. 307.

58. Bustenay Oded, *Mass Deportations and Deportees in the Neo-Assyrian Empire* (Wiesbaden, 1979). Note Tadmor's warning, "The Assyrian royal inscriptions, being by their very nature official documents of self-praise, demand from the historian a judicious critical approach" (H. Tadmor, "History and Ideology in the Assyrian Royal Inscriptions," *Orientis Antiqui Collectio*, 17 [Rome, 1981], p. 13).

59. Oded, ibid., p. 23.

60. See E. F. Weidner, "Jojachin, Konig von Juda, in Babylonischen Keilschrifttexten," *Melanges Syriens Offerts à Monsieur René Dussaud*, 2 (Paris, 1939).

61. Oded, *Mass Deportations*, p. 38.

62. Josephus, *Antiquities*, trans. Ralph Marcus, Loeb Classical Library, 6, p. 212ff.

63. Oded, *Mass Deportations*, p. 46.

64. Ibid., p. 81. In contrast, however, see Oates: "When the King of Assyria says of a conquered nation, 'With the people of Assyria I counted them...' it seems to mean that they were thence-forward privileged to share in increasingly heavy burdens of forced labour and military service. In such circumstances, they would be loyal as long as the

military success of Assyria assured them a certain prosperity, but they had no visible motive for risking their lives in its defense if it was hard-pressed. Once the weakness of Assyria became apparent, then the subject peoples had little to lose by changing sides.... "

65. See the fascinating article on the continued Exile concept in the late exilic and Intertestamental period by M. A. Knibb, "The Exile in the Literature of the Intertestamental Period," *Heythrop Journal,* 17 (1976), pp. 253ff.

66. See Lawrence Stager, "The Archaeology of the Family in Ancient Israel," in *BASOR,* 260 (1985), for archaeological arguments for family size.

67. Heinrich Wurz, "Die Wegführung der Juden durch Konig Nebukadnezzar II," Th.D. dissertation, University of Vienna, 1958 (unpublished), pp. 69 and 74. For example, Isa. 40:9; 44:26; Jer. 4:16; 9:10; 25:18; Zech. 1:12; Neh. 8:15; "cities of Judah," Jer. 7:17; 34:11; 6:13; etc.

68. Ibid., p. 36.

69. Ibid.

70. Albright, quoted in Saul S. Weinberg, "Post-Exilic Palestine: An Archaeological Report," *Proceedings of the Israel Academy of Science and Humanities,* 4 (1971), p. 79.

71. Weinberg, ibid., pp. 80–81; see also Ephraim Stern, *Material Culture of the Land of the Bible in the Persian Period, 538–332 BC* (Warminster, Eng., 1982, Hebrew edition, 1973), esp. p. 229.

72. Noth, *The History of Israel,* p. 296.

73. Enno Janssen, *Juda in der Exilszeit: Ein Beitrag zur Frage der Entstehung des Judentums* (Göttingen, 1956), pp. 17–18.

74. E. W., Nicholson, *Preaching to Exiles* (Oxford, 1970), pp. 116ff.

75. Adam Welch, *Post Exilic Judaism* (Edinburgh, 1935). But see also D. R. Jones, "The Cessation of Sacrifice after the Destruction of the Temple in 586 BC," *Journal of Theological Studies* (Oxford, London), 14 (1963).

76. Jones, ibid., pp. 14–15.

77. Graham, "Vinedressers and Plowmen."

78. Weidner, "Jojachin, Konig von Juda, in Babylonischen Keilschrifttexten," p. 927.

79. A. T. Clay and H. Hilprecht, *Business Documents of Murashu and Sons of Nippur* (Philadelphia); for a full bibliography and helpful introduction, see M. W. Stolper, "Management and Politics in Later Achaemenid Babylonia: New Texts from the Murasu Archive (vols. 1 and 2)," dissertation, University of Michigan, 1974.

80. Samuel Daiches, *The Jews in Babylonia in the Time of Ezra and Nehemiah according to Babylonian Inscriptions* (London, 1912), p. 28.

81. Ibid., p. 35.

82. Naomi Cohen, "Jewish Names as Cultural Indicators in Antiquity," *Journal for the Study of Judaism,* 7, no. 2 (1976–1977).

83. Michael David Coogan, *West Semitic Personal Names in the Murashu Documents,* (Harvard Semitic Monographs, no. 7 (Missoula, 1976), pp. 120–124; see also his "Life in the Diaspora" *Biblical Archaeologist,* 37 (1974), pp. 6ff.

84. Coogan, ibid., p. 85.

85. B. Porten, *Archives from Elephantine: The Life of an Ancient Jewish Military Colony* (Berkeley, 1968), p. 124; see also Ran Zadok, *The Jews in Babylonia During the Chaldean and Achaeminid Periods* (Haifa, 1979), pp. 22–23.

86. Zadok, ibid., pp. 50, 74, and 88.

87. Muhammed A. Dandamayev, "Social Stratification...," in *Acta Antiqua,* 1974; see also "The Neo-Babylonian Citizens," *KLIO,* 63 (1981), p. 98.

88. See J. M. Wilkie, "Nabonidus and the Later Jewish Exiles," *Journal of Theological Studies* (Oxford, London), 2 (1951).

89. Galling, *Studien zur Geschichte Israels im Persischen Zeitalter,* chap. 1, "The Golah List."

90. Igor Kopytoff, "Slavery," in *Annual Review of Anthropology,* ed. A. R. Beals, B. Spiegal, and S. Tyler (Palo Alto, Calif., 1982), p. 209.

91. Ibid., p. 215.

92. Ibid., p. 225.
93. Ibid., p. 220.
94. Ibid., p. 221.
95. Orlando Patterson, *Slavery and Social Death* (Cambridge, Mass., 1982).
96. Ibid., p. 8.
97. Ibid., p. 11.
98. Ibid., p. 40.
99. Ibid., p. 55.
100. See P. Van den Berghe, *The Ethnic Phenomenon* (New York, 1981).

Chapter 2

Sociological/Historical Paradigms

Without attempting a detailed history in chapter 1, I have tried to emphasize those aspects of the context of the Exile that provide significant background for textual analysis. Before turning to selected texts, however, we must consider the social constituents of exile itself, and how these illuminate a view of the Babylonian Exile.

First, the Babylonian Exile was certainly a crisis. Crisis itself has been a fruitful subject for analysis by sociologists. It was also a crisis that centered on a self-consciously *religious* group, and this means that the work of sociologists and anthropologists of religion is relevant, especially their work on the religious response to crisis in terms of intra-group reactions and leadership patterns, but also their analysis of the symbol structures of religion and how these change. As noted above, many Old Testament commentators have referred to these ancient exiles who went to Babylon as "prisoners of war," "refugees," or even "slaves." Each of these terms is associated with socio-anthropological assumptions, which should be examined. We know from the folklore of the post-exilic community, and indeed the activities of Ezra and Nehemiah and the priestly concerns of Ezekiel, that self-preservation was a major concern — preservation not only of traditions and values, but perhaps on occasion even physical survival. The success of this preservation can be considered "reconstruction" and "resistance," that is, reconstruction in the sense of maintaining identity in a new circumstance, and resistance to pressures of a human or ecological nature that would threaten the continued existence of this reconstructed identity.

Furthermore, we know that various kinds of literature were unique to the exilic-post-exilic period. We know of many difficulties and conflicts in the post-exilic community. One could continue with more specific "social" aspects of the Exile event that would lend themselves to analysis. In the following chapters, various specific sociological/anthropological aspects of the Exile will be outlined in relation to secondary literature. By the very nature of this kind of argument, therefore, rather extensive notation of secondary literature will be necessary, as will the patience of the reader.

The Babylonian Exile as Crisis:
Clarifying the Event

In *Disaster and the Millennium* Barkun investigated why certain kinds of crises create significant ideological and sociological behavioral responses, and others do not.[1] He concluded that it is when *multiple* disasters occur that the necessary conditions for a need for religious explanation also occur. Borrowing a term coined by Anthony Wallace,[2] Barkun suggests that the crisis must affect the "mazeway" of the people, that is, *the sense that one has of meaning and order:*

> Disaster, by removing the familiar environment, removes precisely those frames of reference by which we normally evaluate statements, ideas and beliefs. Belief systems which under non-disaster conditions might be dismissed now receive sympathetic consideration.... It is small wonder that among persons so situated doctrines of imminent salvation should find such a ready acceptance. Warnings may mitigate effects, but not if they are not accepted.[3]

The literature on the religious response to crisis has generally focussed on the term "millennialism." This term, however, should not be construed to be an anachronistic reference to the exclusively Christian term referring to the "thousand-year reign" of the book of Revelation. Sociologically, millennialism is most widely defined in terms of mass movements that, while experiencing social uprooting or confusion, seek solace in a religious oriented prediction that these catastrophic changes precede better social conditions. Such movements are associated with various kinds of social change, but the specific aspect of millennialist movements that has maintained the interest of sociologists of religion is the vast number of *cross-cultural cases* consisting of the same pattern of responses. This is most effectively demonstrated in Bryan Wilson's *Magic and the Millennium,* which represents the most sophisticated analysis of religious movements from virtually all kinds of societal, economic, and religious settings.[4]

Wilson redirected sociological interest in millennial-type phenomena by marshalling evidence so diverse as to correct the Western, largely Christian, bias of previous attempts to analyze religious movements as social movements (specifically exemplified in the work of Richard Niebuhr and Ernst Troeltsch).[5] By incorporating phenomena that did not "fit" these previous categories Wilson was able to expand the typology of movements into seven different although often co-existent ideologies. Wilson writes of "ideologies" rather than movements, because, as he has pointed out, a movement's "response to the world" encompasses more varied kinds of dynamics that may not be adequately categorized as organized "movements." Wilson suggests seven different "responses to the world":

1. *Conversionist response:* "The world is corrupt because men are corrupt: if men can be changed then the world will be changed.... Salvation is seen not as available through objective agencies, but only by a profoundly felt, supernaturally wrought transformation of the self."[6]

2. *Revolutionist response:* "Only the destruction of the world, of the natural but more specifically the social, order, will suffice to save men. This process of destruction must be supernaturally wrought, for men lack the power if not to destroy the world, then certainly to re-create it. Believers may themselves feel called upon to participate in the process,... but they know that they do no more than put a shoulder to an already turning wheel."[7]

3. *Introversionist response:* "The world [is] irredeemably evil and salvation [is] to be attained only by the fullest possible withdrawal from it. The self may be purified by renouncing the world and leaving it."[8]

4. *Manipulationist response:* "The manipulationist response is to seek only a transformed set of relationships — a transformed method of coping with evil.... Salvation is possible in the world and evil might be overcome if men learn the right means, improved technique, to deal with their problems."[9]

5. *Thaumaturgical response:* "The individual's concern is relief from present and specific ills by special dispensations. The demand for supernatural help is personal and local: its operation is magical."[10]

6. *Reformist response:* "...recognizes evil but assumes that it may be dealt with according to supernaturally-given insights about the ways in which social organization should be amended. Amendment of the world is here the essential orientation." [11]

7. *Utopian response:* "...to reconstruct the world according to some divinely given principles, to establish a new social organization in which evil will be eliminated. This response differs from the demand that the world be overturned (revolutionist) in insisting that men re-make it."[12]

Wilson states, in his programmatic introduction, that what all people seek is some form of "salvation," that is, deliverance from the present unacceptable conditions. Wilson is furthermore careful to point out that responses must fit the "plausibility structure" of a given society. These must therefore be considered in the *context of society,* not as independent features.

Millennialism, or indeed, Wilson's "responses to the world," require and depend upon alternative explanations being available to explain the tragedies. New explanations, new "mazeways" (Wallace), can lead to possible "revitalization" (renewal movements) in order to restructure society.[13]

This approach to religious/social responses to crises has suggested itself as a paradigm for a consideration of Hebrew prophecy.[14] It is not simply the crises of an individual that create group events, but the presence of crises so devastating that a group turns to the prophet and listens, rather than dismissing him or her. The prophet, after all, is not alone.

But what we are most interested in is conceptualizing the process of restructuring identity in conditions of crisis and the challenge to the "mazeways." "Mechanisms" can be seen at work in conditions of social crisis and interaction. One can assume, therefore, that an analysis of such mechanisms would be a most significant tool for understanding the nature of, and response to, a social crisis.[15]

Barkun and Wallace suggest that a crisis can threaten the very sense of group identity itself. In terms of the exegesis of biblical texts of the Exile, the sociological research on crisis and identity reformulation means that we must be open to dramatic changes in religious symbolism and social structure, even though one of the most important canons of biblical study has been the identification of *continuity* in Israelite faith and practice. For example, questions are asked about the roots of prophecy in Judges, or in Moses, or the attempt to find premonarchical "precedents" for the later kings. These approaches stress continuity. But if we begin our analysis of Exile with sociological studies of crisis, then we must be prepared to see unique mechanisms and dramatic changes, as means of reconstruction in the face of foundation-shaking events. It is only of limited value, therefore, to insist on an exegetical plan guided by the investigations of phenomena of continuity in motifs and institutions. The exegesis of the Exile as a crisis must be open to both change and continuity.

We can see in the book of Lamentations, while a product of those left behind,[16] witnesses to the depth of the crisis that the Chaldean defeat incurred. One of the powerful themes of Lamentations was precisely the unexpected nature of the defeat. The reader of Lamentations, therefore, becomes familiar with what Wallace called "mazeway" disruption. Lamentation literature is common among displaced peoples and a sociological analysis of lament literature would be an important approach to this genre. One could compare, for example, Okihiro's work on the lament literature that was essentially *created* from the Japanese-American internment of World War II[17] and Baskauskas's discussion of the theology of the "Worried Christ" that emerged in American Lithuanian immigrant neighborhoods, which he compared to the crisis of the Ibo of Biafra (Nigeria):

> Just as the Ibo petrified their grief in a posture of misery or ritual lament, always particularly liable to see themselves as victims marked for tragedy, so, too, the Lithuanian refugees focused on the Christ figure as portrayed in the Worrier...and saw a purpose in the vale of tears of their refugee experience.[18]

What we are more specifically interested in, however, are the behavioral responses rather than the ideological or religious responses that such a study of lament literature would deal with. The individual in crisis is a member of a group, and when the group as a whole experiences crisis, as we have seen, the behavior patterns are considerably magnified. In contrast to analysis of the individual, anthropological studies have focused on context analysis, focusing not only on the individual in relation to the group, but the group in relation to other groups.

Once we understand the importance of crisis, we can proceed to an analysis of the kind of crisis that the Exile represented. As we have seen in our historical reconstruction, the Exile represented military defeat and continued military domination, which daily reminded Judeans that they were no longer an independent people. Furthermore, for those deported to Mesopotamia, the crisis added the further dynamics of minority consciousness that continued to create social conflict after the Exile as well. (The "punishment for disobedience" in Deut. 28 describes powerlessness in the face of "foreigners," Deut. 28:32, 43, and 49). The awareness that the exiles were among "foreigners" was very great and continued to be a legacy of the Exile long into the Intertestamental literature (see, for example, the books of Baruch and the Epistle of Jeremiah).

The group nature of the crisis in 587 B.C.E. is important. According to recent research, refugee or minority groups are formed in significantly different ways. If a refugee or minority group is formed by the migration of individuals, the resulting relation of immigrants to each other, and to the host society, is significantly different from a refugee or minority group formed by the migration of groups.

William Petersen has constructed a general typology of migration that summarizes his research on a sociology of refugees. In chart A the agents that interact to cause the migration are listed in the first

Chart A
PETERSEN'S TYPOLOGY OF MIGRATION[19]

	Agents in Relation	Migratory Force	Class of Migration	Type Conservative	Innovative
1.	Nature vs. Man	Ecological push	Primitive	Wander-range	Flight
2.	State vs. Man	Migration policy	Forced or Impelled	Displacement (Flight)	Slave Coolie
3.	Man vs. "His Norms"	Higher Aspirations	Free	Group	Pioneer
4.	Collective Behavior	Social Momentum	Mass	Settlement	Urbanization

column. For example, the need to escape adverse weather conditions ob-viously results in what Petersen calls the "ecological push" to migrate. The "class" of the migration is self-explanatory in all four examples. The final column requires some explanation. Petersen's chart suggests a critical difference between "innovative" and "conservative" types of migration. This does not imply a value judgment, but simply the dif-ference of *who* made the primary decision to move. If the people made the decision, then it is "conservative," that is, they are trying to pre-serve something, or prevent something from happening. If, however, the people had little or no say in the decision to migrate, then Petersen classifies the migration as "innovative." This is clear in no. 2, where the agents are Man and the State. If the decision is *not* made by the people, but forced on them, *as in a military campaign,* then the result, sug-gests Petersen, is a social form, represented in recent history by either "slaves" or "coolie" labor.

Petersen's typology helps us to locate the elements on line 2 that relate to the Babylonian Exile as the result of a military campaign. Fur-thermore, his work helps us to see the significant social-psychological difference between a decision that is ultimately of the individual and one that is of the state:

> The difference is real...between the Nazis' policy (roughly 1933–38) of encouraging Jewish emigration by various anti-Semitic acts and laws, and the later policy (roughly 1938–45) of herding Jews into cattle-trains and transporting them to camps.[20]

This "decision" aspect can also determine the kinds of group structures found in the immigrant community itself and the perceived relationship to "home." Egon Kunz identified three types of social relationship to home among refugees.

The first type is found when individuals feel themselves "with" the majority, in opposition to the events at home that led to their decision to flee; home is desired, but the present political or social reality that led to flight is not.[21] For example, Baskauskas observed the processes of grief in the loss of homeland among Lithuanian refugees in the United States after World War II. This is a most revealing case. The expected need to preserve the culture of home results in a reification of memory in the context of hope:

> A major factor in blocking, or at least delaying, the integration of refugees is their failure to realize for years that departure from their former homes is final, that there can be no return and that they must remain in the country of relocation and rebuild their lives there. They instead fervently believe that their exile is temporary and that all of a sudden a radical change in the international situation will upset the status quo and enable them to return to their homes....
>
> The Lithuanian refugees... continued for years to speculate and anticipate when such an upheaval would occur and would interpret the news of the international arena in the light of such a reversal of their fates. This speculation of the future return and disbelief of the permanency of the present situation occurred while the refugees struggled to meet their survival necessities: providing food, shelter, clothing for their families.... This period of conservatism was further marked by an intense radicalized desire to preserve the totality of their culture in the new milieu.[22]

The second type is the individual who did not identify with the majority at home and includes social and religious *minorities*.[23] Thus, for example, the German or Swiss Mennonites, or the Russian Molokans and Dukhobors, or other religious sects, often have little sense of a national homeland, from which they feel alienated only *temporarily*.

The final category includes exiles who, for various political and/or philosophical reasons, do not feel any kinship with the population: "These self-alienated persons might retain some attachments to the panoramic aspects of their homelands, but their attitudes are overwhelmingly shaped by ideological considerations and their departure is a logical result of their alienation."[24]

As one would expect, those from Kunz's first type are more prone to shock, authoritarian attitudes, and indeed millennial expectations, because they had not previously been in a minority situation, and thus had neither experience nor "mobile identities" to draw upon, as is the case of the minority groups of type 2 (religious minorities as example) or the "experienced alienated" of type 3 (the classic examples being "exile" authors and artists, e.g., Thomas Mann, James Baldwin[25]).

Kunz and Petersen help us to refine contemporary examples for more significant comparison. What emerges from this research on refugee patterns is the important criterion that the Jewish exiles in Babylon did not come from a social situation where they were already a minority, although they had been faced with a military threat for a century or more. The dynamics of the *return* from Exile, quite to the contrary, as well as the Exile itself, take on a different set of sociological aspects, for the returned exiles had two generations of minority existence, and therefore could be expected to exhibit features somewhat different from Kunz's first type, including socio-psychological aspects of "experienced alienated" groups.[26] These socio-psychological elements suggest interesting alignments of social conflict in the post-exilic community, which we will consider below.

Identity and Ethnicity

If a social group is facing the kind of crisis that we have thus far considered, in what way can we refer to the "mazeway," the social construction of reality, that groups have? The most fruitful way to approach this problem is a consideration of *ethnic identity,* including the questions of (1) the preservation of self-definition, (2) identity in a minority context, and (3) a minority under domination. Ethnic identity involves some combination of identifiable cultural patterns such as a combination of kinship patterns, symbol systems, language and other forms of communication, artistic motifs, as well as religious traditions. To understand how to differentiate one group from another, many anthropologists have recently focused on the term "Ethnicity."[27]

Ethnicity is defined in different ways by anthropologists. The work of E. K. Francis is particularly impressive as it is an attempt to synthesize a comprehensive theory. Francis defines ethnicity as:

> ... the fact that (1) a relatively large number of people are socially defined as belonging together because of the belief in their being descended from a common ancestor, ... (2) on account of their belief they have a sense of identity, and (3) they share sentiments of solidarity. Shared ethnicity extends genealogical relationships to a wider population whose precise genealogical nexus is unknown or disregarded. Three basic propositions may be added;
>
> 1. Shared ethnicity becomes salient in social action orientation (*a*) if there is a contrast effect between two or more groups of people interacting in a given social context, and (*b*) if the contrast can be interpreted in ethnic terms.

2. The saliency of shared ethnicity as a principle of societal organization differs with the general type of society. Shared territory may serve a similar function in organizing and legitimizing a societal unit.

3. Where genealogical principles of social organization are dominant, there is a tendency to socially define a population sharing a common territory in terms of shared ethnicity.[28]

The importance of groups in contact is illustrated by the work of Frederick Barth, a Scandinavian anthropologist noted for his field studies on the Swat Pathan of Afghanistan and Pakistan.[29] Barth's difficulty in identifying clear social or tribal units among these mountain dwellers in interaction with other "groups" led to his theory of "boundary maintenance."

Barth criticized the typical anthropological techniques of determining an "ethnic group" or a "culture," which had consisted of listing "traits" that pertain to this or that group, in otherwise arbitrary collections or lists.[30]

As Barth points out, such a process appears to freeze groups in time, not allowing for chronological change, or else explaining change by sometimes doubtful cultural "borrowing" (often without direct evidence). Thus, attention is focused on an assemblage of traits, but this does not take into consideration chronological change in the same selected group.[31]

Related to this is the problem of environmental adaptation to different ecological niches by sections of an otherwise homogeneous ethnic group, thus differentiating groups based entirely on a cultural "trait list."[32]

Barth's deceptively simple suggestion for a new basis of defining ethnicity is to note that: "To the extent that actors use ethnic identities to categorize themselves and others for the purposes of interaction, they form ethnic groups in this organizational sense."[33] This suggestion is based on the observation that:

> it is clear that boundaries persist despite a flow of personnel across them. In other words, categorical ethnic distinctions do not depend on an absence of mobility, contact and information but do entail social processes of exclusion and incorporation whereby discrete categories are maintained *despite* changing participation and membership in the course of individual life histories.[34]

Ethnicity, then, is maintained by a group process. A significant dynamic of the experience of Israel in Exile is their consciousness of being among "foreigners," *irrespective of the outward similarity* of first millennium Palestinian cultural traits and first millennium Babylonian cultural traits, including mutual intelligibility or unintelligibility of the Semitic languages involved. Barth pointed out that a reduction of cultural differences between groups does not break down ethnic boundaries, but remains a matter of conscious attitudes on the part of the groups in question.[35] Such a perspective does not allow hasty conclusions about the extent of "cultural influence" between, for example, the Neo-Babylonian heartland populations, other captive populations, and the Jewish exiles. Barth's work focuses the question of maintaining identity on episodes of contact between cultures. Therefore, we can confidently speak of "ethnic identity" whenever a group in question uses certain terms to differentiate itself from another group, although this is only the opening question in a more complex analysis.[36] The perception of uniqueness serves the ubiquitous need for identity, which, as we have seen, is an irreducibly social process.

In conclusion, the preservation of identity in the context of intercultural contact is an important focus for a sociological analysis of the Babylonian Exile. But there are two further elements of this preservation process for the Jews in Exile that must be considered. First, the Jews were a minority in a foreign environment, and second, they were forcibly settled in that foreign environment. Both of these elements must be considered further.

Identity in a Minority Context

Now that we have considered the term "ethnicity" as lodged in the self-identification of an ethnic group, we want to turn to a more careful definition of the social realities of the ethnic group in question. We have already stated that we are dealing with a group in Exile, and a group that was a minority. What are some of the mechanisms of ethnicity that are unique to an exiled minority?

When the process of establishing relevant ethnic characteristics approaches a point of restoring stability for the social group that has experienced a crisis, then the emphasis changes to a realization of the importance of the "diaspora" itself. The group no longer thinks of itself as a temporary "piece" of the homeland. One way of stabilizing the group in a diaspora is the creation of ghettos. Thus, an immigrant society may insulate itself into a *voluntary* ghetto in order to preserve identity. For example, Abu-Lughod, in her study of migrant adjustment to urban life in Cairo, speaks of the literal creation of "villages" within the city itself as an aid to accommodation to the new location:

[with] a lower capacity for assimilation they tend to build for themselves within the city a replica of the culture they left behind.... It

would take a keen observer indeed to distinguish between a village within Cairo and one located miles beyond its fringe.[37]

The phenomenon of self-chosen isolation as a method of social survival after mass movement can furthermore result in the creation of sub-cultures like those of many religious minorities (e.g., Amish, Jainists, Dukhobors, Hutterites, some Mormon groups, Parsees, Coptic Christians in Muslim countries). When the reconstruction of society is completed, the subculture is then totally independent of the homeland. This can happen in contexts that are relatively "open" as well as explicitly hostile to the subculture of exiles or refugees in question.[38]

The difference between a closed and a more open minority group is clarified by pointing to what some sociologists have called the "institutional completeness" of the groups in question. Groups in severe crisis, in order to maintain themselves, will strive to maintain all aspects of society (not merely language, food, folk culture, and other "indicators").

This creation of high level unity can be dramatic in conditions of threat or interaction. This is illustrated by Jane Murphy's experiences in the Displaced Person Camps after World War II. Murphy referred to "true society" (which is what we have called, after Wallace, "mazeway"), which built up in the camps. There were marked problems of social alienation (alcoholism, loneliness) after release from these camps, because of the lamented loss of the true society, the "mazeway" that had built up in the intensive camp experience.[39]

The political forces that can form primary minority groups is further illuminated by a consideration of Armstrong's typology of "Mobilized and Proletarian Diasporas"[40]:

Mobilized Diasporas	**Proletarian Diasporas**
Situational or Archetypical	Coolies, Slaves, etc.

The subcategories of "mobilized diasporas" are "archetypical diasporas," who have no majority in any homeland (historically Jews and Parsees), and the "situational diasporas" of the Volga Germans, Chinese in Indonesia, Lebanese in Africa, that is, groups who are diasporas only when not "at home."

As Armstrong puts it, the archetypical diasporas have a sense of identity far more invested in sacred categories, sacred languages and myths, and the maintenance of "scriptures." The language skills of diaspora members, whether situational or archetypical, have made them stereotypically "court translators" as well as traders and practitioners of other "mobile skills" requiring linguistic diversity. This has been the case for Jews, Chinese, Lebanese in Africa, Copts, Armenians, and many others who have found themselves in similar social circumstances.[41]

Over an extended period of time, however, the existence of a homeland puts the other subcategory, "situational diasporas," under the suspicion of disloyalty (e.g., Japanese-Americans during World War II). This is especially the case if the homeland is outside the political control of the dominant elite.

So the main differences between mobilized and "proletarian" diasporas, suggests Armstrong, are the relative hope for advantage and the relative freedom of operation.

Because of their lower social status and fewer perceived "needs" beyond low-wage or "coolie" labor, proletarian diasporas tend, in Armstrong's view, to become more and more culturally isolated and suffer continued discrimination. But this begs the question of the role of domination as a social reality.

In their research on modern minorities in the situation that Armstrong would call a "mobilized diaspora," the significance of persecution is highlighted by Turner and Bonacich's discussion of their concept of "middle minorities."

Middle minorities have a number of common characteristics including (1) the propensity to form and maintain a separate community or district in the recipient society; (2) the desire to maintain distinct cultural traits, such as language, values, and religious beliefs; and (3) the propensity to cultivate high degrees of internal solidarity through extended kinship ties, school and religious organizations, and preference for endogamy.[42] But we must also incorporate into our analysis the social tensions, discrimination, attacks, and resentment that often accompany minority existence. This results in a "minority economics of protection" typified by involvement in middle-rank economic roles such as trading and small business, the desire to maintain liquid assets, pooling of kin labor to work long hours, and cooperation between ethnic comrades for mutual benefit.

Finally, the role of discrimination and domination has a clear impact on social formations. Among the relevant aspects of the Babylonian Exile community was the fact that it was not only a minority, but it was a *conquered* minority, *under domination.*

In his essay on the cultural changes of the American Indian, Edward Spicer set out five different "models of contact," where the different types of social response are suggested. The important aspect of these models is the difference between "directed" and "non-directed" contact, "directed" referring specifically to relations of *domination.* Spicer's categories are as follows:

A. Non-Directed Contact   1. The Incorporative Model: Nonthreatening acceptance of selected cultural influences.

B. Directed Contact

1. Assimilative (Replacement) integration

2. Fusion (Synthesis)

3. Isolative Integration

4. Bi-Culturalism[43]

Since we are not concerned with peaceful, or non-directed, contact we proceed to consider Spicer's four points under directed contact. To "assimilate," in Spicer's terms, is to replace one practice native to the minority with a practice that achieves similar results or functions practiced by the majority. This need not result in a loss of identity on the part of the minority.

In "fusion" the minority culture incorporates by choice or force so much of the dominant majority practice, belief system, and symbol system that the resulting "culture" is entirely different from either the majority or previous minority systems.

When a trait, practice, or belief is integrated by "isolation," it is clearly kept secluded from even those areas it resembles in the minority system. Thus, an imported religious practice is not associated with the totality of minority religious concepts, but on the contrary, kept quite separate.

This is illustrated graphically by Graburn in his discussion of indigenous art and the production of artifacts for non-native tourist consumption. Graburn points out that an indigenous tribe can continue to produce copies of what was originally a sacred object, but the tribe is able to keep the facsimile ideologically separate from the original, including the meaning of the original in cult or ritual. It is, in the religious sense, understood as a mere "copy" — with more economic than cultic value. This form of adaptation can preserve the cultural and ethnic boundaries in situations of economic contact.[44]

The final model suggested by Spicer is biculturalism — the attitude where one takes on *two* value systems, depending on where one is ("When in Rome..."). It is important to note that all four of these systems under directed contact leave some degree of independent action for the dominated, even though it may be very small.

F. Barth, too, commented on the processes and conditions of intercultural contact and influence and suggested that the acceptance of many foreign elements into native practice, such as in Spicer's "assimilation" model, need not mean the end of a self-conscious ethnic group. Barth believes that a minority may attempt to take the offensive, assert their ethnic identity, and attempt to forge a new place in society for themselves (as with fusion in Spicer's outline). Barth, however, sees this as a source of creative movements from "nativism to new states." The interesting aspect of this last strategy, which brings it closer to Spicer's "fusion" model, is that a minority group must mould its identity from the raw materials of its "native" culture, *but this identity must be functional in the new situation.*

To summarize thus far, identity formation in circumstances of directed contact may reveal the creativity of a minority group in fashioning a viable counter-culture for survival.

In a recent investigation of the survival of American Indian culture under the directed contact of white colonial and mission pressure, entitled "Strategies for Cultural Autonomy of Massachusetts Praying Town Indians" (a praying town was the result of segregation of religiously "converted" Native Americans into townships apart from their brethren), Elise Brenner discusses the important aspects of cultural resistance:

> The adaptation to...exploitation...is an active and not a passive action. The strategies are usually based on passive resistance and opportunism of the client population coupled with a willingness to experiment with and manipulate the hierarchical society. The native group is able to make choices and implement its own decisions into modes of action. Such was the case among the Cherokees.[45]

Related to this mechanism, Bernard Siegal has written about "defense structuring." We have seen how aspects of native culture can be made significant in the presence of stress or the need for reconstruction. Siegal suggests that the symbols that are selected reflect the societal need for unification and boundary maintenance.[46]

The resulting dominated culture is a synthesis of the former cultural expressions of the colonized people and the colonizer's view. Drawing on the social psychologies of dominated peoples, especially the work of Fanon, Mannoni, Memmi, and others, M. Caulfield calls for a realization that cultural reconstruction under domination is resistance and ultimately leads to the means by which the colonizers are defeated in their attempts to dominate totally.[47] Taking another example from the experience of Native American Indians, Clemmer considered the Hopi American Indian resistance to exploitation by twentieth-century American government interests. The response of the Hopi community is summarized by Clemmer as follows:

> It was determined that younger Hopis were not fulfilling their proper roles in Hopi social and ceremonial activities and that Hopi culture was suffering deterioration as a result. The war had indeed forced many young men into the armed forces, thus leaving performance of traditional religious ceremonies and social functions largely to older men. It was decided...that the chiefs and religious

leaders would make concerted efforts to fulfill their own roles as social and religious pace-setters and revitalize Hopi culture. Results of these efforts were an increase in initiates to religious societies; the passing on of secret knowledge to younger people; the assured continuation of religious ceremonies that were about to disappear; and the start of a counter-campaign to the white man's acculturative pressures that would articulate resistance in political language and action that the white man would understand.[48]

Here Clemmer illustrates motifs we will have occasion to discuss in more detail — the resurgence of ceremony and ritual as well as the forced reorganization of traditions in order to respond to threats against the native system (such as the passing on of ceremonial secrets to younger-than-usual initiates).

The preservation of an identity under threat calls for "defense structuring." If, as we have suggested, "ethnic identity" is preserved by conscious choice in circumstances of intercultural contact (Barth), then an analysis of the social mechanisms of the Judean exiles in Babylon ought to reveal creatively structured identities in order to be "the people of God" in a foreign land.

The Sociology of Return

Finally, we can make some brief comments about the sociology of return. The mechanisms for survival and resistance of minorities in a dominated situation also inevitably lead toward a solidarity of the community and the creation of a "community of crisis."

Part of this solidarity is based on memories of the past. The Lithuanian refugees had a mythic view of their home that perpetuated their dream to return. When some of them finally were able to go back, the shock that the homeland was not the homeland of their frozen memory jolted many of them into a realization that they were a permanent diaspora.[49]

A form of this "shock" can be documented for each of the cases where members of the community exiled were able to return to the geographical situation from which they came. Some Japanese-Americans exhibited a unique socio-psychological post-event reaction to the internment camps that one historian of the camps called "selective amnesia," an unwillingness to talk about their experiences.[50] Kiste reported the shock to the exiled Bikini Islanders, who had mythologized the old island into a Golden Era, only to return and find the Island a ghost of its former state. This brings to mind the words of Haggai, who referred to those who had seen Solomon's Temple and cried at the dedication of the new Temple, because it did not seem as glorious.

However, communal solidarity during a crisis can have further sociological effects. R. J. Lifton's study of the *hibakusha,* that is, the survivors of the atomic bomb in Hiroshima and Nagasaki, revealed that there was a "community of experience," a social boundary, among the survivors of the atomic bomb (similar to the survivors of the concentration camps, who found themselves constantly meeting to re-establish a unique communal tie that was formed). This was perceived by Lifton to be a significant "separating" boundary, which set the survivors off from other Japanese with whom they had virtually everything else in common. Lifton records two different reactions. Some survivors tried to see the physical effects of the bomb as a positive identity marker. More common, however, were those who saw their identity as a "death-taint," which was rejected by other Japanese:

> The young are forthright enough to say what many of their elders feel: the death-tainted are a threat, an enemy, and finally, an inferior breed. Thinking back on the advocacy of sterilization on the part of some hibakusha themselves, we can now understand it as a wish to excise symbolically not only the death-taint, but the entire hibakusha identity in which this taint is enmeshed. But both — as for other victimized groups to whom they may be compared — turn out to be all too enduring.[51]

Furthermore, in a series of important articles on the psychology and sociological effects of refugee movements, Kunz[52] and Wong[53] make reference to the impact of return and resettlement. Kunz stressed the differences between waves, what he called "vintages," of refugees. He pointed out that great differences between refugees from the same geographical area, or even the same ethnic group, can result both from the reasons why they left and the circumstances under which they left:

> In addition to political differences which these vintages represent, they also tend in some instances to unite people belonging to similar types of educational, social, or religious background. Although few vintages are fully homogeneous, vintages leaving a country in a refugee situation *tend to take different proportions of the ingredients of the society they leave behind and thus become distinctive enough not to resemble in their composition another vintage."* [emphasis added][54]

In conclusion, the survival of a minority as a group depends on their success in creating a solid community with social boundaries. This solidarity in exile then creates separation from the population that did *not* endure exile. We have seen this occur with the exiles that did not last over even one generation (e.g., Japanese-Americans, Lithuanians). The final sociological element in the crisis of the Exile, then, would be a possible conflict between those who went into Exile and those who did not. This conflict would not necessarily reflect the "degeneration" of religious faithfulness of those left in Palestine, but only that the crisis led to different social configurations. Thus, an analysis of the social conflicts of the era of the restoration and return must take all of these elements of sociological analysis into consideration. The issues cannot be simply religious, or a matter of class, but may have to do with the formation of communities of disaster as well.

NOTES

1. Michael Barkun, *Disaster and the Millennium* (New Haven, 1974).
2. Anthony Wallace, "Revitalization Movements," *American Anthropologist,* 58, no. 2 (April 1956).
3. Barkun, *Disaster and the Millennium,* p. 51.
4. Bryan Wilson, *Magic and the Millennium* (St. Albans, Eng., 1975).
5. Richard Niebuhr, *The Social Sources of Denominationalism* (New York, 1954), and E. Troeltsch, *The Social Teachings of the Christian Churches,* trans. Olive Wyon, vols. 1 and 2 (New York, 1960). For recent developments of this "church-sect" typology, with excellent bibliographies, see Roger O'Toole, "Underground Traditions in the Study of Sectarianism," *Journal for the Scientific Study of Religion,* 15, no. 2 (1976); William Swatos, Jr., "Weber or Troeltsch?: Methodology, Syndrome, and the Development of Church-Sect Theory," *Journal for the Scientific Study of Religion,* 15, no. 2 (1976).
6. Wilson, *Magic and the Millennium,* p. 22.
7. Ibid., p. 23.
8. Ibid.
9. Ibid., p. 24.
10. Ibid., p. 25.
11. Ibid.
12. Ibid.
13. Wallace, "Revitalization Movements," p. 268.
14. Robert Carroll, *When Prophecy Failed* (New York, 1979).
15. For the concept of "mechanisms," I was impressed with the work of H. H. Mol, *Identity and the Sacred* (Oxford, 1976). Although I do not agree with Mol's entire listing of specific "mechanisms," I agree that such mechanisms, as behavior patterns, provide the most important information.
16. Janssen's arguments, among others, seem convincing. See Enno Janssen, *Juda in der Exilszeit: Ein Beitrag zur Frage der Entstehung des Judentums* (Göttingen, 1956).
17. See Opler's work "Senryu Poetry as Folk and Community Expression," *Journal of American Folklore,* 58 (1945).
18. Liucija Baskauskas, "The Lithuanian Refugee Experience and Grief," *International Migration Review,* 15, no. 1 (1981), pp. 280–281.
19. William Petersen, "A General Theory of Migration," *American Sociological Review,* 23 (1958).
20. Ibid., p. 261.
21. Egon Kunz, "Exile and Resettlement: Refugee Theory," *International Migration Review,* 15, no. 1 (1981), p. 43.
22. Baskauskas, "The Lithuanian Refugee Experience and Grief," p. 280.

23. Kunz, "Exile and Resettlement: Refugee Theory," p. 43.

24. Ibid., pp. 43–44.

25. See R. Boyer, *The Legacy of the German Refugee Intellectual* (New York, 1972).

26. For comparative material, see John S. MacDonald and Leatrice MacDonald, "Chain Migration, Ethnic Neighbourhood Formation and Social Networks," *The Milbank Memorial Fund Quarterly*, 42, no. 1 (January 1964); H.B.M. Murphy, *Flight and Resettlement* (Geneva, 1955); Jacob Eichenbaum, "A Matrix of Human Movement," *International Migration*, 13, no. 1/2 (1975), provides an interesting alternative formulation, but I prefer Petersen's, which is fuller and considers more variables. See also J.J. Mol, "Churches and Immigrants," *Bulletin*, Research Group for European Migration Problems, 9, supp. 5 (May 1961); Schuetz, "The Stranger," *American Journal of Sociology*, 49 (1943–1944); E. Flaschberger, "The Marginal Man and His Marginal Attitude," *Bulletin*, Research Group for European Migration Problems, 10, no. 3 (1962).

27. Ronald Cohen, "Ethnicity: Problem and Focus in Anthropology" *Annual Review of Anthropology*, 7 (1978), p. 389.

28. E. K. Francis, *InterEthnic Relations: An Essay in Sociological Theory* (New York, 1976), p. 17.

29. Frederick Barth, "Introduction," in *Ethnic Groups and Boundaries: The Social Organization of Culture Difference*, ed. F. Barth (London, 1969).

30. Ibid., p. 11.

31. "What is the unit whose continuity in time is depicted in such studies? Paradoxically, it must include cultures in the past which would clearly be excluded in the present because of differences in form — differences of precisely the kind that are diagnostic in synchronic differentiation of ethnic units. The interconnection between 'ethnic group' and 'culture' is certainly not clarified through this confusion" (ibid., p. 12).

32. "The same group of people, with unchanged values and ideas, would surely pursue different patterns of life and institutionalize different forms of behaviour when faced with the different opportunities offered in different environments.... Likewise we must expect to find that one ethnic group, spread over a territory with varying ecologic circumstances, will exhibit regional diversities of overt institutionalized behaviour which do not reflect differences in cultural orientation. How should they then be classified if overt institutional forms are diagnostic?" (ibid.).

33. "It makes no difference how dissimilar members may be in their overt behaviour — if they say they are A, in contrast to another cognate category B, and they are willing to be treated and let their own behaviour be interpreted and judged as A's and not B's; in other words, they declare their allegiance to the shared culture of A's. The effects of this, as compared to other factors influencing actual behaviour, can then be made the object of investigation ... " (ibid., p. 15).

34. Ibid., p. 9.

35. Ibid., p. 32.

36. A. L. Epstein suggests a helpful synthesis: "Just as in the case of the individual the notion of personality is accompanied at the level of self-perception by the sense of ego-identity, so ethos has as its counterpart the sense of collective identity, the consciousness of belonging to a group that exists in time ... " (*Ethos and Identity: Three Studies in Ethnicity* [London, 1978], p. 122).

"It is now commonly agreed that it is meaningful to talk of ethnicity only where groups of different ethnic origin have been brought into interaction within some common social context.... Ethnicity serves as a system of social classification ... in terms of which people structure their environment and govern certain of their relations with others. From a socio-centric point of view, these categories are 'objective,' external to the individual, compelling him to take cognizance of them" (ibid., p. xii).

There is also a perspective that explains ethnic behavior as "proto-nationalism," represented in the work of Anthony Smith and Clifford Geertz: Anthony Smith, *The Ethnic Revival* (Cambridge, 1981); Clifford Geertz, "The Integrative Revolution," in Clifford Geertz, ed. *Old Societies and New States* (New York, 1963). But this presents a biased perspective in the direction of nationalism. Does a social entity have to display certain features of emergent nationalism in order to be an "ethnic" unit? In his analysis of American Indian social leadership forms, Clastres points out that they represent forms of ethnic unity that would be far from Western, political forms that deal with violent power and hierarchical leadership (see Pierre Clastres, *Society Against the State* [New York, 1974], p. 9).

37. Janet Abu-Lughod, "Migrant Adjustment to City Life: The Egyptian Case," *American Journal of Sociology,* 67 (1961–62), p. 23.

In considering the case of medieval Jews in Eastern Europe, Louis Wirth, in his classic study, *The Ghetto* (Chicago, 1928, 1956), suggested that segregation was originally the result of the cultic needs as well as social expediency of Jews who live in close proximity with others: "The ghetto was not, as sometimes mistakenly believed, the arbitrary creation of the authorities designed to deal with an alien people. The ghetto was not the product of design, but rather the unwitting crystallization of the needs and practices of the customs and heritages, religious and secular, of the Jews themselves. Long before it was made compulsory, the Jews lived in separate parts of the cities in the Western lands of their own accord" (p. 18).

It must be added, however, that the medieval ghetto can also provide an example for our discussion in the next section of the dynamics of domination. These examples of isolation, to recall Kunz and Petersen, reveal a minimal level of independent response to otherwise imposed conditions of exile. The voluntary ghetto may well be a form of economic slavery open to exploitation by dominant populations, but it can also be a defensive mechanism to maintain boundaries under pressure. The ghetto may be self-imposed in the beginning, but it can then become sanctioned by the state.

38. Although the social isolation of a minority group may not be symbolized by fences or armed guards, the fears of the minority who have created their strict social boundaries may not be a groundless paranoia. To employ a metaphor from American immigration, the Amish farmer, as a representative of an ideologically closed religious subculture, has a different outlook on surrounding society than a typical Norwegian farmer who immigrated to the U.S.A. because of higher aspirations rather than religious or social persecution. The Amish, too, have a history of "real conflict" with "outsiders," which has led to a theology of separation. The different farmers in the country may be considered foreigners by the surrounding majority culture, but the Norwegian farmers see their Norwegian associations as merely an aid to settle in a new homeland, while the Amish feel much more a constant challenge and conflict, and their isolation is chosen as a means of defense. An indication of this social defense is seen in the Amish attitude toward the use and possession of the modern technology of surrounding society. See especially Marc Olson, "Modernity, the Folk Society and the Old Order Amish" *Rural Sociology,* 46, no. 2 (1981).

39. H.B.M. Murphy, *Flight and Resettlement.*

40. John Armstrong, "Mobilized and Proletarian Diasporas," *American Political Science Review,* 70 (1976), pp. 393–408.

41. The use of two different conceptual models, however, has biased Armstrong's views, since he fails to see the coercive character present in *both* his "mobilized" (whether situational or archetypical) and "proletarian" communities. There appears to be, in historical experience, similarities between the two groups, the only difference being the relative economic success of one group in ameliorating their conditions. But even "better conditions" may not mean that a conflict is absent. Armstrong's view of postcolonial situations as the source of proletarian diaspora conditions fails to see the "colonialist" violence that is often perpetrated upon the more financially resourceful (or simply fortunate) mobilized diasporas. This cannot be illustrated better than by pointing out Armstrong's failure to make reference to the persecutions of virtually every "mobilized" diaspora (whether situational or archetypical) that he uses for examples, such as the Jews, Copts, and Armenians.

42. Jonathan H. Turner, and Edna Bonacich, "Toward a Composite Theory of Middlemen Minorities," *Ethnicity,* 7 (1980), p. 146.

43. Spicer's work is a modification of the 1940 essay produced by Ralph Linton on

the subject of acculturation, but Spicer's views clearly set forth the kinds of influence one can find in intercultural contact situations under various circumstances. This range clearly shows a variety of strategies available. See Edward Spicer, "Types of Contact and Processes of Change," in Edward Spicer, ed., *Perspectives in American Indian Culture Change* (Chicago, 1961). pp. 529–533.

44. Nelson Graburn, "Introduction," *Ethnic and Tourist Arts: Cultural Expressions from the Fourth World* (Los Angeles, 1976). Despite the title of this work, which would indicate a subject far from the concerns of biblical studies, it turned out to be one of the most helpful works that I consulted in the course of this study.

45. Elise Brenner, "Strategies for Cultural Autonomy of Massachusetts Praying Town Indians," *Ethnohistory,* 27, no. 2 (Spring 1980), p. 136.

46. Siegal also believes that strong authoritarian controls are present in threatened groups, maintained by perpetuating a high level of anxiety among the group members. This is softened, however, by a promotion of inward harmony and solidarity. "Defense structuring" is imposed by authoritarian figures within the threatened group. Accordingly, in Siegal's view, the groups engaging in "defensive structuring" create the conditions of isolation. Siegal goes to great pains to stress the "perceived" threat of the group in question. It is difficult, with an emphasis on merely "perceived threat," to see the creative response of a group to *actual* outside threats. This is clear if we look at the factors of boundary maintenance from the perspective of the minority, rather than from that of the dominant population, or what the minority "would normally be" if they were not a minority (i.e., a state like the majority). The work on refugee typologies that we have considered proves that attention to the outside factors is a critical aspect of "defense structuring" of the group, and their statelessness is not implicitly pathological (see Bernard J. Siegal, "Defense Structuring and Environmental Stress," *American Journal of Sociology,* 76 [1970–71], p. 16). For a more critical perspective on similar issues, see G. Balandier, "The Colonial Situation: A Theoretical Approach," in *Social Change: The Colonial Situation* (New York, 1951).

47. See M. D. Caulfield, "Culture and Imperialism: Proposing a New Dialectic," in D. Hymes, *Re-Inventing Anthropology* (New York, 1974). See also W. James, "The Anthropologist as Reluctant Imperialist," in T. Adad, *Anthropology and the Colonial Encounter* (London, 1973); A. Memmi, *Prospero and Caliban: The Colonizer and the Colonized* (London, 1974); Dominique O. Mannoni, *The Psychology of Colonization* (London, 1964); and the classic Frantz Fanon, *The Wretched of the Earth* (London, 1979, reprint). See also the work by Balandier, "The Colonial Situation: A Theoretical Approach."

48. Richard Clemmer, "Truth, Duty and the Revitalization of Anthropologists: A New Perspective on Cultural Change and Resistance," in Hymes, ed., *Re-Inventing Anthropology,* p. 233.

49. Baskauskas, "The Lithuanian Refugee Experience and Grief," p. 282.

50. Tetsuden Kashima, "Japanese-American Internees Return 1945–1955: Readjustment and Selective Amnesia," *Phylon,* 41 (1980).

51. See R. J. Lifton, *Death in Life: The Survivors of Hiroshima* (London, 1968).

52. E. Kunz, "The Refugee in Flight: Kinetic Models and Forms of Displacement," *International Migration Review,* 7 (1973), p. 161.

53. P. Wong, "The Social Psychology of Refugees in an Alien Social Milieau," *International Migration Review,* 5 (1967).

54. Kunz, "The Refugee in Flight," p. 138.

Chapter 3

Case Studies of
"Mechanisms for Survival"

We have established that social groups in minority situations must maintain what Barth called "boundary maintenance." Under conditions of unequal distribution of power, this often means that the minority, or low-status, group must resort to creative mechanisms other than violence or escape in order to secure their identity.

To illustrate these mechanisms, we have selected four case studies (from the dozens that are available). These cases were selected while trying to be aware of the critical elements identified in chapter 2.

Mass deportation is not itself an isolated or unique event in history, but, on the contrary, is a well-attested experience, whether on foot as the American Indian "Trail of Tears," or the tragically familiar historical image of train cars carrying Jews, or the transport of Lithuanians, Estonians, and Latvians in the Soviet Union, Japanese-Americans in the United States, or Zulu tribes in modern South Africa. All of these instances, and many others, make up the long trail of history's deportees to foreign lands.

The selection of cases for in-depth examination is based on two criteria. The first is practical — there had to be sufficient literature that incorporated sociological analysis. This rules out a vast number of cases that are otherwise interesting. Second, the case studies are amenable to the outline. However, it should be kept in mind that we do not claim that any of these cases are "exactly like" the Babylonian Exile, but only that they illustrate patterns of behavior that may contribute to developing hypotheses to direct biblical study. The value of this kind of sociological analysis is to increase the awareness of what may by significant in the textual evidence.

In many details, obviously, the cases are not comparable to the Babylonian Exile material of the biblical texts. But on other points they are strikingly similar. The success of this approach, however, is not the proof that a Jewish pattern of response in the sixth century B.C.E. is "just like," for instance, the Japanese-American response to internment in the twentieth century, but rather, the question is whether a particular biblical exegetical hypothesis suggested by the analogy is in itself true.

The cases that I have given particular attention to include the following:

1. Religious Responses to Apartheid in South African Bantustans: Apartheid has been the official policy of the state of South Africa since the coming to power of the Afrikaner National Party in 1948. It is the political expression of the racial segregation of South Africa's 3 million whites from the over 18 million "non-whites." However, we are particularly interested in the land policies that have resulted in the creation and forced population of "native reserves" (comprising 13 percent of the total land mass) called "Bantustans." Black Africans were declared citizens of these homelands and thus excluded from urban South African society as "foreigners" — except as they are allowed to commute to work. Black South Africans have been systematically deported to the rural Bantustans, both en masse and later as a result of any individual infraction of the laws:

> Poor islands in one of the world's richest countries, the Bantustans were created as a dumping ground for unwanted laborers, a method of population control and a way of defusing black protest. South Africa's infamous pass laws give it the right to send any black back to the Bantustan to which he or she has been assigned; the unemployed, the blacks who are too old or too young to work, and the politically active can be removed from white areas and without appeal sent back to starve, or serve as a reserve for cheap labor for the white South African.[1]

Within the Bantustans, various forms of native government are tolerated on a low level. However, the combination of Christian mission and native traditions has resulted in a classic illustration of "directed contact" resulting in "fusion." The resulting religious expressions of the Bantustans can be summarized as (A) nativist maintenance of traditional forms as much as possible, (B) mission churches, which largely reflect white church practice as much as possible, and (C) the so-called Zionist churches (not related at all to Jewish Zionism), which represent an indigenous combination and synthesis of A and B. Category C is of particular interest because of the information available and because it is overtly synthetic and thus avoids the difficulty of isolating the "pure" aspects of A and B. The focus of our study of this case, therefore, will be on the literature about the Zionist churches of the Bantustans. Even though the Zionist movement itself predates the resettlements, the Zionist churches have increased in response to the resettlement policy and represent a "laboratory" of social mechanisms.

According to Sundklar and West, one of the most important aspects of the Zionist church movement, besides its careful perpetuation of significant Zulu traditions in a new context, is precisely the rise of the Zionist churches at the "borderlands" of social contact between whites and blacks.[2]

2. African-American Slavery: The literature on Afro-American slavery is immense. We are specifically interested in the communities of slaves and their leadership patterns. Although this case probably presents the most obvious factors that cannot be compared to the Babylonian Exile, there are some important ways in which studies of slave societies and slave religion can enlighten study of the Bible.[3] Afro-American slavery presents us with individual points of comparison, rather than a general comparison. That is, individual slave communities, stories, and cultural studies of small units are more interesting than discussions of the historical details of slavery in the New World.

It is not possible to give an accurate figure of the number of slaves imported into the New World from Africa. In eleven years, from 1783 through 1793, Liverpool traders alone were responsible for the importation of 303,737, while in the following eleven years they were certainly responsible for as many. While the closing years of the eighteenth century represented the peak in the slave trade, the preceding two centuries show a steady increase leading to the apogee reached in the 1790s. It has been estimated that 900,000 were imported in the sixteenth century, 2,750,000 in the seventeenth, 7,000,000 in the eighteenth, and 4,000,000 in the nineteenth. These figures represent conservative estimates.[4]

The value of slavery studies for our study has been discussed in more detail in chapter 1.

3. Japanese-American Internment during World War II: Declaring "Once a Jap, always a Jap" (*Los Angeles Times,* April 14, 1943), Lt. Gen. John L. DeWitt, commanding general of the American Western Defense Command, issued his order on March 2, 1942, to evacuate to internment camps the entire Japanese population of Oregon, Washington, and California in reaction to the bombing of Pearl Harbor on December 7, 1941.

A full comprehension of this event is not possible unless one understands the segregationist results of the Oriental Exclusion Act of 1924, which prevented immigrants from becoming U.S. citizens and halted any further immigration to the country on the overtly stated basis that Asians could not be assimilated into American life. This created Japanese-American enclaves of small societies composed of those whose memories of Japan were fast becoming fantasies in the light of

Japan's rapid Westernization following the Russian-Japanese War of 1904–1905, and of second-generation U.S. citizens (the so-called "Nisei"; first-generation Japanese are known as "Issei").

Japanese-Americans were herded, in sealed trains, to internment camps located inland from the coastal states. They were taken on the grounds of fear of cooperation with the enemy, which in turn was based solely on the fact of their Japanese ancestry. Most Americans of German and Italian descent were not in the least subject to official harassment, although local uneasiness to perceived accents was common.

In ten camps, 119,000 were interned. Each camp housed approximately 10,000 Japanese-Americans, with three camps (Tule Lake, Calif., Poston, Ariz., and Gila River, Ariz.) having nearly 20,000. The Canadian policy was clearly even more repressive, as noted in an article by Tomoko Makabe.[5] The Canadians forced 11,500 Japanese, many of whom were Canadian citizens, to British Columbia ghost towns. It was Canadian policy eventually to force every Japanese-Canadian to decide whether to return to Japan, and a surprising 40 percent did; and, of these, 60 percent were Nisei (second-generation) Canadian citizens.

The literature concerning the Japanese-American experience still consists largely of governmental reports, usually not dealing with camp existence itself. More recently, however, some interesting accounts provide important insights into the survival mechanisms and resistance activities of the internment camps.

Kitano cities examples of resistance that included work slowdowns, alcoholism (as escapism), humor, and ritualism. Can we determine these mechanisms more carefully?

The camps were divided socially between the Issei, born in Japan, and their American-born children, the Nisei. It was among the Nisei that pro-American feeling was strongest in the military units from Nisei camps. The crisis of split national loyalty, obviously, was greatest among the Issei. When a "loyalty test" was attempted among the camps, in one camp, Tule Lake, the test was unable to be completed. Tule Lake, in fact, became known for particularly strong resistance to official favors and was eventually chosen as the center to which all "disloyal" elements were brought from the other centers. Our interest in this case focuses primarily on information regarding Tule Lake as a center for particularly strong resistance. This is not to say, however, that Japanese-American internment was met predominantly with one form of resistance.

The particular circumstances of Japanese-American internment that are unique include the fact that prior to forced internment, Japanese-Americans were already a self-conscious minority. Japan served as the mythological homeland for the Issei, but it became the homeland for many Nisei as a rallying point for resistance. Ritual, in the form of Christian and Buddhist traditions, became infused with new meaning.

The full range of archetypical weapons of the powerless were evident, as we have noted, including new identities to resist those imposed from above.

Finally, the internment of Japanese-Americans began to exhibit some of these traits within months, since the entire experience lasted only for three or four years during World War II. While boundary maintenance mechanisms we have noticed had only a minor function in such a homogeneous ethnic detention, contrary to all our other examples, we still have seen responses of reconstruction and resistance.

4. The Bikini Islanders: In 1946, the United States government decided that it would conduct tests of nuclear weapons on the Bikini Atoll of the Marshall Islands. Although previously the Germans and then the Japanese had minimal contact with the Bikini Islanders, Kiste writes that the Bikinians had not had extensive contact with outsiders and were among the least Westernized of the Marshallese.[6]

In order to conduct the tests, the United States military had to relocate the approximately 300 Islanders en masse to another island, at first Kili Island. Because of social unrest, the U.S. military was involved in more than one movement of the Bikini population, sometimes to islands with no population native to them, but also to islands with long-standing native populations.

While the circumstances of removal differ in detail from the Babylonian Exile, the social degeneration, reconstruction, and resistance that occurred within the Islander community in new environments, the availability of information regarding relations between American leaders and indigenous leaders, and internal cultural changes make this case of forced removal important for us. As is clear from a consideration of how negotiations between the Islanders and the U.S. government on the removal from Bikini Island were conducted, the difference between "voluntary" and "forced" removal is, in this case, indeed a matter of official interpretation.

It may be objected that we are focusing only on *successful* resistance in these case studies. It is true, for example, that many Japanese-Americans fully co-operated with American authorities or went back to Japan; many slaves did not resist or revolt in the Southern states and the Caribbean; and many blacks in South Africa appear to accept the Bantustan arrangement. But we are interested in resistance because it is the Judeans *who successfully maintained their identity that were responsible for the biblical texts we are concerned with. This is therefore not the only social reality, but it is the social reality reflected in the texts.*

After reviewing a large portion of secondary literature on these four cases, four behavior patterns, or what we will call "mechanisms for survival," were prominent among the common features of the cases. These are (1) structural adaptation, (2) leadership patterns, (3) ritual patterns of resistance, and (4) the emergence of folk tales as an expression of social existence and the creation of "resistance literature." Let us examine the secondary literature in detail for each of these mechanisms for survival.

Structural Adaptation

Social structure, leadership patterns, and lines of authority may be part of the indigenous culture of a minority, but under conditions of social contact or threat to the social group, a process of adaptation becomes crucial for the survival of the group in a new social, as well as natural, environment. As Brass has pointed out:

> Even if one concedes that all people have certain "given" characteristics of culture and language that are acquired from birth and from family life, it remains the case that the process of creating communities from ethnic categories involves selection of particular dialects, religious practices, styles of dress or historical symbols from a variety of available alternatives and that individual characteristics or cultural forms will become transformed in that process.... It is always the case ... that particular social groups, leaders, or elites stand to benefit and others to lose from the choices that are made.[7]

One of the factors in the survival of the Lithuanians in exile was this preservation of aspects of the previous culture and the social structure that was a part of it. The previous society was maintained. For example, even though a former army official was a manual laborer in the U.S., the community still observed his rank, just as they observed the former status of a poet or aristocrat. Yet the new situation created, slowly, new patterns of interaction that eventually exerted new pressures on immigrant society.[8]

The maintenance of old positions of authority totally apart from the contexts of power and position are significant, but at the same time the experience has a "democratizing" effect as a direct result of the breakdown of authority structures. This may either be "denied" artificially, or it can open the way for a new ethnic elite — such as a prophet or priest, in new positions of authority. There are other examples.

A kind of forced democratization was observed among Yemeni Jews, but the response was a rise of distributed leadership and an inward, general assimilation of purity laws:

> With the absence of printing facilities and the scarcity of books in Yemen, all Jewish males mastered the Bible by memory. Males

had a thorough knowledge of the Old Testament, and in urban settings, some also engaged in Talmudic studies. Every man was the embodiment of the Torah and could recite portions of it in the Yemeni Hebrew Dialect, intonation and pronunciation. In effect, the men were walking books, walking Old Testaments who physically guarded the sacred literacy tradition by memory....

The Yemeni Jewish community was too poor to support an independent specialized social class of religious scholars in the study and preservation of the Torah, intellectuals such as the Yeshiva students of the Eastern European congregations. Instead, it entrusted custody of the sacred tradition to all males in the community.[9]

Barth believes that the structural adaptation in conditions of contact between social groups where power is unequally distributed results in the minority group becoming more like the dominant system, in order to assert or protect itself:

A political confrontation can only be implemented by making the groups similar and thereby comparable, and this will have effect on every new sector of activity which is made politically relevant. Opposed parties thus tend to become structurally similar.[10]

Referring to the changing myths of Malay identity in response to directed contact between groups in Southeast Asia, Nagata makes a similar observation:

The social category or group that is salient for a given interest will be identified by those primordial(ized) characteristics that most effectively differentiate them from the significant oppositional categories in connection with that particular issue.[11]

Thus, the very social structure of the group may evolve new configurations to deal with the new situation. Many of these new configurations have clear, material causes that can be analyzed functionally. To turn to our cases, these patterns can be clearly recognized.

In his monograph on resistance in the Japanese-American camps, Okihiro compares the social responses of preserving selected older traditions and innovating new social structures:

As time progressed, the block, a camp residential unit consisting of fourteen barracks, emerged as a primary unit of ethnic solidarity. Although many families within the block were from different geographical areas prior to evacuation, living in close quarters resulted in a degree of cohesiveness through group endeavors in improving

conditions around their blocks and in self-governance.... The Issei, respected for their knowledge which comes of age, became the
central core of block leadership. That was in direct conflict with
the WRA mandate on internal camp government which had disenfranchised the Issei, but in harmony with traditional Japanese
culture.... The block took on the characteristics of the family in
stressing conformity to the collective will. Thus, block residents
disciplined children who lacked parental control and brought dis-
credit on the collective. The slogan, "Keep children within the
block" was widely circulated.[12]

The expected attempt to recreate one's traditional "mazeway" was evident in the traditional activities of the Issei men in the internment
camps. But this was problematical in the conditions of domination.
The Issei had lost power in the new situations, as they were no longer
the filial power brokers in the family and neighborhood. Residents of the
Tule Lake Camp described this role deterioration for Issei men in contrast to Issei women. The women, for example, found new release from
their traditionally hard responsibilities. Issei women were involved in
classes in subjects from Japanese music to floral arrangement. The Issei
women, under normal circumstances, were not allowed such freedom.
The Issei men, on the other hand, were disenfranchised. The Issei men
were barred from political activity and had understandably little desire
to learn English. Some found comfort in Christianity or Buddhism,
others in alcoholism.[13]

This is related to the phenomenon of democratization, or levelling,
under domination, as we have already seen in other cases:

Financial ruin, together with the camp policies of using American
Nisei citizens in positions of camp responsibility, worked to shift
power and influence away from the Issei and onto the shoulders of
the Nisei.... Other community positions became available for the
first time to adult Japanese.[14]

The Bantu configurations of the Bantu Zionist churches reveal similar
structural arrangements incorporating new adaptations with traditional
forms:

The Bethesda type of church is an adaptation to modern conditions
of essential elements of two of the strongest institutions of the historical development of the Zulus: the temporary huts grouped in
sections according to status recall to any Zulu's mind, the ikhanda,
Shaka military kraal, where the King's followers of both sexes con-
gregated, fulfilling different tasks assigned to them by the king. The

follower's status was enhanced by their being in the King's presence.... The second traditional Zulu institution, on the pattern of which the Bethesda Church is evolved, is the community of diviners.... The Zionist prophet's activities follow the Zulu diviner in fairly minute detail.[15]

The fact that the Bantu churches use traditional leadership forms for new leaders under new circumstances should be noted here.

In his study *Bishops and Prophets in a Black City* (Soweto, Johannesburg), West illustrated the significance of prophet leadership to balance formal leadership of the bishops within the same Zionist church. Conflicts between the two forms of leadership are a constant threat, but the significance of the prophetic leadership (often women prophets) was their ability to draw in new members by an emphasis on non-bureaucratic religious forms, such as spiritual healing. Healing, in fact, is a powerful religious/ritual reflection of the perceived needs of black South African life. The persistence of the prophet-like leadership in league with, or in contrast to, formal leadership, is an important reflection of institutional/social response to material conditions.[16]

Similarly, Kiste noted dramatic changes among the relocated Bikini Islanders:

All of Marshallese society has traditionally been structured in terms of rights to land, and it would seem inevitable that the relocation of any community from its established landholdings would result in significant alterations in those relations between groups and individuals which are either determined or influenced by land rights. Given the competitive nature of the island society when matters of power and land are at stake, relocation is tantamount to the opening of Pandora's box.

For the Bikini Islanders, the resulting configuration was an adaptation of the community. The traditional household and lineage system was reorganized into a new communal structure that was divided by skills to cope with new crises. The traditional leader, the *alab*, lost authority:

As individuals, the alab had little opportunity to exercise any of their traditional authority. The kin groups which they headed were not functional in the alien environment, and the alab had little to do with directing the daily activities of the community. Wages meant an unprecedented degree of economic independence for most adults. As the alab did not control essential resources, others were not dependent upon them.... They questioned the traditional social order which divided Islanders into privileged and commoner classes.[17]

Finally, the new structural landholding groups among the Bikini Islanders were given a pseudo-lineage terminology, *bamli*, "family," thus completing the structural change.

To summarize, the conquest/domination of a social group can lead to a realignment of the group's actual *form*. In the Japanese-American camps, the "blocks" took on a familial form, complete with emerging "extended kin" behavior patterns. Among the Bikini Islanders, the reformulation of society also resulted in a familial fiction. In the form of the Zionist churches, Sundklar identified village patterns.

All these examples are confirmed by recent anthropological work on lineage systems, where fictionalized lineage is cited as a significant source for social cohesions.[18] Finally, the significance of familial cohesion to minorities under domination is illustrated by Spicer's work on Southwestern American Indian family systems and the attempted changes introduced by Spanish and Anglo administrators and settlers.[19]

But family systems, and their "use" in structural reformulation, is only one social response of note. A second is the emergence of new leadership out of the destruction of old systems.

The Rise of New Leadership

One of the most important places to see structural adaptation in conditions of domination is the positions of leadership. In looking for the mechanisms for influence in intercultural contact, Barth (among others) has called attention to the role of "elites" as middlemen in the transformation process. Eisenstadt, too, points to the role of elites in the process of cultural assimilation of Jews coming to Israel from a variety of cultures of origin.[20] But how does this invite structural change?

We can cite many examples for the ambiguous position of colonial attention to spurious leaders, the creation of "chiefs" in African and Polynesian tribes where the office of chief did not really exist before, or the preferential treatment given those who sympathize or cooperate with the conquering regime.

The use of second-generation "Nisei" (younger leaders) in the Japanese camps has already been noted and has been the subject of a great deal of study on the impact of the camps on traditional leadership patterns:

The..."Americanization" policy threatened one of the most basic Japanese cultural institutions, the family. Filial piety — the respect for elders and the role of the father as head of the household and embodiment of the ancestral spirits — was disregarded by the WRA in its "Americanization" of camp government. The WRA maintained that "since the objective of the WRA was to create a community as nearly American in its outlook and organization as possible, policy should conform with American practice, and only citizens should vote and hold office."...The WRA gave the Nisei special privileges and recognition because of their American citizenship.[21]

Kiste noted the case of the imposition on the Bikini Islanders of a "council" with a "chief" to negotiate with the Americans. But the rise of the "chief" in power was solely on the basis of the support of the dominating power and showed little understanding of the subtleties of Marshallese traditions, kin structure, and authority. This created severe tensions within the community itself and invited challenges from among the community members to the imposed leaders.

The creation of a loyal class of leadership is often seen in history. Lewis Coser, in a study of marginal people in foreign courts, pointed out that the Ottoman empire used Christian "slaves" by training young people, "converting" them to Islam, and sending them to the far reaches of the empire. This is compared by Coser to the use of "Court Jews" in the Hapsburg courts in medieval Germany. The phenomenon (so reminiscent of Daniel and his friends in the Babylonian courts) is held by Coser to be comparable to the "eunuchs guarding the harem," i.e., a landless people can be trusted to give total allegiance to the ruler.[22]

Raboteau in his study of American black/slave religious patterns emphasized the role of black preachers as cultural intermediaries between slave societies and white society. While they were considered suspicious agents of white power by some, their role as a new elite in new circumstances is comparable to our other cases of crisis leadership, even in their advice for a new strategies of survival. The black preachers were blamed for "pie in the sky" religion, but Raboteau reveals creative strategies of resistance that are evident in the interpretations of the Bible in sermons, the social significance of meetings, and the hidden social meanings of the spirituals.[23]

In sum, domination creates two levels of leadership within the captive population — those who appear "willing to cooperate" and those who resist this strategy. Both can be seen in roles of symbiotic relation to the dominant interests; *both can also be forms of resistance.* The frequent biblical motif of the loyal court Jew who ultimately does not abandon faith is an indication of this and provides possible insights into the lives of Jews in Exile (see below). Minority elites who act as court Jews are often bitterly resented as turncoat collaborators; they often see themselves, however, as acting on behalf of their people. Cases abound in biblical texts of precisely such figures (Joseph, David among the Philistines, Moses among the Egyptians, Esther, Jeremiah).

The symbiotic relationship between the dominant groups and the minority affects the structure of the entire minority group as well as its leadership. Just as in the case of the elites, such a symbiotic relationship can be a form of resistance and not capitulation.

Finally, we note that cases of directed contact may result in the communal restructuring of society. This is not simply a measure of the influence of the dominant society, but may well reflect creative responses to conflict. If the Babylonian Exile exhibits any of these social mechanisms, then we must look carefully at the form of self-government of the exiles and the returning exiles in Ezra-Nehemiah, in whatever textual evidence we can find, for evidence of the kinds of social restructuring we have illustrated. Furthermore, we will look for conflicts in leadership, created either by the democratizing effects of crisis that lead to a more rational and less traditional leadership based on skills appropriate to the moment, or by differences of strategy toward the ruling power.

Ritual

A significant mechanism of boundary maintenance is ritual. Ritual is often considered merely routinized behavior (Sorokin) or, more disparagingly, as "sacerdotal nonsense" (LaBarre).[24] Such views share an inability to interpret ritual in its own terms and in its societal context, as opposed to its specific association with a certain power group, that is, to interpret ritual functionally.

The most important recent consideration of the social functions and sources of ritual is Mary Douglas's *Purity and Danger*.[25] Douglas began her own work with a review of scholarship on Old Testament ritual texts. Nineteenth-century scholars such as W. Robertson Smith attempted to differentiate "authentic" religion from the primitive "survivals," i.e., ritual and purity laws, which were seen as irrelevant. Their existence alongside the pristine glory of the prophetic religion could only be explained in this way. This bias has maintained itself throughout the evolution of critical studies of the Bible, as we have already noted.

Douglas, on the other hand, believes that purity, and the rituals associated with the fear of pollution, are best understood in relation to society. Fear of pollution represents the "stress points" of a society.

In attempting to elucidate the meaning of the purity of certain animal species over others, Douglas believes that impurity, or pollution, is a threat from those cases that do not fit clear, identifiable categories. In the classification of animals, any animal with a trait that placed it outside well-defined categories — for example, sea animals that appeared to be fish but were without scales or fins — was seen as impure because it was outside the category. The maintenance of these lines, for Douglas, is the maintenance of order itself, or, more precisely, the order of society.

Douglas then applies this theory to the purity laws of the book of Leviticus. In contrast to rationalizing interpretations (reasons of hygiene, etc.), the key, Douglas believes, is found within the texts themselves:

> Pollution behaviour is the reaction which condemns any object or idea likely to confuse or contradict cherished classifications.... Any interpretation will fail which takes the "do nots" of the Old Testament in piecemeal fashion. The only sound approach is to forget hygiene, aesthetics, morals, and instinctive revulsion, even to forget the Canaanites and the Zoroastrian Magi and start with the texts. Since each of the injunctions is prefaced by the command to be holy, they must be explained by that command.... We can conclude that holiness is exemplified by completeness. Holiness requires that individuals shall conform to the class to which they belong. And holiness requires that different classes of things shall not be confused.... Those species are unclean which are imperfect members of their class or whose class itself confounds the general scheme of the world.[26]

It should be noted that Douglas's view does not consider redactional issues in the study of the Levitical material. This is a major consideration in our analysis (chap. 6), but does not necessarily render Douglas's insights invalid. Neither do the observations made by some that the practices of surrounding peoples, i.e., Canaanites, were incorporated into purity laws as practices considered particularly polluting or odious. Davis has suggested, for example, that the raising of pigs by the Philistines may have contributed, historically, to the revulsion against pork. The practices of "outsiders" is just as much a threat to the body politic as other symbolic outside forces that are the subject of Douglas's analysis.[27]

Thus, purity laws would serve a theological, as well as a moral/ethical, purpose:

> The dietary laws would have been like signs which at every turn inspired meditation on the oneness, purity, and completeness of God. By rules of avoidance, holiness was given a physical expression in every encounter with the animal kingdom and at every meal. Observance of the dietary rules would thus have been a meaningful part of the great liturgical act of recognition and worship which culminated in the sacrifice in the Temple.[28]

But ritual and legalism also serve a social-defensive function. This is particularly interesting in reference to the polluting qualities of bodily functions:

> We cannot possibly interpret rituals concerning excreta, breast milk, saliva, and the rest unless we are prepared to see in the body a symbol of society, and to see the powers and dangers credited in social structure reproduced in small on the human body.... Four kinds of social pollution seem worth distinguishing. The first is danger pressing on external boundaries; the second, danger from transgressing the internal line of the system; the third is danger in the margins of the lines. The fourth danger ... [is] ... internal contradiction, when some of the basic postulates are denied by other basic postulates, so that at certain points the system seems to be at war with itself.[29]

Douglas has shown how the priestly concerns with ritual, especially with regard to purity and pollution, are especially evident in situations of danger, i.e., threats to the continued existence of a minority group. Thus, just as the prophet can arise as a messenger of a new "mazeway" composed from the raw materials of the old ways, which are carefully selected for their value in preserving the identity and cohesion of the community in crisis, so too is the work of the priest an attempt to "structure for defense," perhaps to be considered in many ways equally as creative and equally as expedient for the body politic.

Thus, the rituals reflect the relationship between a minority and a majority and serve to verify the predominant relationship.

Related to the threat of impurity is the threat of those "on the borders." Douglas suggested that there are examples of women threatening the order of a largely male defined society:

> Where the social system is well-articulated, I look for articulate powers vested in the points of authority: where the social system is ill-articulated, I look for inarticulated powers vested in those who are a source of disorder.[30]

From Katzir's work on Yemeni Jewish communities, we can cite the significance of the low position of women in Yemeni Jewish society. The low position of women in Yemeni Jewish society is directly linked by Katzir to their function as sources of influence from the margins of their society by their outside contacts, especially with surrounding Arab society.[31] Katzir specifically noted the infusion of Arabic folk songs into Jewish culture, a direct borrowing of tunes and lyrics from Moslem-

Arabic songs. (One is reminded of the dismissal of foreign wives in the post-exilic community of Judah after the return from Exile.)

Taking his cue from Douglas's formulations, J. P. Kiernan has also considered the symbolic significance of ritual in the Zionist Bantu churches:

> One of the foremost concerns of a Zionist band in Kwa Mashu is to protect itself against the township as an African community by drawing and maintaining boundaries setting off its membership from the rest of the population. This separation and closing off is vividly dramatized at each Sunday morning of the band by firmly shutting the doors and the window at certain points in the proceedings, and this in spite of the ghastly mid-day heat which suffuses the crowded room.... The action of shutting the township out may be taken as a statement of exclusiveness. It is accompanied by other observances which make the same point. One of these is the mandatory removal of foot-wear. That there is biblical precedent for this is not a sufficient explanation: it must fit a contemporary frame of meaning. I suggest that it is an act of exclusion for it is not the mere removal of shoes that is significant, but the fact that they are left outside. The point about shoes is that they carry the dust of the township upon them and it is this veneer of township life that is withheld from crossing the threshold of the meeting-room.... Uncontaminated by alien dust, and with his workday clothes completely concealed under a laundered white robe, the Zionist makes the transition from one social universe to another.[32]

Sundklar noted the role of healing as a social ritual:

> The Church ... [cares] ... for them in the crises of life. Ill-health is rampant in the city, and Zionist prophets gather crowds in the hovels of the slum or out on the "veld" to pray for the sick and drive out demons. Just off the main road ... they congregate in their hundreds on the Sunday afternoons, laying healing hands on the sick. [The Church] ... is close at hand, and its fellowship, in a strange and bitter world, is reassuring and full of warmth.[33]

Okihiro mentions the revival of folk beliefs and ritual in the Japanese camps and concludes:

> The functional usefulness of this revival of ethnic folk belief during the period of camp confinement was evidenced in its rapid

decline once the camps had been disbanded. Commented a former... internee: "Oh, those fox and badger stories back in the
Center; well, people used to believe a lot of things in the Center
they never believed before and haven't believed since!"[34]

Raboteau cites a variety of ritualistic "protection" and separation rites
in slave communities, such as placing open pots on the ground around
clandestine meetings to "hold the sound" so that they would not be
detected. Recent studies of Voodoo rites among rebel slave communities
have emphasized their function as part of the weaponry of social conflict
and resistance against the slave masters.[35] Raboteau's main interest,
however, was in how slave religion reinterpreted the adopted *Christian*
symbols and rites into mechanisms of resistance:

> Prayer, preaching, song, communal support, and especially "feeling
> the spirit" refreshed the slaves and consoled them in their times
> of distress. By imagining their lives in the context of a different
> future, they gained hope in the present....
>   Prayer was such an effective symbol of resistance because both
> masters and slaves believed in the power of prayer. Hence the
> desperate need of some masters and mistresses for slaves to pray
> for the success of the Confederacy and hence their anger when
> slaves dissembled or refused outright to do so.[36]

In sum, the role of ritual in minority, dominated contexts may play an
important functional role in the preservation and symbolic resistance of
the group in question. This, too, can form a testable exegetical question
for work on texts from the Babylonian Exile.

Folklore

As we are especially concerned with evidence that is literary in nature,
it is important to identify types of literature that have their sources in
the sociological conditions of minorities in exile, with a relationship of
domination by a majority culture.

Peter Hinton's particular anthropological interest is the Karen tribe
in Burma, who occupy large stretches of borderland between two different cultural areas. They have maintained their identity despite clear
pressures from a variety of ethnic groups. Hinton reports that there was
a unique legend that was popular among the Karen, which involved an
orphan who overcame obstacles to achieve success. Hinton called this
an archetype Karen folktale. This raises the image of the hero as a type
in minority folklore.[37]

In a 1974 article, "Folklore as Culture of Contestation," Luigi Lombardi made provocative comments about the social content of folklore:

> Folk-culture...marks the outer limit of the hegemonic culture, whose ideological tricks it reveals, contesting at times only with its own presence the universality, which is only superficial, of the official culture's concepts of the world and of life....In the subordinate folk-world,...behaviour...is *contestant* of that behaviour produced by the dominant ideology, in other words, [it is] a behaviour which potentially governs itself.[38]

If our particular interest is in hero legends, how would these be related to Lombardi's observation? In 1954, Orrin Klapp wrote of the importance of the theme of the victory of the small hero over the large enemy, usually through cleverness or piety. Following this, Roger Abrahams's theory went further in studying the development of hero stories in their social context. Abrahams's analysis was an attempt to systematize his observations of hero types in American black folklore: written, oral, and cinematic. Abrahams defined the heroic role as "...the attainment of public acclaim by specific figures (whether real or mythic or fictional) whose actions are seen as noteworthy and good, and in most cases, worthy of emulation.... Hero stories are a depiction, a projection, of values in story form."[39]

The unique focus of Abrahams's analysis is precisely the relationship of the theme of the story with the *social event of recounting the story.* Thus hero stories are told among black Americans:

1. to increase the storyteller's prestige;

2. to give the audience a plan of action that is viable in present and recurring situations;

3. to provide the male audience with male deeds in the past or bolster present confidence;

4. to provide for future success;

5. to fulfill manliness by association of teller and audience with the subject of the hero story.[40]

Furthermore, Abrahams believes that hero stories undergo changes as the social basis of the storytelling culture changes. In the stage where the values inherent in the hero story are operative, there is genuine regard for the antagonist. When there is a collapse of the societal possibility of embodying the values of the hero, then the hero becomes a superman, always ready to fight, with no regard for the antagonist. Finally, the hero himself decays, and stories reflect desperation — passive, suicidal, or powerless clowning heros.

Goiten has collected folklore stories from Yemeni Jews, who have a rich and varied tradition. The story of Maimuni especially illustrates the kind of unique literature that has its particular source in the diaspora. In this story, Maimuni is a doctor to the sultan and incurs the jealousy of non-Jews who resent his high position. The sultan is talked into a contest between a master of poison and Maimuni, the winner to be the sultan's physician. But not only does Maimuni know the antidote to each of his opponent's poisons; he responds by encouraging his opponent to *believe* that Maimuni is also poisoning him in return. In the end, Maimuni's opponent dies of sheer fright of imagined poison rather than any real concoction. The sultan is pleased with Maimuni's cleverness and piety (for he would not really kill his opponent, as the Law prevents murder), and he is rewarded. This story illustrates the weapon of cleverness of the powerless, as Klapp noted above, and also serves as an example to illustrate "diaspora ethics." Finally, it includes the essential element of the emphasis on Maimuni's Jewish identity and the jealousy of the dominant ethnic group.[41]

It does not seem to matter whether the stories are traditional or synthesized. Indeed, Geertz notes the role of synthesized tribal histories in Nigeria that helped to galvanize resistance to colonial administration.[42]

Kiste notes the creation of "new histories" of the Bikini Islanders in order to restore a new sense of continuity and strength in their exile.[43]

In a related manner, the often humorous stories from Afro-American slavery illustrate the clever hero motif. Because the literature on African-American slave folklore is vast, a few examples will suffice to make the point:

> The master called the slave to his sick bed. "Good-bye, Jack; I have a long journey to go; farewell...." Jack replies, "Farewell massa! Pleasant journey; you soon be dere, massa — all de way down hill!!"...
>
> Slave named George was informed by his master that he was to be buried in a good coffin and placed beside his master's earthly remains in the same vault with the white folks. George's response to this news is mixed: "I like to have good coffin when I die,... but I 'fraid, massa, when de debbil come take your body, he make mistake, and get mine!"[44]

Lastly, one can point to the rich folklore of heroes and laments that were an aspect of American slavery, taken directly from the biblical motifs of the time period we have under consideration and thus representing a "hermeneutic of the poor":

The story of Israel's exodus from Egypt helped make it possible for the slave to project a future radically different from their present. From other parts of the Bible, especially the Prophetic and apocalyptic books, the slaves drew descriptions which gave form and, thus, assurance, to their anticipation of deliverance.[45]

"O my Lord delivered Daniel.... O Why not deliver me, too ?"[46]

In his research on the cultural expression of the Japanese-American internees, Marvin Opler included striking examples of a revival of interest in the legendary swordsmen of Japanese folklore, the Ninjitsu.[47]

In the methodology and theology of the Zionist movements, we see even further evidence of the theological/social reaction to domination. This is particularly clear in the areas of status reversal. Sundklar identifies the following themes unique to Zionist theology. The first reveals the hero motif again — the black Christ — the true Jesus as opposed to the white Jesus and white God preached by the oppressors; part of this theme involves the reversal of the color bar in heaven. Sundklar quotes the end of a story about the reversal of the color bar:

> There were ten virgins. And five of them were White, and five were Black. The five Whites were foolish, but the five Blacks were wise, they had oil in their lamps. All ten came to the gate, but the five White virgins received the same answer as the rich man received (in Lazarus, Luke 16). Because the Whites rule on earth, the Blacks do so in Heaven. The Whites will go a-begging to dip the tip of their finger in cool water. But they will get as a reply, "Hhayyi(no) — nobody can rule twice."[48]

In his monumental analysis of the hero motif, Joseph Campbell outlined a basic form: The hero leaves the normal world to go to a "supernatural realm" where he encounters forces, wins a decisive victory, and returns from this task able to bestow help on others.[49]

Among the variations of the venture into the unknown world is what Campbell called "the belly of the whale." The endurance of a life-threatening test becomes the focus of the hero's heroism, which results in the conclusion that, after all, there is nothing to fear.[50] Although Campbell's literary analysis is helpful, the absence of any material analysis, social or economic sources of themes, renders his generalized comparisons somewhat questionable. Our interest is in those aspects of a story that reflect social conditions.

The two elements of the hero stories of exiled peoples that appear to be most consistently important are (1) the similarity of the hero's fate to that of the community, and (2) the ability of the hero to overcome his or her circumstances armed with the "weapons" available to the community in their social circumstances (piety, cleverness, etc.).

How these mechanisms can serve as a guide for biblical exegesis of exilic texts is the question to which we now turn.

NOTES

1. Grant McClellan, ed., *Southern Africa,* The Reference Shelf, 51, no. 3, p. 28; see also Bengt Sundklar, *Bantu Prophets in South Africa,* 2nd ed. (International African Institute, Oxford University Press, 1964); Christopher Hill, *Bantustans: The Fragmentation of South Africa* (London, 1964); South African Council of Churches, *Relocations: The Churches Report on Forced Removals in South Africa,* 1984; Martin West, *Bishops and Prophets in a Black City: African Independent Churches in Soweto, Johannesburg* (Cape Town, 1975); M. L. Daneel, *Old and New in Southern Shona Independent Churches,* vols. 1–2 (The Hague, 1971).

2. West, *Bishops and Prophets in a Black City,* p. 4.

3. See John Hope Franklin, *From Slavery to Freedom: A History of Negro Americans,* 3rd ed. (New York, 1969); Orlando Patterson, *Slavery and Social Death: A Comparative Study* (Cambridge, Mass., 1982); Albert J. Raboteau, *Slave Religion: The Invisible Institution in the Antebellum South* (Oxford, 1978).

4. Franklin, *From Slavery to Freedom,* p. 59.

5. On Japanese-American internment, see Dillon S. Myer, *Uprooted Americans: The Japanese-Americans and War Relocation Authority during World War II* (Tucson, 1971); John Model, ed., *The Kikuchi Diary: Chronicle from an American Concentration Camp* (Urbana, 1973); D. S. Thomas and R. S. Nishimoto, *The Spoilage* (Berkeley, 1946); Harry H. L. Kitano, *Japanese-Americans: The Evolution of a Sub-Culture* (New York, 1969), esp. chap. 5, "The Wartime Evacuation"; D. Kitagawa, *Issei and Nisei: The Internment Years* (New York, 1967); Roger Daniels, *Concentration Camps USA: Japanese-Americans and World War II* (New York, 1971). See also the various studies of Marvin Opler on cultural activities in the camps, "Japanese Folk Beliefs and Practices, Tule Lake, California," *Journal of American Folklore,* 63 (1950), and, with F. Obayashi, "Senryu Poetry as Folk and Community Expression," *Journal of American Folklore,* 58, no. 227 (January–March 1945); "A 'Sumo' Tournament at Tule Lake Center," *American Anthropologist,* 47 (1945), pp. 134–139.

I also want to express my appreciation to Dr. Peter Suzuki, himself a scholar of the concentration camps, and Dr. Gary Okihiro, who sent me a copy of his offprint, "Religion and Resistance in America's Concentration Camps."

6. Robert C. Kiste, *The Bikinians: A Study in Forced Migration* (New York, 1974), p. 3. Kiste's bibliography is helpful, although the literature on the Bikini Islanders is not extensive. In 1954, Leonard Mason wrote his Yale University dissertation, "Relocation of the Bikini Marshallese: A Study of Group Migration," which has not yet, to my knowledge, been published in any form.

7. Paul Brass, "Ethnicity and Nationality Formation," *Ethnicity,* 3 (1976), p. 35.

8. Liucija Baskauskas, "The Lithuanian Refugee Experience and Grief," *International Migration Review,* 15, no. 1 (1981), p. 281.

9. Yael Katzir, "Preservation of Jewish Identity in Yemen," *Comparative Studies in Society and History,* 24, no. 2 (April 1982), pp. 273–275.

10. Frederick Barth, ed., *Ethnic Groups and Boundaries: The Social Organization of Culture Difference* (London, 1969), p. 16.

11. Judith Nagata, "In Defense of Ethnic Boundaries . . . ," in Charles Keyes, ed., *Ethnic Adaptation and Identity* (New York, 1979).

12. Okihiro, "Religion and Resistance in America's Concentration Camps," pp. 11–12.

13. Kitagawa, *Issei and Nisei,* pp. 91 and 106–108.

14. Kitano, *Japanese-Americans,* pp. 75–77.

15. Sundklar, *Bantu Prophets in South Africa,* p. 55.

16. West, *Bishops and Prophets in a Black City* p. 50.

17. Kiste, *The Bikinians,* pp. 75 and 90.

18. R. Wilson, *Genealogy and History in the Biblical World* (New Haven: Yale University Press, 1977), p. 54; and David Tait and John Middleton, eds., *Tribes Without Rulers* (London, 1958).

19. Chap. 16, "Community Reorientation," in E. Spicer, *Cycles of Conquest: The Impact of Spain, Mexico and the United States on the Indians of the Southwest, 1533–1960* (Tucson, 1962).

20. See also D. J. Lawless, "Attitudes of Leaders of Immigrant and Ethnic Societies in Vancouver towards Integration into Canadian Life," *International Migration,* 11, no. 3 (1964); S. N. Eisenstadt, "The Place of Elites and Primary Groups in the Absorption of New Immigrants in Israel," *American Journal of Sociology,* 7 (November 1951); Nicholas Tabuchis, *Pastors and Immigrants: The Role of a Religious Elite in the Absorption of Norwegian Immigrants* (The Hague, 1963).

21. Okihiro, "Religion and Resistance in America's Concentration Camps," p. 10.

22. Lewis Coser, "The Alien as Servant of Power: Court Jews and Christian Renegades," *American Sociological Review,* 37 (October 1972).

23. Chap. 4 in Raboteau, *Slave Religion.*

24. See W. LaBarre, *The Ghost Dance and the Origins of Religion* (London, 1972).

25. Mary Douglas, *Purity and Danger* (London, 1966).

26. Ibid., p. 36.

27. Christie Davis, "Filthy Pigs and Holy Cows," lecture, All Souls College, Oxford University, 1984.

28. Douglas, *Purity and Danger,* p. 57.

29. Ibid., p. 122.

30. Ibid., p. 99.

31. Katzir, "Preservation of Jewish Identity in Yemen," p. 277.

32. J. P. Kiernan, "Where Zionists Draw the Line: A Study of Religious Exclusiveness in an African Township," *Journal of African Studies,* 33, no. 2 (1974), p. 82.

33. See Sundklar, *Bantu Prophets in South Africa.*

34. Okihiro, "Religion and Resistance in America's Concentration Camps," p. 17, and Opler and Obayashi, "Senryu Poetry as Folk and Community Expression."

35. Raboteau, *Slave Religion,* p. 238; and see R. Pierre, "Caribbean Religion: The Voodoo Case," *Sociological Analysis,* 38 (1977).

36. Raboteau, ibid., pp. 237ff.

37. Peter Hinton, "The Karen, Millennialism, and the Politics of Accommodation to Lowland States," in Charles Keyes, *Ethnic Adaptation and Identity* (Philadelphia, 1979).

38. Luigi Lombardi, "Folklore as Culture of Contestation," *Journal of the Folklore Institute,* 2, no. 1/2 (June–August 1974).

39. Orrin Klapp, "The Clever Hero," *Journal of American Folklore,* 67, no. 263 (January–March 1954).

40. Roger Abrahams, "Some Varieties of Heroes in America," *Journal of Folklore Institute,* 3 (1966), p. 340. If Abrahams is correct in this three-part evolution, then the diaspora stories of the Bible are clearly between the first and second stage, with the Apocalyptic genre possibly resembling more the second. (See the chapter on folklore of Exile).

41. H. S. Goiten, "How Maimuni Conquered His Adversary or Imagination Kills," in *From the Land of Sheba* (New York, 1947). This story reveals a number of parallels to Daniel-type stories, even in the introduction that establishes the low-status origins of Maimuni as a Jew.

42. Clifford Geertz, "The Integrative Revolution," in Clifford Geertz, ed. *Old Societies and New States* (New York, 1963), p. 127.

43. Kiste, *The Bikinians,* pp. 98 and 148.
44. Raboteau, *Slave Religion,* p. 292.
45. Ibid., p. 312.
46. Ibid., p. 292.
47. Opler, "Japanese Folk Beliefs, " (1950), p. 385.
48. Sundklar, *Bantu Prophets in South Africa,* p. 291.
49. Joseph Campbell, *The Hero with a Thousand Faces* (New York, 1949).
50. Ibid., p. 93.

Part II

Selected Texts

Chapter 4

Structural Adaptation in Exilic Society

In our survey of sociological paradigms, we have seen that mass deportation causes social uprooting that can lead to new social structures, either because the old structures are forcibly broken, and/or new circumstances must be adapted to with innovative means. This process, we stated, involves both continuity (the preservation of traditional forms) and change. In the following section, I will argue that the exilic material from the Bible reveals both continuity and change in various aspects of the social life of the exile community. It should be said, however, that the kind of "social adaptation" referred to here can easily be overstated. In the case of the Japanese-Americans, for example the adoption of the block residential units as significant social units was not an adaptation that lasted beyond the immediate circumstances of exile. In the case of the Bikini Islanders, however, the changes solidified into new forms of social existence. The adaptations that we find in the biblical material must therefore be located on such a spectrum, without overemphasizing the extent of change, or underestimating the possibility of unique social forms for the post-exilic community. In any case, we must begin with the social group.

We can base an assumption that the exiles lived in large groups on many pieces of evidence from the biblical record. The number of the exiles would lead one to suppose that they could not have been scattered so widely that substantial numbers were not together.

Josephus (*Contra Apionem,* 1) records a note by Berossus to the effect that Nebuchadnezzar, "being now master of his father's entire realm,...gave orders to allot to the captives, on their arrival, settlements in the most suitable districts of Babylonia...."[1] Although we cannot assume too much from such a late tradition, we shall see that this passage makes some sense.

But it is needless to speculate along this line, for both Ezekiel and Jeremiah speak of "elders" among the Exile community (Ezek. 8:1; Jer. 29:1), which suggest that groups of exiles were able to organize

93

themselves into a form of self-government. We have already seen how significant local autonomy and self-management is for the survival of identity and group-awareness among displaced or otherwise dominated peoples in recent history. As Eph'al has pointedly indicated, the most important single piece of evidence for successful self-management that preserved identity among the Babylonian exiles was the return itself.[2] In this section, we will consider aspects of social structure of pre-exilic and post-exilic Israel, to assess the extent of structural continuity and change that is evident in the texts; we will illustrate the principle of adaptation in Exile by investigating the self-management of the Babylonian Jewish community; a community that would continue to call itself the *bnê hā-golâ* — "sons of the Exile" — even a generation or two after the end of the Exile itself. It should be understood at the outset that the type of textual evidence for this issue requires careful, and at times perhaps even tedious, discussion.

Elders

The continuous presence of "elders" in ancient Israel represents a major aspect of continuity in the post-exilic community. The Hebrew forms of elder leadership have been the subject of extensive scholarly attention.[3] The book of Judges, chapter 8, cites *sārîm*, "officials," *'anšê*, "men...," and "elders" of Succoth. These terms are used almost interchangeably to refer to the leaders of the city, and they make precise conclusions difficult about the exact use and referent of the term *zᵉqēnîm*, "elders."

Elders, in the book of Judges, are usually the leaders of cities, that is, settlements of substantial size (e.g., Judg. 8:16; 11:5). Sometimes a "savior," like Jephthah (Judg. 11), is called on by the elders when a military leader cannot be found among the elders themselves.[4] But can anything more historically precise be said about elders?

The function of elders is usually provided by the context. Generally, elders are in a representative role. The most common term is "elders of Israel." In Exodus, the elders are constantly in dialogue with Moses as the representatives of all of Israel (Exod. 3:16, 18, 4:29, 12:30). The implication of these passages is that elders gathered for decision making. Elders appear in all the books of the Pentateuch, in all the historical books, in Isaiah, Jeremiah, Ezekiel, and Joel among the prophets, and in Lamentations, Job, Psalms, and Proverbs among the Writings.[5]

Scholars have differentiated between elders of the country and elders of an urban area. There is a variety of functions that elders perform. First, they represent the entire people or a community in political or religious activity (e.g., Exod. 3:16; 4:29; 17:5–6; Lev. 4:15). An interesting comparison is the elders who go to consult Elisha (2 Kings 6:32) and the occasions for the consultation of Ezekiel in Exile (14:1, 20:1, and 8:1). Second, elders can accompany leaders on missions, such as Moses' visit to Pharaoh (Exod. 3:18).[6] Third, elders appear as a governing body (Josh. 9:11, Ps. 107:32) in negotiating treaties (1 Sam. 16:4; McKenzie includes Ezra 5:5 and 6:7 and 14). Fourth, in the monarchical period, elders were part of the royal council (2 Sam. 17:4–16). 1 Kings 20:7f. shows Ahab consulting elders on a decision. Lastly, elders appear as a judicial body or as taking part in judicial processes. In the trial of Jeremiah, priests, prophets, and others are mentioned along with elders. McKenzie further believes that the function of the elders changed over time.[7]

It seems clear that elders are prominent citizens, since they are in constant relation with the high officials like the *sārîm*[8] and are also included in such classic prophetic condemnations of abused authority as Isa. 3:14:

> Yahweh calls to judgement
> the elders and the princes of his people.
> You are the ones who destroy the vineyard
> and conceal what you have stolen from the poor.

It has always been assumed that the root for "elder" comes from *zqn*, "beard," and thus refers to actual old people, but it is uncertain whether the etymology of the word continues to be operative in relation to qualifications for elders throughout the use of the term. Anthropological comparative material leads one to suspect that elders must have been heads of local households or families.[9] The latest version of Joseph in Genesis includes elders of the family of Pharaoh (50:7). There are elders of David's house in 2 Sam. 12:17, yet the passage Exod. 12:21 implies that the elders are based in the *Mišpᵉḥôt* (the next largest unit after the household, sometimes called "clan") for whom the elders will choose sacrifices.

It appears that elders are based on family structures, but whether they were representative of the pre-exilic *Bēt-'Āb* or the pre-exilic *Mišpᵉḥôt* must remain an open question. It seems that the only clear level of representation that the pre-exilic material unquestionably reveals is elders of cities, which may be based on representation of the families within the cities. A further problem is separating the use of *zaqēn*, "old man" with *zᵉqēnîm*, "elders" (see, for example, 1 Sam. 2:31). Does it merely mean "no one will grow old in Eli's house," or that no one will be able to attain the office of elder and represent Eli's house? The important point is that elders, while possibly chosen on the basis of representatives of a household (*Bēt 'Āb*), are most typically associated with cities and settled existence — perhaps, but not certainly, determined as representatives of the families in that city.

Finally, McKenzie believes that the power of the elders was progressively eroded by the power of the king.[10]

Reviv has discussed the significance of "elders" in the leadership of kingless cities in the El-Amarna letters. The elders of Irqata "considered themselves competent to approach Pharaoh directly."[11] Assemblies of elders of cities in other Ancient Near Eastern material have been considered in the discussion brought about by Jacobsen's now famous essay, "Primitive Democracy in Ancient Mesopotamia."[12] Wolf, for example, in dialogue with Jacobsen's views, has suggested that "elders" were not at all representative of the people, but that the typical feature of premonarchical Israel was Jewish self-government by democratic assembly.[13]

Wolf believes, with others, that terms such as "elders," 'am ha-'areṣ, and "all the men of Israel," 'edâ, and qāhal were used interchangeably. McKenzie, however, has strongly objected to Wolf's view on the basis that one cannot assume such imprecise use of various terms, and furthermore such a general assembly is not thought by comparative anthropology to be compatible with representative government (or select-person government).[14] Gordis believes that the evolution of constituent representative government in the ancient history of the Jews would be a natural consequence of settled existence — an evolution that eventually led to centralized leadership under a monarchy. But it was never totally abolished under the monarchy: "New conditions led to the diminution of its functions so that ultimately it was convened only in hours of critical importance."[15]

The prevailing view associates elders with settled existence. This would be confirmed by the typical places of decision mentioned in the biblical material for the *assembly* of elders (Isa. 3:14; Ps. 107:32).

Thus, we have the city gate associated with elders (Ruth, Prov. 31:23, Deut. 22:15, Zech. 8:4, Lam. 5:14), with prophets (1 Kings 22:10), with assemblies of the people and king (1 Kings 21:8, 2 Kings 10:1; 33:1), and with the 'edâ (Lev. 4:13, 15; Num. 35:12, 24–25; Josh. 20:6; 1 Kings 22:10; and probably also in the account of Jeremiah's trial). All these considerations lead to the conclusion that elders had a pronounced urban context and were directly involved with government of the people as a settled unit. It seems a minor step indeed to suggest that the very presence of elders in Ezekiel and Jeremiah indicates a self-managed settlement of Jews able to govern, particularly as Jeremiah's letter refers to a group of exiles by means of addressing the elders. These elders were able to make decisions about their lives with relative autonomy. The combination of the city gate with elders and prophets (not to mention royalty and nobles) is suggestive. Not only are we told of an elders' meeting in the book of Ezekiel; it is clearly an occasion when Ezekiel, as a prophet, spoke, thus suggesting the maintenance of a kind of gathering common to the pre-exilic function of elders.

As we have seen, one cannot discount the influence that the dominant group has on the captive population. We have noted the frequent organizational (as well as cultural) impact that dominant groups can have on the dominated. One cannot, therefore, dismiss the possibility, suggested by cuneiform texts and anthropological comparison, that the rise of the elders to prominence in the self-government of the Jewish exiles had as much to do with the expectations of the Babylonians and the Persians in dealing with foreign populations (the "take us to your leader[s]" phenomenon), as it did with the preservation of a traditional political system of the exiles themselves. Therefore elders may not be mentioned simply because of a continuity with the pre-exilic forms of settled self-government. Furthermore, the use of the term *roš* for communal leaders amounts to a difference in nomenclature that may well signal a new concept of leader (see below). In the case of the Jews, continuity probably had an influence, but this must be seen alongside the needs of the Jews in exile to adapt to their new environment and "authorities." Why, then, are contacts with the Neo-Babylonians not specifically mentioned? This is a misleading silence, because we know that the implication of Jeremiah's "letter" was advice to the exiles to be involved in Babylonian society to some extent by planting gardens and building houses (Jer. 29:5), obviously involving commerce (not unlike the land sale attested to in Camb. 85, involving the Egyptian elders).[16]

In conclusion, the presence of elders suggests that the Jewish settlements governed themselves similarly to pre-exilic urban existence, even to the point of maintaining gatherings for decisions and the hearing of prophets. This would seem to represent crucial aspects of sociological continuity in Exile. Is there other evidence for change as well as continuity? For this, we turn to an examination of the pre-exilic *Bēt 'Āb* and the post-exilic *Bēt 'Ābôt*, beginning with a consideration of the terms for leaders.

Rost had concluded a study of the elders and the "heads" by stating that he believes that a *roš*, "head," stood over the *Bēt 'Āb* after the exilic period, whereas before the Exile, a *zaqēn*, "elder," was over a *Mišpᵉḥâ* (clan?).[17]

Rost points out that the term *roš* is used in the Hexateuch only nineteen times other than in the P source, but twenty times in P alone, and no less than sixty times in the post-exilic literature. The heads of the post-exilic *Bēt 'Ābôt*, said Rost, were these *rošîm*, because the literature seems to drop the office of *zaqēn*.[18] It is incontestable that *roš* became the preferred term, but this term signified someone who had more authority than an elder, even though he was still himself an elder in the post-exilic *Bēt 'Ābôt*, simply because "elders" are still found in Ezra.

Exod. 18:25ff. recounts the selection by Moses of intermediary authorities to act as Judges, which account is repeated in Deut. 1:9ff. The result is the selection of *rošîm*. When Num. 11:16ff. recounts a similar story, the leaders are selected from among the elders. Consistent with this, in Deut. 5:23 the "heads of the tribes" are set *alongside* the elders.

In Josh. 21 the heads of the houses seem to be equated with *Mišpᵉḥôt* (clans?). As early as Micah 3, "heads" of the "house" of Jacob are condemned for the perversion of justice.

Thus, these important examples of the use of *roš*, when placed alongside the use of *zaqēn*, "elder," illustrate that post-exilic redactions of pre-exilic sources reveal the concern to relate the "heads" to the elders of Israel, and that the two *coexisted.*

The *roš* rose to prominence as leaders of the *Bēt 'Ābôt,* not in a direct line with the elders, but rather as a more select group among them.[19] If we are correct in arguing that the post-exilic *Bēt 'Ābôt* is a larger construct different from the pre-exilic *Bēt 'Āb*, then continuity in the development of the *roš* makes perfect sense, as leaders of conglomerates of Jews (that is, larger than the pre-exilic *Bēt 'Āb*). *Rošîm* continue to be leaders of the large, resident segments of Jews in the post-exilic community, who "prove" their functional familial fiction by genealogies, like the Golah List. We will pursue this later below. The evidence does not allow us to suggest that elders in the pre-exilic era are the same as *rošîm*, "heads," in the post-exilic era. "Heads" were earlier leaders of large segments of the Jews in exile and especially of the post-exilic *Bēt 'Ābôt* (the exact nature of the latter term will be discussed below). The stories of the "heads" being chosen from among elders does not allow Rost's simple line from one to the other, but suggests co-existence of the two institutions.[20]

So what is the relation between the elders (in the pre-exilic structure) and what came to be called *rošîm* in the post-exilic structure? To begin with, we return to our question about whether elders were actually the eldest males of pre-exilic *Bēt 'Āb*. McKenzie believes this to be the case, on an analogy with Bedouin sheikhs.[21]

The view taken by McKenzie has been accepted by the scholars who have thought about the connections possible between leaders of the tertiary subdivisions and elders. The very term suggests age; but the lack of an explicit connection in any source requires that we consider other possibilities. It can be argued that while elders are continuous, they are not integrally tied to the social structure and that the structure changed. *In other words, elders in the post-exilic period were speaking for a Jewish people with different social structures in the post-exilic community, and some of them became leaders known as* rošîm, *who eventually had much more significant authority over these larger, changed social groups in the post-exilic period.*

If elders are based in the pre-exilic households known as the *Bēt 'Āb*, then a post-exilic construct known as the *Bēt 'Ābôt* would naturally include these elders if it included the smaller *Bēt 'Āb* units. The plural form of *Bēt 'Ābôt* leads one to suspect that these structures were conglomerates of *Bēt 'Āb* households (individual *Bēt 'Āb*'s). Thus, on the analogy of our displaced peoples who are settled in units that become socially "adopted," the *Bēt 'Ābôt* was an exilic unit that included the smaller *Bēt 'Āb*'s and adopted a familial fiction to use the language of a closer family unit, most likely as an expression of social solidarity. In terms of size and function, the *Bēt 'Ābôt* therefore resembles the pre-exilic *Mišpᵉḥôt*, but the change in terminology (as well as the leaders of the *Bēt 'Ābôt* units as *rošîm*) reveals a process of structural adaptation similar to those suggested by the analogies (e.g., the Japanese blocks). Furthermore, while the *Mišpᵉḥôt* were based on "blood" lineage, the *Bēt 'Ābôt* appear to be more artificial and, if the Golah List is to be trusted, one suspects that criteria other than "blood" lineage were determinative for the construction of these *Bēt 'Ābôt* (i.e., residence together in exile). A further hint that the *Bēt 'Ābôt* were constructs as a result of social adaptation is the problem of those in the Golah List who appear to be unable to "prove their lineage." Let us see if we can maintain this hypothesis.

Units of Social Structure in Pre- and Post-Exilic Israel

The classic passage that lists the breakdown of the social structure of pre-exilic Israel is Joshua 7:16ff.[22] The assumption has always been that Achan is a member of the *Bēt 'Āb* of Zabdi.[23]

In Norman Gottwald's work *The Tribes of Yahweh*[24] and J. Scharbert's essay "Beyt 'ab als soziologische Grösse im Alten Testament,"[25] there are important hints toward understanding the changing nature of the *Bēt 'Āb*. On the basis of Josh. 7, the apparent three-part structure for pre-exilic society includes: (1) tribes, composed of (2) *Mišpᵉḥôt* (clans?), composed of (3) *Bēt 'Āb*(s).

The pre-exilic *Bēt 'Āb* does not have a permanent name, being called by the contemporary living eldest male. In Gen. 24, Abraham's servant quotes Abraham as speaking of Bethuel's household as "my fathers house" *and* "my *Mišpᵉḥâ*" Rebekah cannot be part of Abraham's *Bēt 'Āb*, but is a part of Abraham's *Mišpᵉḥâ*. Bethuel is a part of Abraham's *Bēt 'Āb* as Abraham's nephew (Gen. 24:38), but Rebekah, on the other hand, belongs to the *Bēt 'Āb* of the eldest male, i.e., Bethuel (Gen. 24:23!). Rebekah is too far removed to be in the *Bēt 'Āb* of Abraham. The implication of v. 24 is that Rebekah considers herself of the house of Nahor, but now "headed" by Bethuel, and as noted, both Laban and Bethuel are important figures in the decision of Rebekah to marry.

In his article, Scharbert has estimated the size of the pre-exilic *Bēt
'Āb*s. His estimates range higher than Gottwald's. Since the large numbers (into the thousands) seen in the Golah List contrast to much more
modest numbers in the pre-exilic *Bēt 'Āb*, this is a crucial point. Scharbert, like Gottwald, also cites Josh. 7:17, where Achan is assigned to
the *Bēt* of Zabdi. Since three generations are mentioned here, it is logically assumed by Gottwald that a single *Bēt 'Āb* could include as many
as 150 persons.[26] Scharbert, however, believes that the *Bēt 'Ābôt* could
have been as large as *four* generations of people.

Scharbert equates all the elders of Gilead in Judges 11:2–8 with members of the a single *Bēt 'Āb*, since Jephthah is called a Gileadite. But
Scharbert is surely confusing the name of the place Gilead with a man's
name Gilead (Josh. 17 has both place and person name). When the
"elders of Gilead" are mentioned, Scharbert assumes that all these men
are members of the same *Bēt 'Āb* — that of "Gilead" the father of Jephthah. But this is not clear from the text, although admittedly, it could
be read this way if one did not suspect otherwise on the basis of other
evidence. We think, therefore, that this text shows that the elders are
kept separate from the "brothers" or *Bēt 'Āb* of Gilead. For example,
the demand of Jephthah to be the "head" of Gilead is surely more than
simply a request to resume his rightful place as the leader of the family,
the *Bēt 'Āb*, since this would not be the same line of thought as in the
rest of the stories of Judges, where saviors are chosen by settlements to
fight their battles — and this forms a thematic trajectory that leads to
calls for a king in the stories of Gideon.

Scharbert's second major example for large numbers is the family of
Gideon in Judg. 9. Scharbert says that the *Bēt 'Ābôt* of Gideon (Jerubbaal) must have included seventy men, that is, seventy sons of his many
wives (Judg. 8:29). But this example must not be considered typical.
The point, in 8:29–30, as well as the "epic sounding" phrase in 9:5 —
"... put his brothers, Jerubbaal's 70 sons, to death on one and the same
stone ..." — is surely to emphasize how unusual the circumstances were.
Second, in a typical situation, the family of Gideon (Jerubbaal) would
have *divided* into smaller units upon Gideon's death, but the story continues to refer to the "sons of Jerubbaal" for dramatic effect. The *Bēt
'Āb* was usually considered a family in the biological sense. Dealing with
these two examples suffices to argue against large numbers in the pre-
exilic *Bēt 'Ab*. This, then, is a contrast to the numbers in the Golah
List.

Stager's research on archaeological remains for family compounds,
and the estimates of population numbers, reveal much lower figures
than those suggested by Scharbert, and more in line with the theory that
we are proposing for differences between the pre-exilic *Bēt 'Āb,* and the
post-exilic *Bēt 'Ābôt:*

If we assume that a honeycomb pattern prevailed at Raddana, i.e., an even distribution of contiguous, multiple family compounds throughout the settlement, then there might have been as many as 20 or more such households in the village, totalling ca. 200 persons under high-fertility-low-mortality conditions. But this projection may be too high, and serves only as an upper limit.... These upper estimates do not take into account the various phases of the family cycle within established multiple family households, the establishment of new nuclear households, and the dissolution of others.[27]

Gottwald further analyzes the different social terminology according to different historical sources. Gottwald cites Num. 17:1[16H]–11[26H], where P uses *maṭṭeh* for "rods" as opposed to P's normal use of *maṭṭeh* for the social division traditionally called a *Mišpᵉḥâ*. Since the term is used for rods, P then preferred to use *Bēt 'Āb* as the major subdivision, rather than the term for a clan. But typical of P is this association of the *Bēt 'Āb* with the larger units, and indeed, in P and all the other post-exilic or exilic material, the numbers of people in the basic social units have changed dramatically.[28] Gottwald believes this to be a result of P's attempt, at a later date, to understand the *Mišpᵉḥôt* as lineage units ("*Bēt 'Ābôt* writ large...") rather than "enlarged composites of lineages in residential and regional groupings whose various sociopolitical affirmations of unity are not biologically demonstrable links."[29]

While the size of the post-exilic *Bēt 'Ābôt* compares more favorably to the pre-exilic *Mišpᵉḥôt*, the change is more than merely nomenclature. Let us further consider some texts.

Numbers 1 presents us with some confusing details, which are not made any easier by the problems in transmission. The beginning, v. 2, states that the census in this chapter is to be of all the *ᶜēdâ* of the "sons of Israel." Twelve people are chosen to be with Moses and Aaron, one from each *maṭṭeh* and also *roš* of his "father's house." This implies a double qualification and further implies that the father's house is a subunit of the "*maṭṭeh* tribe." This is so far understandable. But finally, the leaders that are chosen are said to be representing, not the *Mišpᵉḥôt*, but the various *Bēt 'Āb*'s. Although the Hebrew text suggests a probable deletion of the *Bēt 'Āb* in v. 44, it is apparently the case that *Bēt 'Āb* is being confused with the entire tribe. In Num. 2, the "standards" for the fathers' houses are clearly twelve in number, further confusing the situation. During the enumeration in chapter 1 of various tribes, the terms *Mišpᵉḥâ* and *Bēt 'Āb* are in use. But *Mišpᵉḥâ* is not involved in the confusion of larger units (even in the textual variations) — only the term *Bēt 'Āb* is confused with larger units. As Gottwald has noted, this confusion is apparent in Num. 17 as well. Numbers reflects an exilic-post-exilic confusion of structural terminology that we would certainly expect if the basic social structures have changed dramatically as a result of the Exile. *The consistent "mistake" in Numbers is to associate the words* Bēt 'Āb *with the basic large structural units of Israel.*

Eisenstadt, following Alt and Weber, thinks that by the time of the Exile, and *especially as a result of the Exile,* the larger social units had broken down, allowing the rise of smaller family units to positions of prominence.[30] Others have made the same assumption based on the similarity of terms between *Bēt 'Āb* and *Bēt 'Ābôt.* This idea follows a suggestion made already by E. Meyer that lineage was no longer an aspect of Jewish identity in the time of the Chronicler.[31]

The argument would be realigned considerably, however, if the basic subdivisions during and after the exile were not really families at all, but groups of people who use a familial fiction to describe decidedly non-blood relationships. In the language of segmentary lineage systems, we can say that the genealogical information was adapted to fit new social circumstances.[32] If this is true, we aren't then referring to a "breakdown" as Alt, Eisenstadt, Meyer, and Bartlett assumed — a breakdown that led to an emphasis on "smaller units." What we must refer to is a unique post-exilic construct, called a *Bēt 'Ābôt,* similar in *numbers* to the pre-exilic *Mišpᵉḥôt,* but in nomenclature and solidarity more similar to the pre-exilic *Bēt 'Āb,* from which the name obviously comes, suggesting a "collective" of *Bēt 'Āb's.*

To consider this more fully, particularly the possible changes that the Exile may have caused in the societal structure, we must analyze three groups of texts: first, as we have already briefly noted, the Numbers passages; second, some selected passages from Chronicles as a post-exilic "read-back" of pre-exilic history; and third, the nature of the so-called Golah List, which remains our primary source of information about the social structure of Israel in the post-exilic era.

The texts from Numbers, as stated above, consistently mixed the language of *Bēt 'Āb* with larger units of Jews. These units are larger than the *Bēt 'Āb* we know from the pre-exilic sources. In Chronicles, this confusion continues, and this suggests a unique institution called a *Bēt 'Ābôt,* which only "sounds" like the pre-exilic *Bēt 'Āb* (and undoubtedly intends to suggest the closer relationship of the *Bēt 'Āb* in the larger units), but is, in fact, a new construct, under the specific leadership of selected elders who are called *rošîm,* "heads."

The Changes in the Social Structure: Analysis of a Theory

In 1 Chron. 15, there is an expansion of the description of 2 Sam. 7. This is a redrafting that also reflects a concern with numbers and technical organization. In Chronicles, the care taken to enumerate the specific "sons" and "heads" (*rošîm*) and officials (*sārîm*) is well known. The

Chronicler, however, is clearly reading back into history a terminology more applicable to the post-exilic era.

We know that what appears to be genealogical material can often reflect contemporary social realities more than historical lineage. In his analysis of genealogical material in anthropological literature and then its application to biblical literature, Wilson points out that "families" (segmentary lineage systems) can often be changed over time, reflecting changing membership of those "families" and "tribes" especially when groups are "grafted" into a "history."

The "sons" of Levi (and Aaron!) as already enumerated in 1 Chron. 6:16ff., are called *sārîm* of the sons of Levi, but then in 1 Chron. 15 11 David gathers these *sārîm* and calls them the "heads." They are the heads of the *'Ābôt* (1 Chron. 6:19, 24), but 2 Chron. 15:16ff. implies that these *Bēt 'Ābôt* include many heads of groups ("and their brethren"). In short, Chronicles reads back into pre-exilic society the post-exilic dominance of the unit called the *Bēt 'Ābôt,* which are large units with *rošîm* as the heads or leaders.

1 Chron. 23:1–7 has David organizing work on the Temple (note the context of organized labor, which appears to require listing people into groups; see discussion below). What is important to note here is that in v. 8, only one of the sons of Laban, Jehiel, is called "chief," but then they are all called *rošê hā 'ābôt* (heads of the families) of Laban. Clearly, however, we are meant to read *roš* differently in the case of Laban, a "head head" as it were. In 1 Chron. 23:11, we even have the example of the combining of several families into one father's house as a clear construction artificially imposed to make up for the small number of sons in each of the families of Jeush and Beriah.

Finally, in 1 Chron. 26:10, there is an interesting note to the effect that, even though not first born, Shimri was made *roš* by his father, suggesting again the structural connection of *roš* and the *Bēt 'Ābôt.* A "head" is different from an "elder."

The material in Numbers and Chronicles reflects important "confusions" of numbers and units. From the Golah List, we gain more significant information about the nature of the units called *Bēt 'Ābôt* and how they may have arisen.

The Golah List

The list of those returning to Jerusalem is recorded in three places, Ezra 2, Neh. 7, and 1 Esdras 5. The list has given rise to an extended controversy about its origin, composition, and date.[33] In the context of the present investigation, the *components* of the list are important. The list purports to be a picture of the returning exiles by either family (presumably the *Bēt 'Ābôt,* Ezra 2:68) or by place of residence. Rudolph claimed that the change in the sequence of the list from "families of," indicated by *bᵉnê*, and "residents of" indicated by *'anšê*, was a sign that additions were made to the list.[34] For example, priests were added as a unit to the list, Rudolph explained, because they would have come only when the Temple was completed. Rudolph believes that the list was genuine, in that it predated the settled community that came to be called the "sons of the Exile."

Among his reasons were that (1) Jeshua is listed among the leaders of the returning people, but without the title of high priest (note the absence of a high priest to consult the Urim and Thummim); (2) by the time of the writing of Nehemiah, Uriah (son of Hakkoz; Neh. 3:4, 21, Ezra 8:33, and 1 Chron. 24:10) is involved in priestly activities, and thus the sons of Hakkoz *were no longer banned* as they were in the Golah List itself (Ezra 2:61). Rudolph also believes that (3) 2:1b and 2:70 formed an important "head and tail" to the list as a whole and thus helped in dating the list by its association with Zerubbabel. Alt and Galling associated the list with events contemporary to the building of the Temple,[35] while Mowinckel and Albright would date the list at the earliest to the times of Ezra-Nehemiah themselves, although Mowinckel believes that the Artaxerxes in question was, in fact, Artaxerxes II, thus dating Ezra-Nehemiah material at the end of the fourth century B.C.E. Albright took the earlier dating of Artaxerxes I, thus holding the traditional dating of 450 B.C.E.[36]

The list, at first sight, is simply a "roll-call" of *Bēt 'Ābôt* and others organized by living area, with the associated numbers. But already in 1913 Batton (ICC) was doubtful as to its genuine dating to the time of the return. Among his reasons were:

1. the numbers are too large (it was hard to accept a return of this magnitude);

2. the use of place names suggests settlement, i.e., long after the actual return of the exiles "each to his own town";

3. the term *"bᵉnê Mᵉdinôt"* suggests a time when Syria was a regularly instituted satrapy of the Persian empire;

4. the debate about the suspension of priests would only be an issue after the building of the Temple, and

5. it is probable that Ezra-Nehemiah ordered the suspension;

6. Ezra 2:68 shows that the original was after the Temple was built and;

7. the use of the term "all the congregation" suggests a census.

In regard to the order of listing people by family, then place, then families again, Batton believes that these were either additions to the list itself, or simply problems in the tradition history of the list we now have. Batton believes that "it is safe to conclude that it was intended to use 'sons' before personal names, and 'men' before place-names but that there was doubt about some of the names."[37]

It is precisely this confusion of terminology that led Mowinckel to posit the idea of a fictionalized lineage system that came about through the exilic experience. Since Mowinckel believes that the social divisions were already breaking down by the time of settlement in the period of the Judges, he wondered if the removal of the natural organization from settled areas invited the return to familial-tribal division systems.[38]

There are a number of related points made by Mowinckel in his analysis. First, he suggests that, by the time of Ezra-Nehemiah (which he associated with the Chronicles), fictionalized familial terms were common, such as guilds of workers (e.g., "metal-workers guild," Neh. 3:8; one also thinks of Amos's protest that he was neither a prophet nor the "son" of a prophet, i.e., among the guild of prophets, suggesting an earlier use of such familial fiction, cf. 2 Kings 2). Second, the names of the families are fictionalized relations based on a real or fictionalized person. Third, Mowinckel believes that Ezra 8 already gives us an indication of local self-government of Jewish colonies, by calling on the *roš* of Casiphia.[39]

Mowinckel's theory about fictionalized familial units dispenses with speculation about the additions to the list by suggesting little difference between "sons" and "people," in reference to their intended meaning. This casts further doubt on Meyer's original suggestion that the personal names belonged to "wealthier" people, while those listed by place were poor.[40]

An interesting problem is raised in the Golah List in Ezra 2:59–63, where certain Jews were unable to find their names. Among these are the priests of Hakkoz, who are later found to be performing priestly duties and therefore were accepted at some point. If Wilson's observations about lineage systems are trusted, especially the flexibility of those lineage systems according to social realities, then what we see in this passage in not necessarily the determination of "relatives," but the determination of *true Israelites,* or true members of the purified "sons of the Exile." As Japhet has stated, the question raised by the Golah List as a whole is, "Who is the true Jew?"[41] But even more significant is that there was such a problem at all. The need for some returning groups to "prove themselves" reveals the disturbance in the social system and suggests that groups were settled apart from one another in exile so that in the intervening years, some would "grow apart." Furthermore, it strikes one as exceedingly doubtful that the issue here is one of blood relations — surely there would be enough distant relatives to vouch for "long lost relatives" if blood lineage were the question. If, however, the structures of the exiles were only partly "blood," and otherwise social adaptations to the conditions of group settlement of Jews in exile, *then precisely the kind of verification problems we see in this passage would be expected* (Ezra 2:59–63). The Ezra text is testimony to the extent of the social upheaval created by the Exile and suggests (however vaguely) that groups were separated in their settled conditions.

The argument about the Golah List will only be advanced when it is determined just what the list is listing. For this, we need to focus again on the *Bēt 'Ābôt.*

Weinberg's "Citizen-Temple-Community" and the *Bēt 'Ābôt*

Our suggestion of expanded numbers and significant changes from pre-exilic structures to the post-exilic *Bēt 'Ābôt* agrees significantly with the work of the Soviet historian Joel Weinberg, whose important analysis can be summarized.

In an interesting series of essays on this period, Weinberg begins his analysis with the view that the *Bēt 'Ābôt* is a *terminus technicus* of P, as opposed to the earlier, standardized use of the singular *Bēt 'Āb*. As we have noted, the fact that the numbers of the members of these post-exilic *Bēt 'Ābôt* could exceed 3000 rules out any real family units, and Weinberg, too, believes that the *Bēt 'Ābôt,* as opposed to the pre-exilic structures of either the *Bēt 'Āb* or the *Mišpᵉḥôt,* indicates a unique social institution in Judah in the post-exilic period.[42] But Weinberg's analysis goes much further.

The main source, notes Weinberg, remains Ezra-Nehemiah, where the *Bēt 'Ābôt* are mentioned nineteen times. In the context of the *Bēt 'Ābôt* is the overarching concern with the construction of the Temple. From this combination of Temple concerns with the *Bēt 'Ābôt,* as a "collective of the returnees," Weinberg postulates the existence of a post-exilic "Citizen-Temple-Community" based on the leadership of the various *Bēt 'Ābôt.* Weinberg believes that the *Bēt 'Ābôt* was directly involved in administration of property that centrally belonged to the constituent members of the "community." For Weinberg, the *Bēt 'Ābôt,* while clearly the constituent unit of the post-exilic community, cannot be seen as a direct link to the pre-exilic *'Bēt 'Āb* without grossly minimizing the impact of the Exile itself.[43]

Weinberg holds that the Golah List is a source for, and possibly a register of, the kind of social structure upon which the post-exilic Jews organized themselves, while at the same time clarifying its unique status in comparison with the pre-exilic "tertiary subdivisions." The importance of this view is clear when comparing it with the views already stated. But Weinberg's view is also based on a clear relation of the community and work represented by Ezra, and the community work of Nehemiah. Mantel, on the other hand, would separate Ezra from Nehemiah, and also separate the religious communities involved. Ezra would be seen as the leader of an exilic religion that had little connection with the Temple[44] and Nehemiah would be more involved directly with Persian affairs. This set of circumstances becomes very complex. Could it be that Ezra was the one to arrive in Palestine and start a communal religious structure among the "sons of the Exile" that was later incorporated into a "Citizen-Temple-Community" of the sort that Weinberg cites not only for Palestine, but among many other people under the Achaemind administration as well?

If Weinberg's suggested "change through crisis" is right, at what point can we see the establishment of the *Bēt 'Ābôt* as the primary social component of the Citizen-Temple-Community? Weinberg believes it to be firmly established by the announcement of Artaxerxes that accompanied Ezra.[45] This idea is supported by comparative examples of the use of indigenous leadership in the post-Darian Achaeminid empire. Under both Artaxerxes and Cyrus the Younger, we have examples of Egyptian, Greek, and Karian self-governing structures (Xen., *Hell.,* III, 1, 10, *Anab.,* 1, 2, 21, 4, 2; Diod., XIV, 19, 35).[46]

Political Structure: "Internal" or "External"?

Weinberg does not believe that his suggested community was the same kind of institution as an actual provincial government, such as would be the case if Sheshbazzar or Zerubbabel were actual governors of a province of the Persian empire. Noting that no Persian documents deal with a single, recognized authority, Weinberg concludes that Sheshbazzar and Zerubbabel were, in fact, not Persian authorities at all.[47]

Weinberg dates the founding of the Citizen-Temple-Community on the basis of a comparison of the "edicts" of Ezra-Nehemiah, with careful attention to what each of the edicts actually allows or calls for:

The Edict of Artaxerxes included:	But Cyrus's?	Darius's?
1. Permission of return and collection	*Yes*	*No*
2. Support of cult-Temple through funds	*No*	*Yes*
3. Tax-freedom for priests, Levites, Temple, and Temple personnel	*No*	*No*
4. Establishment of jurisdiction and appointment of a Judge	*No*	*No*
5. Punishment of those who break the "Law of your God and the law of the King"	*No*	*No* [48]

Thus Weinberg believes that the Golah List represents the established Citizen-Temple-Community under Nehemiah, now officially recognized by Artaxerxes, although this is not be to confused with the king's making Judah a *province*.[49]

It is clear that Weinberg is making a quite revolutionary suggestion for the nature of the social and political structure in the post-exilic period. But it is worth noting that Weinberg is describing a community that is defined by social boundaries, the kind of definition and differentiation that we have come to expect from our sociological analysis in both maintenance of ethnic identity and the survival of deportation and exile. But Weinberg's "community," if it existed, is made officially secure only at the time of Nehemiah. What happened in the meantime? Weinberg believes that the commune-like structure was in process of developing during an extended period before the time of establishment under Nehemiah.[50]

Weinberg's argument suggests that the elders remained a major force of leadership in the post-exilic community until such time as individuals like Ezra and Nehemiah became officially recognized by the Persian authorities. Eventually, we see that the high priest comes to hold the central authority within the Jewish community itself, as is clearly attested in the Hellenistic era through to the Roman period.

The only major problem with Weinberg's thesis, as I see it, is that the documents of this period, mainly Malachi, Ezra-Nehemiah, and Haggai-Zechariah, are understood as documents exclusively about the *internal* politics of the post-exilic community, rather than having an immediate impact on the "external" politics, i.e., encompassing matters of state concern to the satrapy rulers and the Persian throne. The term *Paḥâ* (governor), for example, becomes an internal office when used of Jews like Zerubbabel with little relevance to the Persian authorities themselves (i.e., Tattenai). *Sārîm, Ḥôrîm, Sᵉgānîm,* are all "depoliticized." While this is reminiscent of our case of the Lithuanian refugees who continued to use the titles of their former existence when they were in exile, this may be pushing the analogy too far. It is clear that before we can proceed any further and make a final judgment on Weinberg's suggestion, we must attempt to clarify the use of the term *Paḥâ* (governor) in reference to leaders before Nehemiah — which inevitably requires a consideration of the issue of the political status and authority of the *mᵉdinôt Judah* ("area of Judah") in the post-exilic Persian era.

The Term "Governor" and the "Province of Judah"

In Old Testament sources the term *Paḥâ* usually refers to a government official. They are rulers over "districts." This is the sense in 1 Kings 10:15 of "governors of the land" (cf. 2 Chron. 9:14). In 2 Kings 18:24, the implication of the Rab-šāqē's speech is that "governors" are less important dignitaries, with a military function (Isa. 36:9). In the oracle against Babylon in Jer. 51, the context of v. 23 seems to suggest a dual military-political role for the *Paḥâ* yet v. 28 has the sense of "under-secretary" under the kings of the Medes; in Jer. 51:57 the list includes political and military figures. Ezek. 23:6 associates "governors," all of whom were "young men," with the military as well (cf. Ezek. 23:12, 13).

In the context of a blistering condemnation of those who do not bring pure animals for sacrifice, Malachi challenged people to consider whether these same people would dare bring a flawed gift to their "governor" (Mal. 1:8). This appears to suggest that such gifts were expected by the governor, and expected to be among the best. Are we here discussing "tax" payments to a representative of a foreign government? This calls to mind Ezra 8:35–36.

Haggai 1:1 calls Zerubbabel the "governor" of Judah, in a stereotypical phrase repeated in Hag. 1:14, 2:2, and 2:21. Esther 3:12, 8:9, and 9:3 are stereotypical collections of officials to whom official correspondence is sent, but the exact connection of area or people to each of the offices listed is somewhat muddled.

The most important passages are those in Nehemiah, especially chapter 5, where Nehemiah compares himself to former "governors" (favorably) and explicitly mentions the requirements of the people to support the governor with money and *animals* (thus confirming Mal. 1:8 and Ezra 8:34b–36). Most intriguing is the mention of the governors "beyond the river" in Neh. 2:7 and 9, but especially 3:7 where those from Mizpah are under the authority of the governor of the province "beyond the river." These references could be taken to refer to those who were now the colleagues of Nehemiah, i.e., other governors, or that Nehemiah was in some sense answerable to them. In any case, the military functions of the officers under Nehemiah's command suggest that the military-political image of "governor" in Jeremiah and Ezekiel passages are confirmed (although we are admittedly dealing with two different political systems, Babylonian in Jeremiah and Ezekiel, and Persian in Nehemiah).

Could it be that we are dealing with a governmental official whose jurisdiction is determined not so much geographically as *ethnically?* Thus, the governor may be a military leader, in charge of a group of soldiers, but also assigned to oversee also the affairs of the immediate area and its population, deriving his sustenance from the people over whom he has supervisory charge. This may be an explanation for the archaeological evidence of Persian type "cist-tombs" from Iran to Palestine, which Stern and Moorey have taken to indicate the presence of Persian troops throughout the Persian empire, including Palestine.[51]

There has been some debate about the political fate of Judah in the restoration period. McEvenue argues that in Ezra 5:2–9, Tattenai does not deal with Zerubbabel and the elders. The term "governor" is not therein specifically mentioned.[52] Galling believes that Tattenai's lack of knowledge about the Temple building, and his questions, should lead us to believe that there was no governor figure present. Nothing is said about Zerubbabel as governor, or authority, even when 1 Chron. 3:17–19 attempts to establish his Davidic descent. The Hebrew term "Medina" can be "area" and not "province," and Tattenai, who is specifically called a *Paḥâ* in the encounter with Zerubbabel, Jeshua, and the elders, does not appear to be merely Zerubbabel's equal.[53] Thus, McEvenue would confirm Alt's earlier suspicion that Judah had no political independence until the time of Nehemiah.

Japhet, while agreeing with those who see Judah's independence beginning with Zerubbabel, points out the unique aspect of life under the Persians. Japhet sees with typical clarity the *social* significance of a growing "democratization" of the post-exilic community:

> The special regime under which the people of Judah lived during the Persian period — autonomic existence under foreign domination — had an important role in catalyzing the process of decentralization, in which the power of local and family leaders gradually grew....[54]

The linguistic arguments for the independence of Judah before Nehemiah are not convincing, nor, for that matter, is the meaning of "governor" clear when applied to Zerubbabel, Nehemiah, and Persian officials.

Some archaeologists, on the basis of work on collected coins, seals (bullae), and jar handle stamps, have argued for an early, separate province of "Judah." A series of stamps and a coin have been in the British Museum since the beginning of the twentieth century, and Sukenik finally correctly identified these as bearing the term *Y-H-D,* Aramaic for Judah.[55] Since that time, Aharoni has reported finding more *YHD* stamps in his digs at Ramat Rahel in 1959–60.[56] In the reports for this find, the stamps were analyzed by Garbini, who concluded that archaeological dating was doubtful because of the lack of a layer-stratified context for the finds. The Ramat Rahel stamps cannot be compared to other *YHD* stamps that were bought on the antiquities market and not found *in situ.* The significance of these coins and stamps for our discussion is twofold. First, they have led some scholars to surmise a province of the Persian empire, under the satrapy reorganization of Darius (but also earlier, according to Avigad, Japhet, and others), that was called Judah, apart from Samaria. Secondly, however, is the discovery on some of the coins and seals of the term *PHW,* or fuller inscriptions, such as the one discussed by Avigad on which is stamped, "Elnathan, Governor," or another interesting example where the stamp inscription reads, "Belonging to Shelomit, maidservant of Elnathan *PH...[W?]*."[57] On the basis of these occurrences of *PHW* and *YHD* on seals and bullae, Avigad has concluded that Judah was an administrative unit with "autonomous internal rule."[58] Avigad has further associated *YHD* jar handle stamps with food and wine taxes, which are specifically mentioned in Neh. 5, and which Avigad says are post-exilic manifestations of the now famous "LeMelekh" jar handles of the monarchical era.[59] Finally, Avigad has reconstructed a series of governors from archaeological sources as follows:

- Sheshbazzar, "governor [*phh*]" (Ezra 5:14); "prince of Judah" (Ezra 1:8): ca. 538 B.C.E.

- Zerubbabel, son of Shealtiel, "Governor of Judah [*pht yhwdh*])" (Hag. 1:1, 14): 515 B.C.E.

- Elnathan, "governor [*phw*]" (bulla and seal): late sixth century B.C.E.

- Yeho'ezer, "governor [*phw*]" (jar impression): early fifth century B.C.E.

- Ahzai, "governor [*phw*]" (jar impression): early fifth century B.C.E.

- Nehemiah, son of Hacaliah, "the governor [*hphh*]" (Neh. 5:14, 12:26): 445–433 B.C.E.

- Bagohi (Bagoas), "governor of Judah [*pht yhwd*] (Elephantine Papyrus 30:1): 408 B.C.E.

- Yehezqiyah, "the governor [*hphh*]" (coins): ca. 330 B.C.E.[60]

What we are faced with, in the archaeological material, is seal impressions, jar handles, and coins from the Persian period reading both *YHD* and *PHW*. Does this mean that the governor was given authority, not only to oversee the collection of taxes in kind (food and wine, Neh. 5, Mal. 1:8) but also to strike coins? The significance of a political independence that allows a people/governor to produce monetary units is not to be dismissed lightly, as Herodotus' discussion of the Darian silver standard, as well as later Jewish coinage, clearly attests.[61] But there is a curious problem about the onomastica of the Persian period coins. Avigad already suggested, in an article analyzing the stamp seal from Jericho, that the *priests* were involved in the autonomous economy of the province of *YHD*. On the Jericho seal, Avigad identified "Urio" with Uriah, son of Haqqoz, who is mentioned in Neh. 3:4 and 21 and was a

member of the priestly family of Haqqoz (Ezra 2:59–63). On the basis
of this, Avigad assumed a governor-Temple administration:

> In a little semi-autonomous theocratic state like Judah, where both
> religious and civil affairs were concentrated in the hands of eccle-
> siastics, there could scarcely have been a division between temple-
> and state-administration. The autonomy granted to Judah by the
> suzerain power was of a religious nature, and the temple incor-
> porated the interests of the whole community. As we can gather
> from Neh. 13:13, needy persons got their share from the temple
> treasuries.[62]

But in his 1976 study of bullae and seals, the discovery of *YHD* and
PHW stamps and coins led him, as we have seen, to reconstruct the
names of the governors of his hypothetical pre-Nehemiah province.[63]

In a survey of the stamps that contain (in most probable interpretations) the term *PHW,* Weinberg points out that the names associated
with it (Ahyo/Ahzai, Hanana, Yeho'ezar, and 'Uriyo) are all related to
the biblical names of priests.[64] Barag has now corrected an earlier reading of Mildenberg and found the word *H'CHN* (the priest) next to the
name Yohanan, thus adding weight to the theories of both Avigad and
Weinberg.[65] Weinberg noted the prominence of the office of high priest
in the late Achaeminid period, especially in Hellenistic times, and suggested that the authority of the *Pahâ* of Judah was transferred to the
high priest.[66] This is logically possible only if we do not consider the
governor as an administrator of a geographical unit, but primarily as
administrator of a population, i.e., an "ethnarch." Coinage associated
with the priesthood would appear to support an administration of a
group connected to the Temple. What, then, do we make of Haggai calling Zerubbabel the governor of Judah? While the use by Haggai of *Pahâ*
is problematic for our thesis, it is clear that the alternative explanation
of an actual administrator of a land sector in the Persian empire also
involves the problems mentioned earlier. We conclude that the "governor" was a Persian official under the satrap who was a semi-military
officer in charge of a specific area or particular population. A more
precise view of leadership terminology is necessary.

Further Terms for Leadership

Zucker has contrasted what he believes to have been the "internal" organization of the Jews with the "officials" who are associated with the
Persian regime itself. Zucker does not believe that Ezra or Nehemiah
could have acted without Persian authority vested in them, but neither

could they overstep their authority in dealing with matters within the jurisdiction of the internal politics of the elders and the high priest.

In Neh. 8:13, it is the elders who approach Ezra, as though they are an essential presence necessary for the study of the law. Ezra 10, on the other hand, shows that dissolution of marriage could not be successfully accomplished apart from Ezra's authority. A possible key is Nehemiah's careful distinction between the officials called *sᵉgānîm* and the *ḥorim*. It has been suggested that terms like *sar, sᵉgānîm, ḥōrîm,* and *rošê 'ābôt* all mean the same thing. Yet Nehemiah is careful in apportioning blame for certain problems among the Jewish community. In Neh. 13:17, the *ḥōrîm* are blamed for Sabbath violation, *ḥōrîm* being among the internal leadership of the Jewish people. While *ḥōrîm* are listed with *sᵉgānîm* on many occasions (Neh. 2:16), Zucker believes that the *sᵉgānîm* were Persian officials under Nehemiah's direct command.[67]

Both *ḥōrîm* and *sᵉgānîm* are blamed for abuses in Neh. 5:7, although it can be argued that corruption in both internal and Persian authorities is being condemned here. Certainly, economic matters, especially the raising of silver in the Darian Persian tax system, was an official matter in which Nehemiah has a direct interest. Neh. 12:40 associates the *sᵉgānîm* directly with Nehemiah's authority, especially considering the exclusive condemnation of the *sᵉgānîm* for failure to carry out a Persian official mandate in supporting the Temple.

In Jer. 51:28, 57, and 51:23 the *sᵉgānîm* are clearly considered officials of the nations, especially Babylon. Ezek. 23:6 (and 12, 14, 23) makes the same association with the "Assyrian" officials and warriors.

Ḥōrîm, on the other hand, are associated with elders in 1 Kings 21:8, 11, and Neh. 6:17. Isa. 34:12 seems to suggest an inability to arrive at decisions and also associates *ḥōrîm* with the normal function of "higher citizens" and elders. The *ḥōrîm* among those taken, or punished, by the Babylonians, are mentioned in Jer. 27:20 and 39:6.

Nehemiah also uses the term *sar,* which has a very rich usage in the Old Testament text (some 450 occurrences). In the vast majority of cases, the term has military or royal associations. Zucker, however, regards *sar* and *sᵉgānîm* as virtually synonymous. This is possible, but only because *sar* appears to have a generic application to any position of leadership. Ezra, for example, refers to the *sarê haCohenim* (*sar* "of the priests") and the *sarê Ābôt* (*sar* "of the Fathers').

In any case, the internal affairs were administered by the priests and elders, while the Persian-appointed Ezra and Nehemiah had to work with their *sᵉgānîm* or in cooperation with the elders. The internal self-administration then eventually led to the predominance of the high priest, whose power rose as that of the Persian authorities declined, until in the Hellenistic era it was the high priest who was officially recognized. With this, however, we are far beyond the specific time of our concern.

I would thus agree that Judah was not a separate administrative division of the Persian Empire until Nehemiah. Until then it was an administrative division of the Syrian area, which included many groups of stationed troops who depended for their livelihood and support on the population or area to which they were assigned. This suggestion is really a call to be less precise about political boundaries and jurisdictions in an attempt to be *more* precise about *social* authority and jurisdiction. We can conclude that the textual evidence of "previous governors" (as Nehemiah referred to them), and Zerubbabel in particular, is not so clear as to remove our original theory that the leaders of the post-exilic community were the elders and "heads" of the "Citizen-Temple-Community," which was divided into units using a familial fiction from the Exile itself. These leaders continued to function as leaders until the advent of the governor's power, whose own decline, in turn, made way for the rule of the high priest.

A similar picture of Israelite social structure can be found in a Hellenistic source, "Hecataeus of Abdera," which is extant in Diodorus Siculus, XL, 2. Mendels has argued that this reflects post-exilic attitudes that emphasize Moses over David, the place of the high priest, and the prominence of elders. Stern believes that this discussion clearly reflected Nehemiah's reforms and considered Neh. 5:15 to be evidence for this. The source is dated to the late fourth century and the relevant passage is as follows:

> He [Moses] led out military expeditions against the neighboring tribes and after annexing much land apportioned it out, assigning equal allotments to private citizens and greater ones to the priests, in order that they, by virtue of having received more ample revenues, might be undistracted and apply themselves continually to the worship of God. The common citizens were forbidden to sell their individual plots, lest there be some who for their own advantage should buy them up, and by oppressing the poorer classes bring on a scarcity of manpower. We required those who dwelt in the land to rear their children....
>
> [Moses]...picked out the men of most refinement and with the greatest ability to head the entire nation.... These same men he appointed to be judges in all major disputes, and entrusted to them the guardianship of the laws and customs. For this reason, the Jews never have a king, and authority over the people is regularly vested in whichever priest is regarded as superior to his colleagues in wisdom and virtue.[68]

This late passage may be based on a late etiological saga for the rise of the *rošim* and appears to be a description of an ethnic, autonomous unit, both in its total neglect of the monarchical traditions and in its emphasis on internal leadership and, finally, the shift to the authority of priests.

Summary

In summing up this wide-ranging survey of social structures of the exilic period, we can reach only tentative conclusions. The prominence of the organizational divisions of the *Bēt 'Ābôt* in the face of the uncertainties regarding the individual authority leads us to conclude that the *rošîm* as "heads" of the constituent *Bēt 'Ābôt* became the most prominent form of self-government in the exilic period, arising from the elders of the people. The elders, while always present, appear to have become less involved. The growing representative strength of the other offices, especially the *rošîm* and, after the restoration, the other offices mentioned in our discussion of the Nehemiah materials, e.g., "princes" and officers, would support this view. It is possible that Ezra himself was among these *rošîm,* as was Iddo in Casiphia.

Whatever the *externally validated* authority Zerubbabel, Ezra, Sheshbazzar, and Nehemiah may have had through their relationship with the Persian authorities, the internal social structure of Israel was the division into the new *Bēt 'Ābôt* led by "heads." This is confirmed by comparing the Golah List (Ezra 2 ‖ Neh. 7 ‖ 1 Esd. 5) from the late sixth century with the list of those who accompanied Ezra in the mid-fifth century (Ezra 8; see also Chronicles), which *still lists social units by the nomenclature of the Bēt 'Ābôt,* although in smaller numbers than the Golah List. That there is a difference between the internal and external leadership was indicated by Zucker's study of terms and Weinberg's study of a Citizen-Temple-Community.

Furthermore, while I do not believe that the post-exilic *Bēt 'Ābôt* was continuous with the pre-exilic *Bēt 'Āb,* which was a smaller, real biological family unit, the use of the *Bēt 'Ābôt* terminology to refer to a structure that was, in fact, more similar in size to the pre-exilic *Mišpᵉḥôt* (clan) is itself highly significant. The familial terms and "close-knit" nature of the pre-exilic *Bēt 'Āb* were used to impose a familial fiction on a sociologically necessary unit of survival — the bands of "remnants" in Exile who settled together. Post-exilic sources show such changes occurring for social and political reasons (cf. 1 Chron. 23:11). I submit that this is similar to the function of social restructuring found in our case studies.

The work of Wilson on segmentary lineage systems and social change provides precedent — not only in Ancient Near Eastern and contemporary anthropological records, but in other biblical records as well — for changes that reflect social and/or political realities. The confusion comes from the use of "houses" and "fathers" for two different units, but anthropological work on lineage "mythologies" leads us to suspect that the "confusion" *is not a mistake.*

Those scholars who argue that the post-exilic *Bēt 'Ābôt* are exilic forms of the *Mišpᵉḥôt* will have to consider the terminological changes, and the meaning of those changes — especially in the context of *other* familial fictions in the post-exilic period, such as the terms used of the entire Israelite community (or even more significantly, "sons of the Exile") and the use of such terms in guilds and trades.

There remains one last suggestion that can be made regarding further reasons for these structural changes. In the sociological paradigms, we were able to see the function of the structural adaptation of groups in exile and minority situations. Since we cannot draw conclusions about such functions among the biblical exiles without more data, we can only speculate on the basis of our analogies. What is finally significant in this investigation is not, however, what the *function* of the structural change was (though it would be good if we did know), but the fact that a major structural change occurred.

A Materialist Theory of the Post-Exilic *Bēt 'Ābôt*

An aspect of post-exilic identity is the consciousness of having been a part of an exilic event, either by being a "son" of a returning collective, or by separating oneself from the "others" and becoming one of these "sons." This expansion of familial terminology may be significant. We have noted, with Weinberg, that the *Bēt 'Ābôt* did not evolve directly from the pre-exilic *Bēt 'Āb*, but rather appears to be a form, in both number and structure, of the pre-exilic *Mišpᵉḥâ.* But in maintaining a terminology from the pre-exilic extended family, the *Bēt 'Ābôt* expanded the familial fiction, even to encompass *all the people* as "sons" of the Golah, as "sons of Israel." This is best understood as a socio-psychological response to the crisis of exile. Not only is this an expression of solidarity (equivalent to "brother" or "comrade"), but it is an indication of a new divisional principle. On the basis of our analogies from sociological investigation, we might suspect that the relations with outsiders intensified the familial bonds and at the same time the worries about purity. Finally, there are socio-economic factors that we must consider in the adaptation and reformation of post-exilic Israelite society.

If we begin with the late monarchical formation of society that consisted of herding and orcharding in the Judean hills, we find a diversified, but certainly not strongly centralized, economic system based on smaller familial units.[69] While centralizing tendencies were certainly evident in the Israelite monarchy, they were, according to textual evidence, strongly resisted (1 Sam. 8; 2 Sam. 24; 1 Kings 5:13). In any case, Judeans were still able to own land, and the usurpation of this landed independence (as in the case of Naboth's vineyard) was bitterly condemned. As long as ownership of land was connected with the *Bēt 'Āb*, the numbers of these familial units could be smaller (indeed, smaller units meant more surplus). It was from this surplus that international trade of the crown was fueled.[70]

If the post-exilic *Bēt 'Ābôt* ("House of the Fathers") were fictionalized sibling groups, why, then, would the social units of the Judeans (called the "House of the Father") increase in size during the Exile?

To pursue this question, we must consider certain aspects of the economics of Babylonian society in this period. Wittfogel's now classic work, *Oriental Despotism,* was an attempt to relate the organization of society to the economics of a regime under which that society lived and worked.[71] His basic thesis was a theory of centralization of state control through the maintenance of water rights and canal systems. Wittfogel suggested that a "hydraulic society" was the result of an economic requirement of centrally organized canal/water systems for the good of society. Ultimately, this central organization would result in despotic rule. Wittfogel's thesis has been severely criticized as too legalistic and overarching, particularly when it is considered to be a "law" of social development applied to all societies. But Wittfogel was *not* as dogmatic about this as critics sometimes suggest. Wittfogel recognized, for example, that:

> too little or too much water does not necessarily lead to governmental water control; nor does governmental water control necessarily imply despotic methods of statecraft. It is only above the level of an extractive subsistence economy, and below the level of a property-based industrial civilization that man, reacting specifically to the water-deficient landscape, moves toward a specific hydraulic order of life.[72]

The necessary condition, in short, is the building of a canal system on what Wittfogel calls a "monumental style," a single large mass. The necessity for centralized control in a single project seems self-evident.

More specific for our purposes, however, is his conclusion about slave labor in "hydraulic society":

> The costs of supervision inhibited the use of great numbers of slaves in the most typical of all public works in hydraulic society: the construction and maintenance of canals, embankments, roads and walls. It was only in spatially restricted enterprises such as mines and quarries, the building of palaces and temples, and the transport of bulky objects that slave labour could be easily supervised and therefore advantageously employed.[73]

So, if we have suggested that hydraulic centralization, under "monumental project" conditions is a valid application of Wittfogel's insight
(as opposed to a general validity of all water/agricultural base societies)[74]
what does this mean for our thesis? The significance lies precisely in the
fact that the Chaldean kings embarked on a massive building program
at about the same time as their campaigns in the West, which included
the deportation of the Jews to Mesopotamia. In his important study of
building trends in the Ancient Near East, according to the evidence of
ground surveys, Adams has concluded:

> There is no doubt about the rapid, continued growth that got under
> way during, or perhaps even slightly before, the Neo-Babylonian
> Period. This is most simply shown by the rising number of sites.
> ...The total increases from 143 in the Middle Babylonian period
> to 182...in the Neo-Babylonian period, to 221 of Achaeminid
> date.... The available documentary evidence suggests that large
> masses of people were involuntarily transferred as part of inten-
> sive Neo-Babylonian efforts to rehabilitate the central region of a
> domain that previously had suffered severely.[75]

Furthermore, work that was controlled centrally had especially to do
with major, larger canals. Smaller communities were left to work out
the projects on their own.

It is clear that the Jewish exiles were, at least in the community where
Ezekiel was present, on Kabur, a large canal near the major city-center
area of Nippur. Thus, we could suggest that the formation of the post-
exilic configuration of the *Bēt 'Ābôt* was the result of a combination of
social crisis and the centralized economic policies of the Chaldean land
resettlement and possibly even labor needs.

The tendency for centralized political control to favor larger social
units can be illustrated in Israelite history as well, and may well be the
basis for the resistance to the census in 2 Sam. 24. The mustering of
troops in Numbers 1–2 assumed large constituent units, able to supply
manpower and infantry needs to a single, unified central government.

Nehemiah's reconstruction of the Temple, unlike Solomon's construction, was based on a division of labor according to large, constituent
social groups (as his resettlement policy also reveals) as indicated by
the "guild members" listed in the same context. In Jewish history,
too, "monumental labor" required larger social units and centralized
leadership.

By analogy, Adams's survey would strongly suggest that settlements
larger than the settlements of the size typical of pre-exilic *Bēt 'Āb*'s were
encouraged, as we have argued above. It is likely that these settlements
provided workers for Neo-Babylonian building projects. In a building

inscription, Nebuchadnezzar II, the conqueror of the West, listed his conquered people in the context of all those of his realm that he pressed into service on the Temple projects:

> ...the governor [-] of the lands of Hattim from the upper Sea to the lower sea, the lands of Sumer and Akkad, the land between the two rivers... the rulers of the land of Hattim across the Euphrates towards the setting of the sun, whose rulers on the order of Marduk my Lord, I rule over, and the mighty cedars from the mountains of Lebanon I brought to my city, Babylon. All the different nationalities, people from far places whom Marduk my Lord had given me I put them to work on the building of Etemenanki and I imposed upon them the brick-basket...[76]

Finally, the term "yoke" is commonly used to refer to labor and service to ruling authorities in the Old Testament. In fact, it is more frequently used in this way than in the context of "yoked oxen" (1 Sam. 6:7; Num. 19:2; Deut. 21:3). Isa. 10:27, 14:25, and 9:3, if dated earlier than the Babylonian period, could therefore refer to the figurative "yoke" of Assyria (the service to Assyria, as we have seen, could be expensive), much as the Northern Israelites spoke of the yoke of the Southern Davidic house (1 Kings 12 ‖ 2 Chron. 10:4, 10). But in the Babylonian period, the yoke is often combined with forced service, e.g., Ezek. 34:27 ("those that enslaved you") and Isa. 47:6 (where the yoke was made heavy on the "aged"). The language is figurative, but the color is darker in the Babylonian period.

Many scholars have protested that we know nothing of the conditions of exiles and thus have not been able to talk of "slavery" or "forced labor."[77] Most references go directly to Jeremiah's letter, pointing to a situation that does not sound overly oppressive. But J. M. Wilkie calls into question this assumption of "easy living" in the Exile. Wilkie points out that Deutero-Isaiah contains many references to suffering (40:2; 41:11–12; 42:7, 22; 47:6; 49:9, 13, 24–26; 51:7, 13–14, 23; etc.).[78]

In oracles such as Isa. 13; 47:6; and Jer. 50–51, there is strong expectation of the punishment of Babylon for abuses. It is furthermore well known that Babylon remained the symbol of the oppressor, even into the New Testament era (Rev. 14:8). Zech. 5:5–11 is an early oracle reflecting this tendency, and Rome was later to be symbolically represented by Babylon. One of the most important sources for this is the "Satire on a Fallen Tyrant" of Isa. 14:4–21. Finally, there is the image of the Suffering Servant itself, certainly an image of suffering after catastrophe.

The emerging picture from this brief analysis is that of a social reconstruction of the *Bēt 'Abôt,* which was built on pre-exilic foundations, but was constructed not only as a result of crisis, but also in the "context of empire." It thus represents a *mechanism of survival* of the Judeans in Exile and afterwards. This thesis gains strength in the light of our sociological paradigms of a dominated population. Previous exegesis of the structure of the Judeans both during and after the Exile has not been in the context of a full appreciation of the social significance of the crisis and domination of the Judeans after the fall of the Judean state. The Exile was an experience of a dominated minority who reformed societal structures in response to a social ecology of domination by pulling together into tightly knit groups — which assumed a familial fiction. Such an explanation, while not accounting for *all* the evidence, most certainly accounts for most evidence and unravels a number of long-term puzzles in the study of this period What we have seen in this chapter was that there was structural change. What we propose to argue in the following chapters is that this change occurred in the context of domination.

NOTES

1. See also S. Mowinckel, *Studien zum Buche Ezra-Nehemia,* 1, *Die nachchronische Redaktion des Buches, Die Listen* (Oslo, 1964), pp. 75ff.

2. See I. Eph'al, "The Western Minorities in Babylonia in the 6th–5th Centuries BC: Maintenance and Cohesion," *Orientalia,* NS 47 (1978).

3. M. Weinfeld, "Elders" (entry), *Encyclopedia Judaica;* J.L. McKenzie, "The Elders in the Old Testament," *Analecta Biblica,* 10 (1959); Johannes Pedersen, *Israel: Its Life and Culture,* vols. 1–4 (Oxford, 1940); R. de Vaux, *Ancient Israel: Its Life and Institutions,* trans. J. McHugh (London, 1961), pp. 69ff. See also W. Zimmerli, *Ezekiel 1* (Philadelphia, 1979), pp. 236ff.; H. Reviv, "Elders and Saviours," *Oriens Antiquus,* 16 (1977); idem, "On Urban Representative Institutions and Self-Government in Syria-Palestine in the Second Half of the Second Millennium B.C.," *Journal of Economic and Social History of the Orient* (Leiden), 12 (1969).

4. Reviv, "Elders and Saviours," p. 203.

5. McKenzie, "The Elders in the Old Testament," p. 398.

6. This, however, does not take into consideration that the elders may be performing unique tasks in the P material as a result of later insertions (such as Exod. 24:14, Num. 11:28, and, perhaps, Exod. 3:18[?]).

7. McKenzie, "The Elders in the Old Testament," p. 392.

8. Ibid., p. 394.

9. Ibid., but cf. R.A. Fernea, *Shaykh and Effendi: Changing Patterns of Authority among the El Shabana of Southern Iraq* (Cambridge, Mass., 1970), pp. 400–401.

10. McKenzie, "The Elders in the Old Testament," p. 405.

11. Reviv, "Elders and Saviours," p. 288.

12. See Th. Jacobsen, "Primitive Democracy in Ancient Mesopotamia," *Journal of Near Eastern Studies,* 11 (1943).

13. C.U. Wolf, "Traces of Primitive Democracy in Ancient Israel," *Journal of Near Eastern Studies,* 6 (1947), pp. 100ff.

14. McKenzie, "The Elders in the Old Testament," p. 405.

15. Robert Gordis, "Democratic Origins in Ancient Israel — The Biblical *Edah,*" Alexander Marx Jubilee Volume, JTS (New York, 1950), p. 388.

In 1946, Smith proposed that the threshing floor was a place of assembly to be associated with the city gate. Based on Ruth 3:2, Smith suggested that the threshing floor was near the city gate to provide guard over grain left there by the workers overnight. Smith thought that the combination of the threshing floor and city gate was important. He cited a passage of Aqht which referred to the Ugaritic Dan'el taking his place with the dignitaries "on the threshing floor." A lively debate ensued about Smith's translation from Ugaritic, but it is clear that the association with elders, city gates, and probably threshing floors was a valid one. In 1962–1963, Evans further pointed out, with reference to 1 Kings 22:10, that meetings at the gate may have been the occasion for prophets to prophesy on the threshing floor of the gate.

Furthermore, there is an interesting note about the archaeology of the Solomonic Gates at Hazor, Megiddo, and Gezer, in Madeline S. Miller and J. Lane Miller, *Harper's Encyclopedia of Bible Life* (New York, 1978), p. 242. The suggestion is that there were chambers with benches to accommodate various "courts" of the elders.

See S. Smith, "The Threshing Floor at the City Gate," *Palestine Exploration Quarterly* (1946); G. Evans, " 'Gates' and 'Streets': Urban Institutions in Old Testament Times," *Journal of Religious History,* 2 (1962–1963); idem, "Ancient Mesopotamian Assemblies," *Journal of the American Oriental Society* (New Haven) JAOS, 78 (1958).

16. Eph'al, "The Western Minorities in Babylonia," p. 76. On the basis of a reading of a cuneiform text, Camb. 85 (25 Dec., 529 B.C.E., in the first regnal year of Cambyses), Eph'al refers to a sale transacted in the presence of "the elders of the Egyptians." The term used for elders is related to *sbim*, which is well attested in Ezra 5:5, 9; 6:7, 8, 14, used in comparison with the Hebrew *zᵉqēnîm*. It is furthermore notable that Tattenai, the "governor," deals with these elders and not with any other leaders among the exiles in Ezra 5:9ff. Eph'al has argued that all the various ethnic groups that he and others have identified in sources such as the Murashu Tablets had councils of elders in their "diaspora." Eph'al's arguments, other than his appeal to the single tablet Camb. 85, however, would seem less than convincing if it were not for Dandamayev's essay on the elders among the Neo-Babylonians themselves. Dandamayev cites numerous texts that refer to the elders of cities such as Sippur, or simply "elders of the city." He further cites inscriptions of kings (e.g., Nabonidus) who state that they assembled the "elders of the city, citizens of Babylon." Such elders may have been called in lieu of the entire gathered assembly of free, full-right citizens. It was Dandamayev who first pointed out Camb. 85, and the Egyptian assembly of elders and proposed the analogy with the elders mentioned in the books of Ezekiel and Jeremiah, which Eph'al then elaborated further. See M. Dandamayev, "The Neo-Babylonian Elders," in *Societies and Languages of the Ancient Near East* (Wiltshire, 1982).

It must be considered, however, whether evidence from the Persian era (that is, specifically the elders in Camb. 85, and in Ezra-Nehemiah) represents conditions that are significantly different from the conditions under the Babylonians. In his study of ancient Jewish self-government, Zucker made reference to the Persian ruling methods that came into existence with the Darian redivision of satrapies. Zucker's main source was Christensen's "Die Iranier," which in turn depended significantly on Meyer's classic *Geschichte des Altertums* of 1901. In his work Meyer had investigated the relevant sections of Xenophon and Diodorus. The assumption, based also on a reading of the Elephantine Papyri, was that the Persians allowed a great deal of local autonomy to ethnic and cultural units, often allowing one of their own number to rule (A. Christensen, "Die Iranier," in Alt, Christensen, Götze, Grohmann, Kees, and Landsberger, *Kulturgeschichte des Alten Orients,* 3 [Munich, 1933], p. 270).

The question is whether the Persian system reflects a uniquely Persian governing philosophy, or whether Camb. 85 can actually be combined with evidence of elders in the Neo-Babylonian documents to support our conclusion that elders were the self-government authorities of the deported populations throughout the exilic period. It could be that the system of elders came into being with the satrapy system of Darius. But we know that local leadership was trusted by the Chaldeans, who placed Zedekiah and Gedaliah on the thrones of Palestine to rule for the king (2 Kings 24:17–18; 2 Kings 25:22ff.). We may assume that indigenous leaders were trusted, and thus the references to the elders in Babylon during the Chaldean reign, as attested in Jeremiah and Ezekiel. I would argue that the Jewish community in Babylonia was able to approach Cyrus regarding a rebuilding of the Temple, and later under Darius to organize an actual return, only on the basis of social community that had organized itself during the Chaldean reign to such an extent that correspondence could be carried on between the community in Palestine and the community in Babylon; the community in Babylon included not only elders, but the prophets whom Jeremiah condemned as well. Permission given to rebuild the Temple, according to Ezra 6:7–8, specifically mentioned "the elders of the Jews." Throughout the Persian period, as recorded in the documents that now make up Ezra-Nehemiah, the Persians address mainly the elders.

See Hans Zucker, *Studien zur Jüdischen Selbstverwaltung im Altertum* (Berlin and New York, 1936); E. Meyer, *Geschichte des Altertums* (Berlin, 1939).

17. Leonard Rost, *Vorstufen zur Kirche und Synagoge im Alten Testament, BWANT* (Stuttgart, 1938), pp. 68–69.

18. Ibid., p. 62.

19. Bartlett cites Job 29:25 and the story of Naboth's vineyard (1 Kings 21) to show that the head was originally a judge in the tribe and later in the city. But it is interesting to note that Bartlett argues that the *roš* became associated with families, *Bēt 'Ăbôt,* that he thought were "smaller" in the post-exilic period, because of the breakdown of the monarchy. See J. R. Bartlett, "The Use of the word *roš* as a Title in the Old Testament," *Vetus Testamentum* 19 (1969), p. 10.

20. If we could go along with recent doubts about the date of some of the stories of Moses and especially the selection of the seventy "helpers" in Exod. 18:25, Num. 11:16ff., or Deut. 1:9ff., we might be able to suggest that this story was in circulation as an important etiological saga of the rise of the "heads" in the post-exilic community that eventually would become a council of seventy and lead to significant later developments in the Hellenistic era. For coins bearing references to "councils," see Ya'Akov Meshorer, *Ancient Jewish Coinage* (New York, 1982), pp. 47–48).

21. McKenzie, "The Elders in the Old Testament," p. 400.

22. Norman Gottwald, *The Tribes of Yahweh* (Maryknoll, N.Y., 1979), p. 285ff. Josh. 7 is usually dated as pre-exilic, which justifies our use of this passage: "...E traditions" (Gottwald, ibid., p. 258); "...a combination of J and E..." (O. Eissfeldt, *Introduction to the Old Testament* [Oxford, 1965], p. 253); "...pre-Deuteronomic redactor..." (J. Gray, *The Century Bible: Joshua, Judges, and Ruth,* new ed. [London, 1967], pp. 80ff.).

23. While not immediately relevant to our discussion, it is possibly significant to note that there is a textual variant, from Syriac texts, which suggests that the "house" of Zabdi was itself called up "house by house," rather than "man by man" (Josh. 7:17). But the question is, what is meant by "man by man"? Achan may well have been a head of household himself.

The suggestion that a "GBR" was a head of a household is supported by Ps. 127:5; Judg. 5:30; Isa. 22:17; Jer. 22:30; 44:20; 31:22; Mic. 2:2; Hab. 2:5, Ps. 128:3–4. The blessing that Jacob fooled Isaac into giving him was a blessing that made Jacob *Gᵉbîr over his brothers,* i.e., inheriting the right to be over the house of Isaac (Gen. 27:29). In Gen. 16, the feminine form refers to the female head of household, Sarah. Thus, we are justified in concluding that the *Bēt 'Āb,* before the Exile, referred to the household of living males who were the leaders or prominent males often referred to in the older material as the *GBRim.* There are occasions, such as in Job, where the term simply means "male," but this is clearly in a different context from our above cited instances, where more than simply a male is implied ("male" would, indeed, make little sense in Gen. 27:29, and 1 Chron. 5:2). If a *GBR* is a head of a small household, then is the *GBR* the only "elder" from the *Bēt 'Āb?* There is no evidence that this is the case, although it would make sense. However, in the case of Rebekah's marriage, Laban *and* Bethuel appear to make a decision jointly. While in the pre-exilic source (and sources that discuss pre-exilic events) the term implies a head of household, in post-exilic sources (such as Job) the term has no particular meaning other than "male person." I would like to suggest that the term was not associated with the post-exilic *Bēt 'Ābôt* because, as I will argue, the post-exilic *Bēt 'Ābôt,* while similar in nomenclature to the pre-exilic *Bēt 'Āb,* was not the same structure at all; this would explain the loss of the more prestigious meaning of *GBR* in later texts.

24. Gottwald, *Tribes of Yahweh.*

25. See J. Scharbert, "Beyt 'Ab als soziologische Grosse im Alten Testament," in Delsman, Nelis, Peters, Romer, van der Woude, eds., *Von Kanaan bis Kerala* (Neukirchen, 1982).

26. Gottwald, *Tribes of Yahweh,* pp. 25ff.

27. L. Stager, "The Archaeology of the Family in Ancient Israel," *BASOR,* 260 (1985), esp. pp. 22–23.

28. I am assuming that the Golah List is trustworthy in the numbers that it provides for a social unit.

29. Gottwald, *Tribes of Yahweh,* p. 290.

30. S. Eisenstadt, "Paralleleinblicke in das jüdische und römische Familien und Erbrecht," *KLIO,* 40 (1962).

31. E. Meyer, *Die Entstehung des Judentums* (Halle, 1896), p. 163.

32. See, on this, the analysis in R. Wilson, *Genealogy and History in the Biblical World* (New Haven and London, 1977), esp. p. 54: "... oral genealogies usually have some sociological function in the life of the society that uses them. Even when genealogies are recited as part of a lineage history, they are likely to reflect domestic, political, or religious relationships existing in the present rather than in the past. The purpose ... is to legitimize contemporary lineage configurations."

33. R. Klein, "Old Readings in 1 Esdras: The List of Returnees from Babylon," *Harvard Theological Review* 62 (1969). However, Batton also noted an interesting variation in the use of terms for family and place names. Ezra has $b^e n \hat{e}$, before all the names except Netophah, Anathoth, Michmas, Bethel, and Ai (that is, up to v. 35), whereas 1 Esdras 5, in the LXX, has the equivalent υἱοί before the last three only. Interestingly, in the LXX text, following the standardized υιοι βαιτηρ ους, there is the insertion of a separating term that suggests an awareness of a problem: υιοι εκ βαιθλωμων and thereafter, οι εκ. In Nehemiah, the term *'anšε* stands before all the terms from Bethlehem to Nebo. Batton believes that the intent was to associate $b^e n^ε$ with personal names and *'anšê* with place names, but that confusion surrounded terms like Magbish, Harim, Senaah, Azmaweth, and Nebo. See Loring Batton, *Ezra and Nehemiah,* International Critical Commentary (Edinburgh, 1913).

34. W. Rudolph, *Esra und Nehemia,* Handbuch zum Alten Testament (Tübingen, 1949), pp. 16–20.

35. Ibid., p. 16.

36. C. Schultz, "The Political Tensions Reflected in Ezra-Nehemiah," in Evans, Hallo, and White, eds., *Scripture in Context* (Pittsburgh, 1980), pp. 225ff, where various views are listed.

37. Batton, *Ezra and Nehemiah,* p. 73.

38. Mowinckel, *Studien zum Buche Ezra-Nehemia,* p. 75.

39. Ibid., pp. 75–76.

40. Meyer, *Die Entstehung des Judentums,* p. 152.

41. S. Japhet, "People and Land in the Restoration Period," *Das Land Israel in biblischer Zeit* (Göttingen, 1981).

42. On the P terminology, see S. R. Driver, *An Introduction to the Literature of the Old Testament,* 7th ed. (Edinburgh, 1898), p. 133. See J. Weinberg, "Das Beit Avot im 6–4 Jh. v.u.z.," *Vetus Testamentum,* 23 (1973), p. 400. See also Weinberg's other essays, "Demographische Notizen zur Geschichte der nachexilischen Gemeinde in Juda," *KLIO,* 54 (1972); "Bemerkungen zum Problem Des Vorhellenismus in Vorderen Orient," *KLIO,* 59 (1977); "Zentral — und Partikulargewalt im achamenidischen Reich," *KLIO,* 59 (1977); "Der 'am ha'ares des 6–4 Jh. v.u.z.," *KLIO,* 56 (1974); "Netinim und 'Söhne der Sklaven Salomos' im 6-4 Jh. v.u.z.," *Zeitschrift für die Alttestamentliche Wissenschaft* (Berlin), 87 (1975).

43. J. Weinberg, "Das Beit Avot im 6–4 Jh. v.u.z.," p. 400.

44. H. D. Mantel, "The Dichotomy of Judaism During the Second Temple," *Annual of the Hebrew Union College* (Cincinnati), 44 (1973).

45. Cross's reconstruction of the restoration may be helpful here. He refers to three different versions of the Chronicler's history. Chr A contained a retelling of the royal history (1 Chron. 10–2 Chron. 34) and the material celebrating the restoration of the Temple and a celebration of Zerubbabel as the chosen servant of God (1 Esd. 1:1–5:65 ‖ 2 Chron. 34:1–Ezra 3:13). Read within these limits, Cross notes that "the future is open, and the work of restoring the ancient institutions is well begun; all is anticipation" (F. M. Cross, "A Reconstruction of the Judean Restoration," *Journal of Biblical Literature,* 94 [1975], p. 13).

The story of Ezra, with a preface to explain the troubles (Ezra 5:1–6:19) was added by Chr B, and finally Nehemiah's memoirs were added by Chr C, although Kellerman argues convincingly that the Nehemiah tradition also came in stages (see Ulrich Kellerman, *Nehemia: Quellen, Überlieferung, und Geschichte* [Berlin, 1967]). The interesting point is that the addition of Ezra, says Cross, changed the attitude toward leadership: "When the record resumes with the narrative of the mission of Ezra, the messianic themes of the earlier narrative are no longer to be heard. Hierocracy supplants the dyarchy of king and high priest. We hear nothing of the Davidic prince either in the Ezra-narrative or in the memoirs of Nehemiah" (p. 15). With Ezra, we have a priest-scribe whose religious attitudes are decidedly "exilic." Religious worries about purity become the main and most significant concern.

46. See Weinberg, "Zentral — und Partikulargewalt im achamenidischen Reich."

47. Ibid., p. 33.

48. Ibid., p. 39.

49. Ibid., p. 36.

50. Ibid., p. 34.

51. See Ephraim Stern, *Material Culture of the Land of the Bible in the Persian Period, 538–332 B.C.* (Warminster, 1979); P.R.S. Moorey, "Iranian Troops at Deve Huyuk in Syria in the Earlier Fifth Century B.C.," *Levant,* 7 (1975).

52. S. McEvenue, "The Political Structure in Judah from Cyrus to Nehemiah," *Catholic Biblical Quarterly* 43 (1981).

53. Ibid., p. 363.

54. S. Japhet, "Sheshbazzar and Zerubbabel" *Zeitschrift für die Alttestamentliche Wissenschaft* (Berlin), 94 (1982), p. 87.

55. See Sukenik, quoted in N. Avigad, "Bullae and Seals from a Post-Exilic Judean Archive," *Monographs of the Institute of Archaeology* (Jerusalem), 4 (1976).

56. Y. Aharoni, ed., *Excavations at Ramat Rahel* (Rome, 1962).

57. N. Avigad, "The Governor of the City," *Israel Exploration Journal,* 26 (1976); idem, "Bullae and Seals from a Post-Exilic Judean Archive"; idem, "A New Class of Yehud Stamps," *Israel Exploration Journal,* 7 (1957).

58. Avigad, "Bullae and Seals from a Post-Exilic Judean Archive," pp. 4ff.

59. Ibid., p. 35.

60. Ibid. Alt had originally suggested that the districts of Judah after Nehemiah's time were (in his view under Nehemiah for the first governor) similar in breakdown to Josh. 15–19. Also, on this basis, Aharoni suggested that Neh. 3 (the persons and their homes) implied the following breakdown of areas:

Mizpah	Capital: Mizpah; subdistrict: Jericho
Jerusalem	Capital: Jerusalem; subdistrict: Gibeon
Beth-Haccerem	Beth-Haccerem (Ramat Rahel)
Beth-Zur	Capital: Beth Zur; subdistrict: Tekoa
Keilah	Capital: Keilah; subdistrict: Zenoah

Aharoni's plan, however, is one of many that have recently been surveyed by Stern (*Material Culture of the Land of the Bible in the Persian Period, 538–332 B.C.,* pp. 243ff.). The problem, as Stern notes, is that the list in Neh. 3 is not complete and does not appear to match all the areas where *YHD* stamps were found. Stern's work attempted to align cities mentioned in Ezra-Nehemiah and the locations of the *YHD* and *PHW* seals and bullae that have been found; there is not an exact parallel between the two, although the comparison is very interesting.

Furthermore, also on the basis of the wall construction of Neh. 3, some have suggested an organizational breakdown that follows this pattern:

> *Paḥâ:* Governor
> *sar Pelekh:* District governor
> *sar hesi Pelekh:* Sub-district governor

Demsky, however, calls into serious question the use of the term *pelekh* to be "area," upon which is built the above three-tiered divisions of the province of Judah. Demsky cites the term *pilku* in Akkadian, which means "work duty" or "work tax" in the form of conscripted labor, and thus challenges the idea of "area":

Nehemiah organized the project, which had been approved by the Persian authorities, into work battalions composed of local citizenry and occupational units, groups of volunteers, and levies fulfilling their tax obligations in the form of physical labour. Accordingly, these latter groups, working the rougher terrain of the lower city, were placed under overseers designated *sar(hesi) pelekh* (A. Demsky, "Pelekh in Nehemiah 3," *Israel Exploration Journal,* 33 [1983], p. 244).

In conclusion, we cannot be certain of reproducing the subsections of a province of Judah, much less the actual existence of a province before Nehemiah.

61. See Ya'akov Meshorer, *Ancient Jewish Coinage, 1, Persian Period through Hasmoneans* (New York, 1982); B. Kanael, "Ancient Jewish Coins and their Historical Importance," *Biblical Archaeologist,* 26; L. Y. Rahmani, "Silver Coins of the Fourth Century," *Israel Exploration Journal,* 21 (1971); Leo Mildenberg, "Yehud: A Preliminary Study of the Provincial Coinage of Judaea," *Greek Numismatics and Archaeology,* 1979.

62. Avigad, "A New Class of Yehud Stamps," p. 152.

63. "Since this title of governor has been discovered on the coins of Tell Jemme, this identification has been doubted. Even so, it might not present any discrepancy: the governor mentioned on this coin could have served prior to the conquest of the province by Alexander, and when Ptolemy seized power, Yhezqiyah was already an old man, having continued in office as high priest even after his title of "governor" had been abolished by the new authorities" (Avigad, ibid.); see also his article "Bullae and Seals from a Post-Exilic Judean Archive." It was earlier thought that a coin bearing the name Yehezqiyah was identical with one Ezekias, the high priest mentioned in Josephus.

64. Weinberg, "Zentral — und Partikulargewalt im achamenidischen Reich," p. 41.

65. Personal letter from Dr. Barag, November 5, 1984 (Hebrew University).

66. Weinberg, "Zentral — und Partikulargewalt im achamenidischen Reich," p. 41.

67. Zucker, *Studien zur Jüdischen Selbstverwaltung im Altertum,* p. 24.

68. See Menahem Stern, ed., *Greek and Latin Authors on Jews and Judaism* (Jerusalem, 1974), pp. 23ff. See also the analysis by D. Mendels, "Hecataeus of Abdera and a Jewish 'patrios politeia' of the Persian Period," *Zeitschrift für die Alttestamentliche Wissenschaft* (Berlin), 95 (1983).

69. See H. Kreissig, *Die Sozialökonomische Situation in Juda zur Achamenidenzeit* (Berlin, 1973), esp. pp. 39ff.

70. "Foreign trade was in fact initiated by the Crown and conducted on its behalf. It owed its existence to two factors: in the first place to the existence of agricultural surpluses in Palestine, which were, in turn, the result of favourable climatic conditions and the diligence of the people in developing and husbanding the land. Trade in these surpluses was mainly with the kingdom of Tyre, a natural customer because of its unique economy and its proximity to Israel. In the second place, there existed particular geopolitical conditions which allowed Judah and Israel to participate in international trade by virtue of their

control over international routes or parts of them. This, however, was largely a transit trade which was conducted by the Crown; while it produced profits for the royal court that enabled it to strengthen the military force of the kingdom and to raise the standard of living of the royal family and those close to it, it had only a limited influence on the national economy or on the occupational distribution of the country's inhabitants" (M. Elat, "The Monarchy and the Development of Trade in Ancient Israel," *State and Temple Economy in the Ancient Near East,* Orientalia Lovaniensia Analecta 6 (1979).

71. See K. Wittfogel, *Oriental Despotism* (New Haven, 1957).

72. Ibid., p. 12.

73. Ibid., p. 322, which is confirmed by Dandamayev from the Neo-Babylonian texts; see "Social Stratification in Babylonia," in Harmatta and Komoroczy, eds., *Wirtschaft und Gesellschaft im Alten Vorderasien* (Budapest, 1976).

74. See the fascinating collection of papers on this theme, Downing and Gibson, eds., *Irrigation's Impact on Society,* 1974, especially Eva and Robert Hunt, "Irrigation, Conflict and Politics: A Mexican Case," which amends Wittfogel helpfully.

75. R. Adams, *Heartland of Cities Surveys of Ancient Settlement and Land Use on the Central Floodplain of the Euphrates* (Chicago, 1981), p. 177.

76. F. H. Weissbach, *Das Hauptheiligtum des Marduk in Babylon* (Leipzig, 1938), pp. 47f. See also Stephen Langdon, *Building Inscriptions of the Neo-Babylonian Empire,* Part 1, Nabopolassar and Nebuchadnezzar (Paris, 1905), p. 59 and p. 149.

77. "Once settled, however, it appears that they enjoyed considerable economic well-being. This may be gathered from Jeremia's letter to the Babylonian captives" (Irving Zeitlin, *Ancient Judaism* [Oxford, 1984], p. 259).

78. J. M. Wilkie, "Nabonidus and the Later Jewish Exiles," *Journal of Theological Studies* (Oxford, London), 2 (1951).

Chapter 5

Jeremiah and Hananiah: The Crisis of Leadership

It was noted above that defeat and mass movement gave opportunities for new "spokespersons" to arise in times of crisis. Significantly, leaders would clash over the issue of what the group must do to face the future. In the Babylonian Exile, one of the most important conflicts of advice was between the prophets Hananiah and Jeremiah. The main focus of this analysis is therefore Jeremiah 27–29, the final chapter of which contains two "letters" attributed to the prophet Jeremiah and one from the exilic community in answer to Jeremiah's first letter. The context of this entire section is the debate between Jeremiah and Hananiah.

Jer. 29 is written in prose, but the entire book of Jeremiah is composed of two general literary forms, prose and poetry. Since the poetry is all obviously supposed to be the words of Jeremiah, and Jeremiah is talked *about* in the third person in the prose materials, debate has often centered on the compositional history of Jeremiah, particularly the date and origin of the prose sections. Nicholson dates the original compilation of the sayings of Jeremiah ca. 605–604 B.C.E.[1] In Nicholson's view, the events surrounding Nebuchadnezzar's victory at Carchemish led Jeremiah to believe that his prophecies about the "Foe to the North" were about to be fulfilled. Thus, it would seem a good occasion for Jeremiah to call on Baruch to write his "memoirs." Since the prose material specifically mentioned Baruch the scribe as involved in writing some of the sayings of Jeremiah, it has generally been thought that Baruch wrote down Jeremiah's own words, and then himself composed the prose material in a biographical work about Jeremiah.

Mowinckel, in 1914, separated out three layers of tradition: (A) the poetic prophetic words, (B) prose narrative, and (C) prose sermons. Many scholars have commented on the sermons, noting especially their form and literary resemblance to the Deuteronomic speeches.[2] Indeed, Nicholson believed that *both* the sermons and the prose narratives assumed their present form at the hands of the Deuteronomists, and he does not believe that there is a convincing reason why sections B and C should be separated.

Wanke believes that it is unlikely that Baruch was responsible for the historical section (Jer. 37–44), since there is no information about Jeremiah after his leaving Palestine.[3] We know that Jeremiah was taken to Egypt, but the information stops there. More specific to our text, Wanke believed that Jer. 27–29 were composed together, because of the similarity in method and theme, and then attached to Jer. 26.[4] Others, like Giesebrecht, are confident in assigning this section to the hand of Baruch.[5] However, T. Seidl, in two meticulously detailed volumes, has argued against the *compositional* unity of Jer. 27–29.[6] There are many reasons often cited for the unity of these chapters, and their differentiation from Jer. 26. For example, Jer. 26 is set in the time of Jehoiakim, while 27:1ff. is in the time of Zedekiah. The MT has "Jehoiakim" in 27:1, but this is clearly an error, in view of 27:3 and 12, and the fact that v. 6 assumes Nebuchadnezzar's conquest. The Syriac (7th–8th century A.D.) and Arabic texts have corrected the text to "Zedekiah" in 27:1.

Jeremiah is in the third person in Jer. 26, while most often in first person in 27–29. The spelling of Jeremiah is *yirm*^{e}*yâ*, in 28:5, while it is the fuller *yirm*^{e}*yāhû* in Jer. 26. Jer. 27–29 contain "Nebuchadnezzar" rather than "Nebuchadrezzar" as elsewhere. Finally, the theme of yoke, yoke-bars, prison, and restraint are connectors for 27–28 especially. Prophetic conflict is more the theme of Jer. 27–29 than Jer. 26, and it is clearly the internal thematic principle.

Seidl does not believe that these chapters were produced at the same time, but they came to be a unit because of the subject matter that was common to all the sections.

Jeremiah's Letter in Ch. 29

The "letter" of Jeremiah to the exiles is contained in material considered highly controversial from a literary point of view, but also from a historical perspective. Does it, for example, give indication of the issues and circumstances faced by the exiled Jews in Babylon?

Let us begin with some critical comments on the relevant portions of Jer. 29, before examining the social issues involved.

This is the text of the letter that the prophet Jeremiah sent from Jerusalem to those who were left of the elders in exile, to the priests, the prophets, and all the people whom Nebuchadnezzar had deported from Jerusalem to Babylon. This was after King Jeconiah had left Jerusalem with the queen mother, the eunuchs, the chief men of Judah and Jerusalem, and the blacksmiths and metal-workers. The letter was entrusted to Elasah son of Shaphan and to Gemariah son of Hilkiah, whom Zedekiah king of Judah had sent to Babylon, to Nebuchadnezzar king of Babylon. The letter said: "Yahweh Sabaoth, the God of Israel, says this to all the exiles deported from Jerusalem to Babylon: Build houses, settle down, plant gardens and eat what they produce; marry and have sons and daughters; choose wives for your sons, find husbands for your daughters so that these can bear sons and daughters in their turn; you must increase there and not decrease. Work for the good of the city to which I have exiled you; pray to Yahweh on its behalf, since on its welfare yours depends.... " (Jer. 29:1–8)

It is interesting to note that the Greek text (LXX) has already caught the significance of the theme of Jer. 27–29, because the "prophets" are called, in 29:1: "pseudoprophets" ($\psi\epsilon\upsilon\delta o\pi\rho o\varphi\eta\tau\alpha\varsigma$).

In 29:3 of the LXX (which is chap. 36 in the different arrangement of the LXX) there is no mention at all of Nebuchadnezzar.

In 29:4, the LXX has only "from Jerusalem"; the Hebrew text adds, "to Babylon."

In 29:8, again, the LXX has "pseudoprophets."

The most important variant, however, is the omission of vv. 16–20 altogether from the LXX text. Most commentators therefore speculate that 16–20 should be omitted from critical consideration of the earliest forms of Jer. 29. It is clear that vv. 16–20 are Deuteronomic in influence, if not origin. To begin with, the concept of the "throne" of David, as a symbol of authority, is Deuteronomic (cf. 1 Kings 1:13, 17, 20; 2:12, 24; 8:20 [throne of Israel]; 2 Kings 10:3; but cf. Jer. 17:25, which talks of kings and nobles on the throne of David). Where the concept of the throne of David occurs in Jeremiah, there is obviously the presence of a formulaic sentence (cf. Jer. 17; 22; 29:16; and 36:30).

The "trilogy" of sword, famine, and pestilence and the figurative use of "figs" both relate directly to the prose section, chap. 24, and obviously were either introduced at the same time as chap. 24 (although this is doubtful if the LXX does not have vv. 16–20), or 16–20 was composed on the basis of chap. 24. Giesebrecht thought that they were from the same hand. (I do not accept this.) The fig imagery, it is interesting to note, is used elsewhere only in Jotham's fable, in Judg. 9:7ff.

Finally, the charge of disobeying the many prophets that God sent (Jer. 29:19) is a common Deuteronomic theme, frequent in Deuteronomic sermons.[7]

Vv. 16–20 are thus not considered integral to the message to the exiles by commentators such as Nicholson, Weiser, Duhm, Volz, Giesebrecht, and Rudolph.

Is There a Letter in Jeremiah 29?

Since Duhm, most commentators attribute to the original "letter" only Jer. 29:5–7. The first few words of v. 1 are probably the earliest redactional introduction to the letter, since the list of people probably depends on latter additions. Further, much of v. 2 is deleted because it is assumed to be influenced by 2 Kings 24:12. The most interesting variation at this point, however, is that the LXX has "bound and free" rather than the Hebrew text's "craftsmen [woodworkers?] and smiths" in the list of exiles.

Duhm believed that Jer. 29 contained portions of a real letter, which he believed to be composed of vv. 4a, 5–7, and 11–14. After removing what he considered further additions, Duhm read the letter to *mean*:

> When you call me and come and pray to me, I shall listen to you.
> When you search for me, you will find me; when you search whole-
> heartedly for me.... (NJB)[8]

Within vv. 5–7 Duhm believed that the addition of "choose wives for your sons; find husbands for your daughters so that these can bear sons and daughters in their turn" came from an exilic concern to lengthen the generations in keeping with the (in his view, late) tradition of a length of stay of "seventy years." Thus, vv. 8–10 were also considered from a late hand.

Volz also believed the letter to be genuine and accepted the basic limits of the text reconstructed by Duhm. Volz added that the "seventy" of v. 10 is undoubtedly to be taken symbolically as "a long time" so may also have an early date. Furthermore, Wanke noted that the promised "good" of the future in 29:10 is reminiscent of 33:15, but the latter, along with the entire 12–26 passage of chap. 33, which contains future promises of good, is absent from the LXX, raising doubts about its presence in 29:10.

Seidl, too, believed that vv. 8–10, with its great hope for the future, is *"unjeremianisch."* Rudolph, on the other hand, disagreed with those who would omit v. 10. He accused Volz of wanting to read Jeremiah's letter as advice for a permanent settlement and religious life without the Temple, a desire which Rudolph suspected to have faintly "protestant" motives.[9]

In the light of the growing significance of the seventy-years theme,[10] it seems most likely to me that the "original letter" did not contain reference to the hoped-for return; for had it done so, it would have had the effect, as Volz has argued correctly, of undercutting the impact of Jeremiah's advice. The original letter could even have come to serve other purposes entirely; Duhm comments that one could easily find in

v. 7 the intention of certain Babylonian Jews to have the prophet's authority behind their wish to remain in Babylon.[11]

Furthermore, the anger expressed in the "response" to the letter was because Jeremiah had claimed that the stay would be long, but the response quoted only the content of v. 5. One would have presumed some mention of a return if Jeremiah had mentioned one.

As for vv. 8–9, Nicholson believes that they are also products of the Deuteronomic redactor, since they are so reminiscent of Deut. 18:10–14, while vv. 13–14 are paralleled by Deut. 6:29 and 30:1–5.

Finally, Wanke, Nicholson, and Duhm, all point to the execution of the prophets Ahab and Zedekiah, described in such graphic terms in vv. 20–22 and 23, in all probability *ex eventu*. The burning by fire, also recalled in the tales of Daniel, must have been a terrifyingly vivid recollection of a Neo-Babylonian practice.[12]

We are left with vv. 5–7 as the essence of the letter from Jeremiah. There is virtual unanimity among commentators that this letter is authentic, or based on an authentic tradition. The most cautious note, however, is Seidl's view that the present form of the letter is simply a shortened message based on a spoken message or a tradition of the prophet Jeremiah.[13]

But do we, in fact, have a *letter* in vv. 5–7? Recent analysis of Aramaic letters from the time of Jeremiah reveals common forms for the "letter type." As recently, and conveniently, enumerated by Pardee, they are as follows: (1) *praescriptio:* address formula, sender-recipient, greeting; (2) transition to body; (3) body of letter; (4) closing formula (late).[14]

Duhm believed that we have portions of a real letter, and Volz added that such a letter, sent by authority (or certainly with the permission) of King Zedekiah, would have served as good propaganda in assuring the Babylonians of Jewish cooperation. Further, Rudolph assumed that the writing of such a letter in the first place proves that the Jews could not have been living in a "concentration camp" (*Konzentrationslager*) atmosphere, but must have had free movement within their settled area.[15] How Rudolph arrives at such information from Jer. 29 is not clear. All of these views add to our understanding of Jeremiah, but do not, I believe, focus on the social context.

Volz assumed the letter's purpose was to advise on an ordered, settled existence on the land from which God would still hear their prayers, despite the view expressed in Amos 7:17 and Hos. 9:1ff. that foreign land was unclean and impious. Weiser considered the letter's purpose to be twofold. Noting first its context, Jer. 27–29, where prophetic conflict is the theme, he believes that it spoke out against fanatical prophets who predicted a quick return, but also against desperation and faithlessness.[16] Finally, Nicholson believes, in regards to vv. 5–7, that "in both content and language [it]...has all the appearance of being authentic."[17]

The Meaning of Jeremiah's Letter: Nonviolent Resistance

If the letter is genuine, or refers to a genuine exchange of ideas between Palestine and Babylonia, then aspects of Jer. 29 become significant. Perhaps most significantly, the letter represents an important political document. This is particularly clear when we note that Jer. 27–29 is concerned in the main with prophetic conflict, between those prophets who advocated God's sure and quick end to the Exile and Jeremiah's teaching of long endurance.

But was the issue of chaps. 27–29 merely the issue of true and false prophecy? In a very interesting article about Jer. 27–29, Overholt argues that Hananiah must be seen as a prophet who preached an orthodox message containing allusions both to the inviolability of Zion and God's trustworthy protection and aid through a quick return from Exile. *Hananiah was not perceived as a false prophet by the people during his confrontation with Jeremiah.*

Indeed, the message of the prophets in the exilic community proves, if not Hananiah's own influence, then the wide range of similar prophetic views. As Overholt comments: "The message of Hananiah had its roots sunk deep in the promises of security of Yahweh's positive action on behalf of his people, embodied in the nation's cultic establishment."[18]

While making interesting observations on the specific details of Hananiah's conflict with Jeremiah, Overholt is interested in the wider question of "false prophecy" and its determination.

This is also the subject of Crenshaw's survey and analysis in his work *Prophetic Conflict.*[19] Crenshaw detailed the many attempts to determine biblical criteria for "false prophecy" but ended up supporting the notion that true and false prophecy are two sides of the same coin: they cannot be easily separated because of the nature of prophecy itself.

One of Crenshaw's most helpful generalizations, however, is that biblical "true" prophets inevitably found themselves in conflict with the "standard religion of the people." Aspects of this standard religious view included, according to Crenshaw: (1) confidence in God's faithfulness (Jer. 5:12, 23:17); (2) satisfaction with traditional religion; (3) defiance of prophets who disagree; (4) despair when hope seems dead; (5) doubt of the justice of God (Ezek. 12:22f., 18:25); (6) historical pragmatism (Jer. 44:16–19).[20]

The important thing to note, especially regarding point 1, is that many of the attitudes here enumerated could, *in other circumstances,* be orthodox in the strict sense — thus justifying Buber's insight (echoed by

Overholt) that false prophecy is simply "the right word for the wrong time."[21]

It is fair to observe, however, that even these comments on prophetic conflict do not focus enough attention on the historical occasion for this particular conflict, the Exile and the response to it. This is the specific issue that divided Jeremiah and Hananiah.

Most commentators assume that Hananiah was preaching some form of noncooperation and resistance to the Babylonian conquerors, perhaps with the assumed support of Egypt. This is similar to the message of Ahaz, Shemiah, and Zedekiah in the exilic communities. Similarly, Lang has argued that Ezekiel, far from having little political perspective, was actually preaching against Zedekiah's planned revolt in Jerusalem.[22] Was Jeremiah, therefore, preaching against revolt or resistance in Babylon?

The answer comes from focussed attention on vv. 5–7, which is the essence of Jeremiah's message to the exiles. As we have seen, the consensus is that these words probably represent a genuine tradition of a letter to the exiles. Let us consider the language of vv. 5–7.

Build, Plant, and Marry

In 1961, Bach analyzed the images of "build and plant" and concluded that these were a well-known theme in Old Testament tradition.[23] Bach sought to find the probable *Sitz im Leben* of this image. Since it is usually mentioned in the context of future well-being and represents landed existence as well as *one-time* activities in a man's life (connected with houses and vines, or olive trees on rare occasions), Bach suggests that the phrases originated as parts of a "wish" for future success at the birth of a son.[24] This was confirmed in Bach's thinking by the fact that another "one-time life activity" was occasionally added to "build houses" and "plant gardens/vines," namely, marriage.[25]

Shalom Paul also believed that this phrase was traditional, but he said that these words of encouragement are "no more than a well-known stereotypical formula for future bliss."[26] Paul was particularly interested, however, in Jeremiah's relationship with Deutero-Isaiah, and related Jer. 29 to Isa. 65, where "build, plant, and marry" is also found. Even the theme that God hears the people when they call is common to both passages (Isa. 65:23, 24).

While Paul did not relate the three images to Deut. 20 and 28, neither did Bach relate Jer. 29 or Deut. 20 and 28 to Isa. 65. Bach considered his three passages that mention the three images to be different enough in context to justify his assumption that the "birth wish" probably came to have marriage associated with it in some traditions.

But we can take issue with Bach's view that Deut. 20 and 28 and

Jer. 29 are three different contexts, then add Paul's inclusion of Isa. 65, and so consider together the context of all four occurrences of the three images, build, plant, and marry. "Build" and "plant" is a well-known combination. Bach's idea of a birth wish may be granted as a feasible etiology; but when "marry" is added, to make a three-point image, *the context is always warfare;* that is, the three are things that are protected, or lost, in warfare.

The context of Deut. 20 is clear. These are the Deuteronomic military "exemptions" from Holy War. Von Rad, Weinfeld, and Dion have commented on the Holy War language of this passage, such as "fear not," and 1 Macc. 3:55f. attests to the continued observance of these exemptions:

> Next Judas appointed leaders for the people, to command a thousand, a hundred, fifty or ten men. He told those who were building houses, or about to be married or planting vineyards, or who were simply afraid, to go home, every one of them, *as the law allowed.*

Carmichael comments that the dedication upon building a house symbolized and anticipated an individual Israelite's residence in the land in a secure place.[27] Regarding the planting of vines, in Lev. 19:23–25 it is clear that the ritual process of purification of fruit takes five years, which would make it by far the longest exemption implied in Deut. 20, unless house dedication took a length of time we are not now aware of. Deut. 24:5 implies that the marriage exemption was one year. Keil and Delitzsch's summary of these exemptions is instructive:

> The intention of these instructions was neither to send away all persons who were unwilling to go into the war, and thus avoid the danger of their interfering with the readiness and courage of the rest of the army in prospect of the battle, nor to spare the lives of those persons to whom life was especially dear, but rather to avoid depriving any member of the covenant nation of his enjoyment of the good things of this life bestowed upon him by the Lord.[28]

Deut. 28 describes the punishment for not living according to the law given by God. The punishment includes not being able to live in one's house; not being able to enjoy one's vineyard; or not being able to marry one's wife because of defeat in war by the enemy (Deut. 28:25). Furthermore, Isa. 65, with its parallels (although not as striking as the other three) concludes the section with a typical Isaianic motif of peace:

> The wolf and the lamb will feed together, the lion eat straw like the ox, the dust will be the serpent's food. They will do no hurt,

no harm on all my holy mountain, says Yahweh. (Isa. 65:25; cf. Isa. 11 regarding the return from Exile, esp. vv. 10ff.)

On the basis of these parallels, and their context in warfare, and especially the *cessation or exemption from warfare,* it is clear that Jeremiah is not simply advising a settled existence, but that he uses the Deuteronomic exemptions from warfare to declare an "armistice" on the exile community. This is confirmed by the martial language of Hananiah, who proclaimed God's deliverance in decidedly militaristic terms: "I have broken the yoke of the king of Babylon. . . . I will bring back Jehoiachin the son of Jehoiakim king of Judah. . . . I will break the yoke of Nebuchadnezzar king of Babylon from the neck of all the nations within two years" (Jer. 28:3–4, 11). If Jeremiah's advice is proclaimed in the traditional context of warfare, then we are quite clearly dealing with a prophetic conflict on the issue of the appropriate action toward Babylon. Jeremiah's call to seek the *shalom* of the city/country would then be a direct call to abandon revolt in Babylon and Palestine and would be as appropriate to this section as Isaiah's ending is appropriate in the section of that book where the same three elements are mentioned; both are understood in the context of holy war. This would also strengthen Volz's view that Zedekiah allowed the message to be sent to reassure the Babylonians of his sincerity and loyalty. The issue is not God's action, but the exiles' response to God's plan as announced by the prophets, either Jeremiah or Hananiah.

Once the issue is seen in terms of conflicting advice on *strategy* for exilic existence, then the division between Hananiah and Jeremiah is an example of a split between two political spokespersons in a community under domination and control. The split is between those who advocate a limited cooperation and those who advocate open, and frequently violent, rebellion. The frequency of this split appears to be in the nature of the social configurations resulting from domination and minority existence. Finally, since revolution was contemplated in a prayer for an "exodus-like" delivery, the comparisons of Babylon to Egyptian servitude indicate that the circumstances of the Exile could hardly be described as "not so bad" (even if the strong terms of Jer. 50ff. are ignored as ahistorical).

Vv. 5–7 reflect Deut. 20 and 28 , and less dramatically, Isa. 65. This however, raises the question of whether this "letter" is in fact from the Deuteronomic redactor of Jeremiah rather than an actual letter. If Nicholson's thesis, for example, is that strong Deuteronomic language in Jeremiah invariably signals an actual Deuteronomic hand as the author, one fails to see why the letter itself, i.e., vv. 5–7, should not be a prime candidate for such a Deuteronomic editor! Thus, Jeremiah the prophet finally disappears from the entire chapter, and at best we have a faithful retelling of attitudes that are (no doubt) historically attributed to Jeremiah himself and his work. The enigmatic Lachish Letters, which complain of a prophet who is opposed to resistance, prove that a partisan conflict existed in regard to the war against Babylon, even if the prophet in question is not Jeremiah.[29] I do not believe that there is reason to doubt that vv. 5–7 represent a faithful tradition about Jeremiah, even if edited by a knowledgeable Deuteronomic hand. The chronological sequence of the latter additions to Jer. 29 and the way they develop the thoughts of 5–7 — i.e., the addition of a hoped-for return (*ex eventu?*), the seventy years time span, the traditions regarding Ahab and Zedekiah — would indicate this. Finally, the section containing vv. 16–20 represents an addition that connects with the dramatic imagery of Jer. 24, and was added at a time when the split between the exiles and those remaining behind was growing. We tentatively place this period before the destruction of 587, when hope for a return would have added to the animosity of those who wanted something to return to.

This must be tempered, however, by insights on the continued social conflict in the exilic period, noted in Ezekiel's references to conflict over property rights and the use of the term "thieves" in reference to those who hold land in Palestine that formerly belonged to exiles! In the same vein, an addition like vv. 16–20 could be dated virtually any time during the Exile, at about the same time that an idea of a "seventy-year" stay was current.

The whole of Jer. 29, therefore, gives us insights into the social psychology of a group under stress. We hear in this chapter about rumors, emotional upheaval, and divisions of leadership with their conflicting strategies for survival and faithfulness. Indeed, it may be that the additions to vv. 5–7 in Jer. 29 give us a chronological "history" of the ideological development of the attitude of the Exiles to their fate, beginning with the advice to seek the peace of the city, progressing to the upheaval of occasional rumors of imminent freedom (e.g., the "seventy-year" figure), and finally the word about the treatment of property "back home."

Hananiah's opposition to Jeremiah was the opposition of a Zealot, the violent revolutionary who called on Israel to draw their swords to end the yoke of Babylon. The argument between Jeremiah and Hananiah was both political and theological: how to be the people of God in a foreign land.

In his commentary for the Anchor Bible series, John Bright goes to great pains to exorcise Jeremiah of the demons of "pacifism" and "cowardice":

How one's country is best to be served is a question upon which men may at any time legitimately disagree.... [Jeremiah]... advised submission to Babylon, but to mark him down as a Babylonian sympathizer, or a collaborationist, would be to do him a grave injustice.... To suppose that Jeremiah spoke as he did because of pacifistic leanings, or from personal cowardice, would be, if possible, even more unfair.[30]

Despite the fact that those who advocate violent resistance consider other options to be "unpatriotic," "unfaithful," or ineffective, we can see that the other means of resistance, e.g., nonviolent social resistance (which represented Jeremiah's strategy), are not prescriptions for suicide or acceptance of evil, but alternative means of faithfulness and mechanisms for survival. The intent of Jeremiah's advice was to ensure that the Jewish community "...multiply there: do not decrease!"

That this was seen as a significant model of Hebraic resistance is clear from the themes of "spiritual" resistance to foreign influence (especially idolatry), which later traditions associated with Jeremiah's influence, i.e., the books of Baruch and the Epistle of Jeremiah (parts of which date as early as the fourth century B.C.E.).[31]

NOTES

1. E. W. Nicholson, *Preaching to the Exiles: A Study of the Prose Tradition in the Book of Jeremiah* (Oxford, 1970), esp. pp. 20ff., "Literary Considerations."

2. S. Mowinckel, *The Composition of Jeremiah.*

3. Gunther Wanke, *Untersuchungen zur sogenannten Baruchschrift,* Beihefte zur Zeitschrift für die Alttestamentliche Wissenschaft, 122 (Berlin, 1971).

4. Ibid., pp. 43ff.

5. F. Giesebrecht, *Das Buch Jeremia,* Handkommentar zum Alten Testament (Tübingen, 1907), p. xx.

6. Theodor Seidl, *Texte und Einheiten in Jeremia 27–29,* Arbeiten zu Text und Sprache im Alten Testament (Munich, 1977), and *Formen und Formeln in Jeremia 27–29,* Arbeiten zu Text und Sprache im Alten Testament (Munich, 1978).

7. Nicholson, *Preaching to the Exiles,* pp. 99f.

8. B. Duhm, *Das Buch Jeremia,* Kurzer Handkommentar zum Alten Testament (Tübingen, 1901), pp. 229f.

9. W. Rudolph, *Jeremiah Handbuch zum Alten Testament,* 12 (Tübingen, 1947), p. 155.

10. Michael Knibb, "The Exile in the Literature of the Intertestamental Period," *The Heythrop Journal,* 27 (1976).

11. Duhm, *Das Buch Jeremia,* pp. 229ff.

12. Rudolph, *Jeremiah Handbuch zum Alten Testament,* pp. 155f.

13. Seidl, *Texte und Einheiten in Jeremia 27–29,* p. 301.

14. Dennis Pardee, *Handbook of Ancient Hebrew Letters,* SBL Series for Biblical Study, no. 15 (Chico, Calif., 1982), chap. 4, "Formulaic Features of the Hebrew Letters." With the sole exception of the Hebrew term for "letter" (or "document") in v. 1, nothing in the content itself suggests a letter form. But by including v. 23 in the original letter, Holladay has suggested that the mention of God as "witness" suggests a "technical term for

'counter-signatory'" (W. L. Holladay, "God Writes a 'Rude Letter,'" *Biblical Archaeologist,* 1983). Further, Holladay believes he has found in 29:4 the typical "from PN to PN" portion of the "praescriptio." (As a reference to Westermann's "Basic Forms of Prophetic Speech" will confirm, however, this is part of a standard messenger formula for prophetic pronouncements). Lastly, Holladay notes that some form of *shalom* is typical of greetings in the letters and suggests that since the mention of "peace" is not found until further in the letter, the letter is "rude"; instead of the sender wishing peace, the sender is saying that peace is up to them! Holladay's attempts are somewhat strained, and at best one can say that the tradition that included this material as a letter may have been aware of a letter form in the construction.

15. Rudolph, *Jeremiah Handbuch zum Alten Testament,* p. 155.

16. A. Weiser, *Das Buche des Propheten Jeremia,* 4th ed., Alte Testament Deutsch (Göttingen, 1960), p. 253.

17. Nicholson, *Preaching to the Exiles,* p. 98.

18. T. Overholt, "Jeremiah 27–29: The Question of False Prophecy," *Journal of the American Academy of Religion,* 35 (1967), p. 245.

19. J. Crenshaw, *Prophetic Conflict: Its Effect Upon Israelite Religion,* Beihefte zur Zeitschrift für die Alttestamentliche Wissenschaft (Berlin, 1971).

20. Ibid., pp. 24ff.

21. Davidson, similarly, also believed that Jeremiah was actually criticizing the generally held Deuteronomic "tests" as themselves inadequate: "There is no reason to doubt the religious sincerity of the men who opposed Jeremiah on these issues. Viewed in the light of Deut. 8:1–6, Jeremiah was a false prophet inviting his people to 'go after other gods' (Deut. 13:3), a politico-religious fifth columnist proclaiming treason against the noblest reformed tradition of his people" (R. Davidson, "Orthodoxy and the Prophetic Word," *Vetus Testamentum,* 14 [1964], p. 412).

22. See B. Lang, *Kein Aufstand in Jerusalem* (Stuttgart, 1981).

23. R. Bach, "Bauen und Pflanzen," in R. Rendtorff and K. Koch, eds., *Studien zur Theologie der altestestamentlichen Überlieferungen* (Berlin, 1961). The varied instances used by Bach are helpfully set out on p. 16 of his work.

24. Ibid., p. 22.

25. Bach speculated that houses and vineyards are typical of landed existence, which may be significant in the light of the traditions like Deut. 6:10f., Josh. 24:13, and in regard to the Rechabites, Jer. 35:7.

26. Shalom Paul, "Literary and Ideological Echoes of Jeremiah in Deutero-Isaiah," in P. Peli, ed., *Fifth World Congress of Jewish Studies* (Jerusalem, 1969), p. 119.

27. C. Carmichael, *The Laws of Deuteronomy* (Los Angeles, 1974); G. von Rad, *Studies in Deuteronomy* (London); M. Weinfeld, *Deuteronomy and the Deuteronomic School* (Oxford, 1972); Paul-Eugene Dion, "The 'Fear Not' Formula and Holy War," *Catholic Biblical Quarterly,* 32, no. 4 (1970).

28. C. F. Keil, F. Delitzsch, *Biblical Commentary on the Old Testament,* vol. 3, *The Pentateuch* (Grand Rapids, 1951).

29. See D. W. Thomas, *The Prophet in the Lachish Ostraca* (London, 1946).

30. John Bright, *Jeremiah,* Anchor Bible (Garden City, N.Y., 1965), pp. cviii–cix.

31. See Carey Moore, "Toward the Dating of the Book of Baruch" *Catholic Biblical Quarterly,* 36 (1974), pp. 312f., and his Anchor Bible commentary, *Daniel, Esther and Jeremiah: The Additions* (Garden City, N.Y., 1977).

Chapter 6

The Ritual of Survival

The Character of the Priestly Redactors: Dating the P Document

Since the Kuenen-Reuss-Graf theories and Wellhausen's systematic revision and formulation at the turn of the twentieth century, it has been largely accepted in Christian scholarship of the Old Testament that the final redaction of the Pentateuch was from the hand of an exilic or post-exilic writer (or writers) whose predominantly cultic interests and literary style earned them the name "the Priestly writer(s)."[1]

Major exceptions to this view come largely from scholars such as Kaufmann, Weinfeld, Japhet, and Hurvitz.[2] Since the chronological arguments form an important presupposition to the following section, we will briefly consider some of the major directions of this argument.

Wellhausen's arguments, as noted by many critics who nonetheless share his general views, are based on an assumption of a religious/historical development along the general line of:

Nomadic stage → Building (Urban) stage → Prophetic → (decline to) Legalistic Religion

The final stage is an encrustation of the vitality of the penultimate stage. As Wellhausen himself unfortunately remarked:

> The Mosaic theocracy, the residuum of a ruined state, is itself not a state at all, but an unpolitical artificial product created in spite of unfavourable circumstances by the impulse of an ever-memorable energy: and foreign rule is its necessary counterpart. In its nature it is intimately allied to the old Catholic Church.... If the Priestly Code makes the cultus the principal thing, that appears to amount to a systematic decline into the heathenism which the prophets incessantly combated and yet were unable to eradicate.[3]

In recent scholarship, the general tendency has been to place the compo-

139

sition of the priestly writer *during* the Exile, in a time of *preparation* for the return,[4] and we see no reason to doubt this on the basis of recent arguments.[5]

Kilian argues that, since the central core of "P" ends with the death of Moses, it does not include the taking of the land. With Vink, Kilian also notes the "demilitarized" nature of the P narrative, which sought to emphasize the knowledge of God rather than military might as the strength of a nation. Kilian notes specifically that Exod. 14:1–14 emphasizes the protection of Israelites during the wilderness escape from Pharaoh; he also mentions the family nature of the Passover, which had become the diaspora festival par excellence.[6]

The cultic legislation, in Kilian's view (shared by Elliger[7]), was totally invented in the Exile, intended for the time when "you come into the land" [again!] (Lev. 19:23, etc.).

Brueggemann also looks for a theological basis for the priestly writer's task, concerning himself with identifying the "kerygma" of the priestly writer. This central kernel is found in its first and fullest form in Gen. 1:28 and is repeated in whole or in part in Gen. 9:7, 17:20, 28:1–4, 47:27, and Exod. 1:1–5, 7. It can be viewed systematically as:

Be Fruitful	no more barrenness
Multiply	no more lack of heirs
Fill the earth	no more being crowded out
Subdue	no more subservience
Have dominion	no more being dominated[8]

This is, in Brueggemann's terms, the word that is spoken to the landless people in the circumstances of the Exile.

Supporting such theological arguments have been detailed studies of textual evidence, such as Kapelrud's study of Deutero-Isaiah[9] and Auerbach's arguments that P material exhibits the Babylonian month-chronological system, rather than the pre-exilic Israelite chronology.[10] (The different month system, Auerbach suggested, is indicated by the use of a number for each month, in contrast to the pre-exilic use of month-names. These studies are only more recent examples of what Driver, in his Introduction, attempted to identify, namely, a unique terminology of the P writer.[11])

The consensus is still that P is an exilic document with additions even in the post-exilic period.

P as a Redaction of Old and New Sources

Recently, scholarly work on the priestly source has moved in the direction of seeing the P source as a compilation of layers of historical tradition. One such layer in P, for example, is the Holiness Code ("H"), so named by Klostermann in 1877 and consistently considered to include Lev. 17–26.[12] In his overview of the central issues at his time, Elliot-Binns listed some of the reasons that the Holiness Code had been considered a separate tradition that was later incorporated into P: (1) H does not mention "camp" or "tent of meeting"; (2) in H, priesthood is general, not divided or limited to Aaron and sons; (3) there is no high priest (but compare Lev. 21:10 with Ezra 3:2 and Neh. 3:1); (4) there is no distinction between "holy" and "most holy"; (5) the sacrificial system seems less developed; (6) the slaughter of domestic animals for food is still regarded as sacrificial in H; (7) H connects festivals with agriculture, while P otherwise has tried to connect festivals to historical events.[13]

Reventlow believes that the Holiness Code raises considerable problems for the older documentary hypotheses, since the legal material in the Holiness Code includes both old cultic and civil law and, in common with Deuteronomy, reflects settled existence.[14] Elliot-Binns, however, despaired of dating the Holiness Code any more exactly than its being simply earlier than the traditional date of the priestly writers, i.e., pre-exilic.[15] As we shall see, a form-critical study of priestly laws greatly intensifies the difficulty of certitude about the date of P material.

A Redactional View of Cultic Law

Form critical investigations question, even more substantially, the generalizations that view the legal material as a final stage of the development of Israelite religion. *Form critical* analysis of law essentially began with Alt's ground-breaking theories presented in his essay "The Origins of Israelite Law" (1934). In this article, Alt separated "apodictic law" from "casuistic law." (Casuistic law generally has the form of cases, i.e., "If a man....") This formula for legal material is known outside the Israelite material, and Alt assumed that the use of this form by Israel was a result of Canaanite influence. Alt pointed out that there was nothing inherently Yahwistic about casuistic formulations. Apodictic law, on the other hand, takes the form of *command,* usually directed to humanity from God, i.e., "Thou shalt... " in the imperative or forms of the second person. *This* legal form was genuinely Israelite, so Alt maintained. Alt's views have given rise to an important trajectory of form critical analysis of law that we must consider before making exegetical comments on the function of law in Exile.

In 1936, Begrich tried to apportion priestly legislation between what he called "priestly Torah" and priestly *Da'at* (knowledge).[16] To begin with, Begrich notes that earlier traditions from prophetic sources (Mic. 3:11, Jer. 18:18, and Ezek. 7:26) suggest that "speaking Torah" was the exclusive right of the priests.[17] Torah was the "Word of Yahweh," which the priests taught and maintained (or, in the views of some prophets, failed to teach and maintain). The place of Torah instruction was undoubtedly the Temple. The main content of the priestly Torah was concerned with the maintenance of the difference between the holy and the profane, the pure and impure. (Note in this context Haggai's question directed to the priests in Hag. 2 on the question of purity and holiness.) The common form of this priestly Torah is the short imperative-command claiming to be the word of Yahweh, but Begrich also included more "casuistic" forms as containing the specific subject matter of priestly Torah (Lev. 19:7).[18]

The other form of priestly law is not in the imperative with the Israelite as subject, nor does it claim to be (in form) the oral speech of God. This is information that is *not* for the laity, but consists of legal material that the priest must himself know in order to carry out priestly duties (Lev. 13:50–56; 14:3–7, 11–20, 24–31, 36–45, 48–53; 15:30; etc.). The *subject* is often a member of the cult personnel, lower altar and temple helpers. The predominance of Alt's casuistic form is notable here. Before the Exile (Hos. 3:4) the difference between the two is clear, but Begrich suggested that the term "Torah" later came to mean everything that the priest was involved with.[19]

Begrich's work, like Alt's, focused attention on the form, function, and development of early Israelite law, specifically cultic law. Recent works have taken this investigation further and elaborated the forms of law more clearly. Feucht, for example, specified a more detailed set of forms for legal material in a brilliant work of analysis, which attempted to enumerate metric as well as syntactic differences between legal statements. In all, Feucht suggested twelve different forms.[20] Although Feucht was specifically interested in the Holiness Code, the form critical results of this kind of investigation have led to the search for the beginning of the tradition of cultic law and its *Sitz im Leben*. Thus, the works of Rendtorff[21] Koch,[22] Kilian,[23] Feucht, and Reventlow converge on the form critical task of working on the priestly cultic material and have lent considerable weight to the objections (which form critical arguments had already raised) to the general viability of the documentary hypothesis and specifically that part of it which claimed a late date for all the legal material.

Rendtorff's work is concerned with the law outside the Holiness Code, specifically with sections such as Lev. 1–7. Rendtorff believes that chaps. 1–5 deal with law for Israelites, and 6–7 are specifically for Aaronite priests. This is reminiscent of the distinctions drawn by Begrich.[24] Koch, in a different direction, identifies long series of short sentences of legal material, such as Exod. 25:1–9; Gen. 9:1–5; Gen. 17:1f., 10–14. By investigating the nature of these series of laws on cultic matters, Koch believes that he can identify Temple cultic laws from Israelite practice that precedes the centralization of worship at the Jerusalem Temple; these were later reworked for post-Deuteronomic and exilic writing by the P-redactor.[25]

Kilian's work makes this line of investigation clearer, although one must remember a complex series of redactors that Kilian claims to have identified in the process of analyzing the literary history of the legal material. Kilian's main concern is the Holiness Code, and thus can best be illustrated by his approach to Lev. 17.

Kilian locates the "Urform" of the laws in Lev. 17, for example, by isolating them into three-part passages such as the following two:

v. 3	Part 1	Any man who slaughters a bull, lamb or goat...
	Part 2	...and does not bring it into the Tent of Meeting to make offering to Yahweh
	Part 3	...that man will be outlawed from his people.
v. 8	Part 1	Any man...who offers a burnt sacrifice
v. 9	Part 2	and does not bring it to the Tent of Meeting...
	Part 3	...will be outlawed from his people [26]

With these two examples of Urform laws (he would also include laws from vv. 10 and 13–14) isolated from the redactional layers in the rest of the chapter, Kilian reveals legal material with a setting and worldview different from the final version of Lev. 17. Most significantly, there is no hint of centralization; these laws apply to any sacrifice and seem to imply sacrifice *wherever it is conducted*. Once the phrase about blood guilt is removed from v. 4 (on the basis that it is an additional punishment clause, when the original is most likely the clause that is at the end of this section, as well as in vv. 9 and 14), then the sense of this law is to prohibit sacrifice to other gods. This can hardly be exilic, therefore, and Kilian argues for a very early context for such a law, perhaps even premonarchic or early monarchic.[27]

Interestingly, both Rendtorff and Kilian have located terms such as "sons of Aaron" and "sons of Israel" in the layers that they have peeled away in the Levitical material, as indicative of the very last layer of redactional activity. We have already noted the significance that this term has for the post-exilic communal structure (*b*ᵉ*nê, Yisrael, b*ᵉ*nê, Hagolâ,* etc.) and thus the presence of this term may be yet another hint about the exilic-post-exilic dating of this material.

These processes reveal that a form-critical consensus on Levitical law (among German scholars, at least) is emerging, that the priestly writer was a commentator on legal material that already had a considerable history as cultic law for Yahwistic worship in pre-exilic Israel.

This view makes a great deal of sense. The idea that the entire corpus of priestly legislation was an original concoction of the exiled priests who had nothing to do for two generations but spin out a fantasy of detailed cultic regulations strains credibility. The more recent historical image of priestly redactional activity reveals the intent to *preserve* the older traditions under the threat of Exile and the destruction of the Solomonic Temple; this makes sense not only textually but sociologically as well.

It should be clear, however, that our interest is precisely in the latest priestly redaction of this material and not the "Urform" of the laws. It is in the final layer of redaction that we see the clearest evidence of the sociological impact of the exilic existence on the Jewish minority in Babylon. Furthermore, these later additions often change the force of the whole section to which they are appended, and therefore are arguably the most important level for an investigation of the intentions of exilic authors.

The Ritual of Resistance: A Functional Perspective

There have been many theories about why the cultic regulations were of such concern to the exilic compilers of the priestly material, but most of them are essentially theological. Gispen, for example, wrote that holiness was to be a symbol of a holy *people* who must abstain from sin.[28]

We have already considered the view that these laws were a "hardening" and "breakdown" of the vitality of prophetic religion just prior to the Exile and have argued that this view was dictated by presuppositions regarding the desirable state and role of religion in late nineteenth-century Germany rather than in Israelite communities in exile in the sixth century B.C.E. But this concern is also clearly exemplified in a modern author like Vink, who tries to show how "ecumenical" the P writer is, in clear contradiction to P's decidedly "anti-social" teachings about *avoiding* objects or persons that threaten to pollute holiness![29]

Another theological interpretation is that P is a "utopian plan for the future" — an idea often used in relation to the final chapters of Ezekiel (40ff.). This view has more to recommend it, although it tends simply to put a positive face on the exilic work of the priests, which is still seen as essentially unrealistic, rather than considering it a "decline" into legalism. This view also carries considerable contemporary theological baggage with it.

Koch's view is, in practice, similar to this, although he relates the priestly work far more to the pre-exilic legal materials that the editors worked from. Thus, the ideal can be summed up: "as it was so should it be again."[30]

A sociological perspective, however, provides a strong critique of the prevailing *theological* nature of all these arguments. Theological perspectives do not advance matters much beyond the rather vague suggestions that the collection and editing of ritual law was a form of encouragement in the despair of Exile. However, Kapelrud's view of the Sabbath begins to suggest another direction by investigating the concrete social *function* for the exilic legal material, even though Kapelrud himself did not develop this idea further.[31]

In chapter 2, I referred to the work of Mary Douglas, whose theories about laws of purity proposed that worries about order, separation, and purity are a reflection of social anxieties about the survival of the body politic; "body" hygiene was a symbol of "social survival." This view begins to suggest a *function* within the exilic community *during the Exile* itself, namely, collecting, editing, and indeed propagating cultic regulations as identity-markers *in a minority context.*

We know that the post-exilic community exhibited what can surely be described as xenophobic behavior, particularly evident in the dissolution of mixed marriages, as seen in the work of Ezra after the "return" to Palestine.

In Hag. 2, which I deal with in a slightly different context below (see chap. 8), there is clear indication of a concern for purity in relations between groups. But we can point to a number of other examples where exilic metaphors of the behavior of social groups is couched in the priestly language of the pure and impure.[32]

The entire chapter of Ezek. 8, which deals with the defilement of the Temple during the Exile, is another example, reflecting the horror of impurity among the exiles themselves and their cultic concerns. The purification of Joshua in Zech. 3 is also a reflection of the need in the post-exilic community to be cleansed for cultic purity.

In this context, the concern for the purity of the "holy seed" in the exilic and post-exilic community makes perfect sense. By an examination of levitical passages with late additions (according to form critical analysis) we can show how the *dissolution of mixed marriages, the levitical concern for pure categories, and the fear of transfer of pollution are interrelated and reflect the concerns of an exiled minority people.*

Leviticus 11: Animals in Their Categories and the Pure and Impure

The commentators are agreed on the redactional, stereotypical heading for each of the legal precepts of Leviticus, placing it in the context of the Sinaitic laws of Moses. Note $b^e n\hat{e}$ (sons of) Israel in Lev. 11:2.

Rendtorff isolates 2b–3 as the "Urform" of this law — the positive command regarding animals that can be eaten. This law is "framed" by the second-person permission, "you *may* eat...."[33]

Lev. 11:4 begins a restrictive clause and is considered a second (or latter) elaboration in the negative. The original form reveals a grazing-agricultural setting of cattle and sheep. The clarifications, however, involve animals that do not fit the defined categorization of animals with cloven feet or that chew their cud.

In v. 9, we have another short, positive command, followed again by detailed elaboration. The difference between these two types of legal material, that is, between the short, positive command and the long, detailed negative elaborations, follows Begrich's suggestion of a difference between "Torah" and "knowledge" — knowledge being a "technical commentary."[34]

Because of the similarity of Deut. 14:1–20 to Lev. 11:2–23, Elliger supposes an independent source for these legal materials, which means that the laws and the elaboration must have existed in pre-Deuteronomic priestly practice.[35]

What is significant, however, is that *only* Leviticus continues this section with the material found in 11:24–47, with its detailed elaboration of laws and regulations regarding the transfer of pollution and the means by which this pollution is removed. Hag. 2, as I argue below, is concerned with the *transfer* of pollution, not the *inherent* uncleanness of certain entities. This difference is a significant and reveals a change of emphasis from the first half of Lev. 11.

The final redactional elements in the latter half of Lev. 11 are vv. 46–47. Here a summary is provided of the concerns of the entire section. (As Rendtorff suggests, each legal precept consists of a basic law much older than P, its elaboration, an introduction placing it in the frame of Sinai, and a summary at the end.) These verses provide an essential key to understanding the exilic significance of levitical legislation about the pure and impure:

> Such is the law concerning animals, birds, all living creatures that move in water and all creatures that swarm on the ground. Its purpose is to distinguish the clean from the unclean, the creatures that may be eaten from those that may not be eaten. (JB)

The key term is *bādal* (to "distinguish" or "separate"). In Lev. 19:19, there is another use of this term in the context of preventing the mixing of species, which Kilian considers a late addition.[36] In a related passage in Lev. 20:22ff., the warning that the land will "vomit out" the unclean inhabitants is associated with the call to maintain separation (*bādal*). Note especially Lev. 18:24–30, where the pollution caused by *strangers* is the key concept.[37]

Bādal is generally used in *late* biblical material. Although not in itself a technical term, the vast majority of instances appear in a cultic context. Sometimes the sense is "selection" or "setting apart" to perform a duty, such as David's selection of the Gadites (1 Chron. 25:1; 12:8 [9]), or the setting apart of the cities of refuge (Deut. 4:41; 19:2, 7); or Ezra's selection of elders to rule in the community (Ezra 10:16); or finally the choosing of people to bury the dead (Ezek. 39:14). Even in some of these cases, however, especially in the last, with its overtones of maintaining purity by choosing special people to handle the dead, a cultic implication can be argued. Generally, the above examples represent all the possible exceptions to our argument about the use of the term *bādal,* and they do not amount to a substantial stumbling block.

An older term, typical of J, is *pālâ,* as noted in Exod. 33:16 and Exod. 9:4 (the distinction between the cattle of Israel and of Egypt) and Exod. 11:7 (the distinction between Israelites and Egyptians). This material is generally reckoned to be J/E and this term is *not* used by P.

The main passages in P that use the root *bādal* are as follows:

Num. 16:21	A call to Moses and Aaron to separate themselves before the Israelites are destroyed.
Num. 16:9	Levi to be separated out to be servant of God.
Exod. 26:33	Veil to separate the Holy from the Most Holy.
Num. 8:14	Separation of Levi.
Lev. 20:24	"I am the Lord Your God, who separated you from all the peoples."
Lev. 20:25	Separation of animals as commanded.
Lev. 11:47	Take a distinction between clean and unclean.
Gen. 1:4,6,14,18	The priestly creation story (separation of land and water, etc.)
Lev. 10:10	"You are to distinguish between...."
Lev. 20:26	"You are to be separated from the peoples...."

These are the main examples of non-P, but exilic, uses:

Isa. 59:2	Evil that separates humanity from God (social impurity).
Isa. 56:3	Righteous converts should not worry that they will be separated from the community of Israel.
Ezek. 42:20	The place in the Temple to separate clean from unclean.
1 Chron. 23:13	Aaron to set apart the holy things.
1 Kings 8:53	Solomon's prayer: the separation of Israel from others.
Ezek. 22:26	Condemnation of priests who make no distinctions.

These may be compared to use of this term in Ezra-Nehemiah:

Ezra 9:1	Those not separated from the *'amê ha-'arṣôt* ("people of the land").
Ezra 6:21	Those who separated themselves from the *gôiê-H'areṣ* ("aliens of the land").
Ezra 10:11	Those who separated from their foreign wives.
Ezra 10:8	Those separated from the Golah.
Neh. 10:29	Those who separated from the "peoples of the land."
Neh. 9:2	Separate the holy seed from all the "sons of foreigners."
Neh. 13:3	Those who separated from those of foreign descent.

Finally, the imagery of Israel as a metal to be smelted into purity is found in Amos 3:12, Ezek. 27:12, 22:18, 22:20; note especially Isa. 1:25, where the Exile becomes a refining fire.

What emerges from this summary is P's use of *bādal* to emphasize clear categorization: the cultic use of separation to ensure and preserve purity and, most significantly, *the separation of Israelites from foreigners, because they are selected by God.* This use is then mirrored by the use of the term in Ezra-Nehemiah to describe the separation of the pure Israel from foreigners, and especially foreign wives. The key concepts are fear of *transfer* of pollution and maintenance of the group.

While not claiming a technical meaning for *bādal* (which is clearly ruled out by a few more common uses, e.g., 1 Chron. 25:1), I think it is clear, on the basis of the vast majority of its uses in the exilic and post-exilic material, that *bādal* was a key term in the post-exilic *concept of a separated and pure people.* Sociologically, such a theology of a separated people chosen by God corresponds to a "xenophobic" concern to maintain the boundaries of the Israelite minority community in Exile.

One passage that deserves comment is Isa. 56:3, which is a reassurance to "converts" that the exilic fervor will not necessarily (or perhaps should not, in Trito-Isaiah's view) mean that they are rejected. Was this a protest on the part of a member of the Isaianic "school," which had always been notable for its more universalistic, "Jonah-like" sentiment? Related to this, was Ezra 9:12 a reaction to the possible misunderstanding or overzealous literalness of some exiles who took Jeremiah's "letter" rather too literally to mean marry *anyone*, not just Jews, and thus endanger the integrity of the pure Israelite community? (Notice the combination here of marriage and seeking the "good" of the foreign element, so reminiscent of Jeremiah's letter.)

The purity/identity concern of the exilic community is thus reflected in the xenophobic concerns of the priestly writer/redactor. The priests' steady rise to power (note the monarchical language associated with Aaron in Exod. 29 and Lev. 16:32) is associated with their function in preserving the collective solidarity of a minority people, maintaining the social (in this case specifically religious) boundaries of separation that are ordained in Creation itself (Gen. 1) and thus in the separation of peoples. While using the term "xenophobia," we do not mean to imply *irrational* concern by any means!

From the perspective of a dominated minority, this mode of behavior is readily explicable. Just as the South African black Zionists ceremonially shake off the dust of the "outside world of sorrows" before entering their place of worship; just as black American slaves incorporated an entire phantasmagoria of ritual protections into their religious life; just as the Japanese-Americans in internment began to emphasize the pride of Japanese ceremonial culture, physical traits, and religious practice — so did Israel conduct the creative rituals of survival and resistance reflected in the carefully elaborated laws of the "pure" and "impure," and especially in the concern about the transfer of impurity through contact with the impure, whether animals or people. It was not the *formulation* of laws of purity that represented the most creative response to Exile by the priestly writer, for we have seen that form-critical analysis reveals many of these laws to rest on older traditions. It was rather the *elaboration* of these laws to emphasize *transfer* of pollution and the association of holiness with *separation*. While the post-exilic community reflected the results of these concerns, the most logical *Sitz im Leben* for their primary function was the Exile itself. The presence of these ritual elaborations of the meaning of separation lends more weight to our thesis that the Exile represented a threat to the Jewish minority. In sum, what we see in the development of purity law is a creative, Priestly mechanism of social survival and maintenance. To dismiss this creativity as "legalism" is to forget, or ignore, the sociopolitical circumstances in which it was formulated. Majority cultures rarely understand, much less appreciate, the actions of minorities to preserve and maintain identity.

NOTES

1. For the opinion that Kuenen was in fact the first to suggest the idea of the documentary hypothesis, see James A. Loader, "The Exilic Period in Abraham Kuenen's Account of Israelite History," *Zeitschrift für die Alttestamentliche Wissenschaft* (Berlin), 96 (1984).

2. Külling has gathered together a number of objections to the standard arguments about the P document, many of which have been raised in the work of those such as Kaufmann. For example, Külling objects to the logical necessity of the *argumentum ex silentio*, that is, that the P material was not mentioned by the early prophets or in the materials

normally identified with J or E. One could argue that the prophets did not know of a priestly collection, or simply did not refer to it. Furthermore, there is no reason to assume that because all the cultic material is now arranged together, it all necessarily originated in the same period (S. Külling, *Zur Datierung der "Genesis-P-Stucke"* [Kampen, 1964], p. 140ff). Külling also argues against the anthropological and philosophical assumptions specifically noted above in Wellhausen. The value of Külling's work, I believe, is that it serves as an important reminder of such assumptions and also provides a careful examination of the logic of many common arguments. But Külling makes reference only to the more general arguments about P, which minimizes the usefulness of his work in the modern context, where analysis is growing increasingly sophisticated. The objections of others are more technical. Hurvitz, for example, aims in his linguistic studies at "establishing the thesis that P is totally unaware and independent of the terminology characteristic of distinctly exilic and post-exilic literature, in regard to fundamental priestly practices and regulations" (Avi Hurvitz, "The Evidence of Language in Dating the Priestly Code," *Revue Biblique*, 81, no. 1 [January 1974], p. 26). For example, the common term for genealogies in the late material, in such places as 1 Chron. 9:1, Neh. 7:5, and a variety of rabbinic sources listed by Hurvitz, is not found in P material, despite its well-known liking for lists and genealogies. Some of Hurvitz's examples seem weaker than others. Hurvitz does not pay much regard to the possible complications in his argument, e.g., whether a word appears in a specific historical *layer* of the P tradition.

See also Y. Kaufmann, *The Religion of Israel from Its Beginning to the Babylonian Exile* (Chicago, 1949), esp. pp. 175ff.

3. J. Wellhausen, *Prolegomena to the History of Ancient Israel* (New York, 1957), pp. 297ff.

4. See P. Ackroyd, *Exile and Restoration* (London, 1968), pp. 84–85.

5. J. G. Vink, *The Date and Origin of the Priestly Code in the Old Testament*, Oudtestamentische Studien 15 (Leiden, 1969).

6. R. Kilian, "Die Priesterschrift Hoffnung auf Heimkehr," in Josef Schreiner, ed., *Wort und Botschaft* (Würzburg, 1967), pp. 229–232.

7. K. Elliger, "Sinn und Ursprung der Priesterlichen Geschichtserzählung" (1952), in *Kleine Schriften zum Alten Testament* (Munich, 1966).

8. Walter Brueggemann, "The Kerygma of the Priestly Writers," *Zeitschrift für die Alttestamentliche Wissenschaft* (Berlin), 84 (1972), pp. 397ff.

9. A. Kapelrud, "The Date of the Priestly Code (P)," *Annual of the Swedish Theological Institute*, 3 (Leiden, 1964).

10. E. Auerbach, "Die Babylonische Datierung im Pentateuch und das Alter des Priester-Kodex," *Vetus Testamentum*, 2 (1952).

11. S. R. Driver, *Introduction to the Literature of the Old Testament* (Edinburgh, 1891).

12. The exact point where the Holiness Code is supposed to begin is less certain that the "ending" in chap. 26. See the interesting suggestions on this problem by C. Feucht, *Untersuchungen zum Heiligkeitsgesetz*, ed. H. Urner, no. 20 (Berlin, 1964). Feucht considered chaps. 18–24 to be pre-Deuteronomic and chaps. 25–26 to be post-Deuteronomic, but before the Exile. Among his reasons was the appearance of the Levites in Lev. 25:32–34, when they are frequently the subjects in Deuteronomic literature, and the concern for continuation of the family line reflected in both Deut. 25 and Lev. 25.

13. L. E. Elliot-Binns, "Some Problems of the Holiness Code," *Zeitschrift für die Alttestamentliche Wissenschaft* (Berlin), 67 (1955), pp. 28f.

14. H. G. Reventlow, "Das Heiligkeitsgesetz formgeschichtliche Untersucht," ed. Bornkamm and Von Rad, *Wissenschaftliche Monographien zum Alten und Neuen Testament* (Neukirchen, 1961), pp. 13–19.

15. Elliot-Binns, "Some Problems of the Holiness Code," p. 37.

16. J. Begrich, "Die priesterliche Tora," *Werden und Wesen des Alten Testaments*, ed. Volz, Stummer, and Hempel, Beihefte zur Zeitschrift für die Alttestamentliche Wissenschaft 66 (Berlin, 1936).

17. Ibid., pp. 64f.

18. Ibid., pp. 73ff.

19. Ibid., pp. 81ff.

20. Feucht, *Untersuchungen zum Heiligkeitsgesetz,* pp. 173ff.

21. R. Rendtorff, *Die Gesetze in der Priesterschrift* (Göttingen, 1963).

22. Klaus Koch, *Die Priesterschrift von Ex. 25 bis Lev. 16: Eine Überlieferungsgeschichtliche und literarkritische Untersuchung* (Göttingen, 1959).

23. R. Kilian, *Literarkritische und Formgeschichtliche Untersuchungen des Heiligkeitsgesetzes,* Bonner Biblische Beitrag (Bonn, 1963), pp. 9ff.

24. Rendtorff, *Die Gesetze in der Priesterschrift,* pp. 5f.

25. Koch, *Die Priesterschrift von Ex. 25 bis Lev. 16,* pp. 9ff.

26. Kilian, *Literarkritische und Formgeschichtliche Untersuchungen des Heiligkeitsgesetzes,* pp. 9ff.

27. Ibid.

28. W. H. Gispen, "The Distinction between Clean and Unclean," *Oudtestamentische Studien* (Leiden, 1948). See also the discussion of tabu as early as 1903 in B. Baentsch, *Handkommentar zum Alten Testament* ed. Nowack (Göttingen, 1903), pp. 355ff.

29. Vink, *The Date and Origin of the Priestly Code,* pp. 22ff.

30. Koch, *Die Priesterschrift von Ex. 25 bis Lev. 16,* pp. 97ff.

31. Kapelrud, "The Date of the Priestly Code," p. 59.

32. In an important article recently published in the Festschrift for D. N. Freedman, Tikva Frymer-Kensky has dealt with "Pollution, Purification and Purgation in Biblical Israel." She deals specifically with pollution of the Temple (Ps. 79:1; Ezek. 9:7; Jer. 7:30, 32:34; Ezek. 5:11) and the pollution of the Holy Land by means of the people becoming polluted (Ezek. 14:11). Frymer-Kensky argues that the holy act of "cleansing" the earth in the flood account is a paradigm of Exile, which would relate purity concerns with an entire literary stratum of the Bible. See *The Word of the Lord Shall go Forth,* Festschrift for the 60th Birthday of D. N. Freedman (Winona Lake, 1983), esp. pp. 409f.

33. Rendtorff, *Die Gesetze in der Priesterschrift,* p. 39.

34. Ibid., p. 45.

35. M. Noth, *Leviticus: A Commentary,* Old Testament Library (London, 1965), p. 91. Koch believes that Leviticus reflects more "programmatic" concern with purity than Deuteronomy. Leviticus, on the other hand, is far more the form of "extended Torah." See Koch, *Die Priesterschrift von Ex. 25 bis Lev. 16,* p. 91.

36. Kilian, *Literarkritische und Formgeschichtliche Untersuchungen des Heiligkeitsgesetzes,* p. 46.

37. It is interesting to note Elliger's belief that 20:25 is a badly placed insertion into the flow of thought of 20:22–26. The emphasis in Elliger's comments is on the "be holy because I am holy" passages in 11:44, 20:7, and 20:26, into which concerns with animal purity appear to "intrude." But if we consider the typical instances of *bādal* in the Bible, another perspective emerges. See Elliger, *Leviticus,* pp. 271f.

Chapter 7

Folklore of Hope

In this chapter, two aspects of exilic literature are illuminated by considering them in the context of the sociological mechanism of literary expressions of resistance. One of these literary products of the Babylonian Exile has come to be called the "diaspora novella." Our discussion focuses on the stories of the Book of Daniel as a basis for comparison with Esther and the late version of the Joseph story (although one could include Tobit and other apocryphal traditions). Second, however, I will argue that the phenomenon otherwise generally known as "messianism"[1] is in fact a literary and *social* phenomenon related to the diaspora novella, and that taking these two elements together will serve to further illumine the experience of the Exile.

Obviously these points must be treated within a limited focus. It is not our task to consider the diaspora novella, messianism, or the other themes in and of themselves, but to subject them to analysis in reference to the task of understanding the sociology of Exile.

The Diaspora Novella

In his survey of the history of scholarship on the question of the unity of the book of Daniel, Rowley wrote that, as early as Spinoza, there was a suggested division of the book of Daniel between the first and second halves, roughly corresponding to the change from "court stories" to visions.[2]

Recent scholarship can be summarized by a consideration of the now famous debate between Ginsberg and Rowley on the unity of Daniel. In 1948, H. L. Ginsberg divided Daniel into "Daniel A" and "Daniel B." He included only chaps. 1–4 in Daniel A and then suggested that Daniel A may well come from an early era, before the time of Daniel B, which he dated in the Maccabean, late Hellenistic era in common with those scholars who date *all* of Daniel in this time.[3]

In 1950–51, H. H. Rowley defended the unity of Daniel in his response to Ginsberg. Rowley agreed that there are three "seemingly natural" forms of dividing the first half of Daniel from the second. These include the changes of (1) language from Aramaic to Hebrew, (2) court stories to visions, and (3) story narratives to first-person descriptions of visions. But these three criteria do *not* divide Daniel in the same place or in the same way. Furthermore Rowley points out that there has never been agreement on where the supposedly earlier stories are to be dated; and this confusion led to serious doubts about resulting theories of development.[4]

Rowley believed that the entire book is contemporary with the Maccabean era and refers to the persecutions under Antiochus Epiphanes.[5]

Asked to explain how stories of someone named Daniel could reflect Maccabean oppression when they refer to Daniel serving in the court of this hated ruler, Rowley responds in a weak manner that "a story told to [give] a message does not have to be an exact parallel to all particulars."[6]

Many answers have been given in response to Rowley. First of all, in regard to the relation of the "four kingdom" motif in Dan. 2 and 7, Ginsberg already pointed out that 2:44 presumed a time when there was a coexistence of three kingdoms, that is, he thought, Media, Persia, and Babylonia. This final kingdom must have been Alexander's Macedonian empire. Thus, Ginsberg gives this a date of ca. 307 B.C.E., when such a political configuration existed. This argument, however, is somewhat strained. Much more compelling is the analysis of P. R. Davies.

Davies believes that the motif of Dan. 2 is similar to Deutero-Isaiah, i.e., Babylonian gods vs. the one true God. Although Davies cites the terminological similarities, he believes that the dream *interpretation* narrative itself should be separated from its context, thus adding a more literary objection to Rowley's comparison of Dan. 2 and 7.

Davies points out that the "toes" in Dan. 2:41–43 were not in the original dream as given in 2:31–35. The stone cut "with no human hand" in 2:34 becomes a mountain in 2:35, but in the interpretation the stone is cut *from a mountain* (Dan. 2:45ff.). The statue itself is made of progressively inferior metals, while the interpretation (like Dan. 7) suggests progressively stronger kingdoms. In the dream, the four metals are destroyed together, while in the interpretation a succession is implied. Thus, the interpretation of the dream is in accord with Dan. 7, because, like Dan. 7, *it is itself an instrusive product of the Maccabean time.* Because the rest of Dan. 2 assumes a beginning and decline from Nebuchadnezzar, Davies believes that the roots of Dan. 2 come from the end of the Exile, four monarchs from Nebuchadnezzar, i.e., the end of the reign of Nabonidus.[7] Finally, Davies cites the narrative similarities between Dan. 2 and the Joseph story, suggesting the awareness of a model diaspora story:

		Gen. 41	Dan. 2
1.	King has a dream	v. 8	v. 1
2.	Dream troubles king	8	10–11
3.	King's wise men fail	8	10–11
4.	Member of court introduces obscure Hebrew captive	9ff.	10–11
5.	Hero expresses confidence that God will reveal to him the dream's meaning	16	25
6.	Hero states that God has revealed to the king what will happen in the future	25, 28	45
7.	The hero is successful and is promoted to high office	39–40	48

Rowley's argument about the Greek instrument in Dan. 3 (*symphonia*) is an interesting point, but one that is not final. It could, for example, have been inserted in redactions of the story when it was added to the other chapters — or it could have been inserted as a part of a list of instruments. Unless one is trying to argue that the *final* form of Daniel is early, then these terminological arguments are not the strongest.

Finally, we come to the presumed "Maccabean relevance" of the court stories themselves. First of all, we have shown that dietary regulations, as an aspect of purity laws, are indicative of all minority and exilic experiences and would therefore suggest an early, as easily as late, diaspora setting. That "purity" is also an issue in the Maccabean era is hardly a surprise or a unique, and thus dateable, event.

This view comes directly from our sociological/anthropological evidence that Rowley could not have been aware of. Ginsberg also noted that Dan. 1 intends no malice against Judaism and its purity laws *per se*.[8] The citation of the Hellenistic worship of rulers in the time of Antiochus can be countered not only by the probability of religious conflict in the early Exile (as we have discussed), but also by the fact that the story in Daniel does not reflect *Temple* worship at all. This also carries for the profanation of the Temple vessels. We can already see in Ezra 1, Ezek. 8, and Hag. 2 that there was concern for the purity of the Temple and the replacement of Temple vessels. The point of mentioning Temple vessels in Belshazzar's feast is the "exile" of the vessels themselves, their inevitable profanation in the hands of foreigners (like the Ark among the Philistines), which is similar to the cult paraphernalia captured by the Assyrians and Babylonians. No compelling reason for a necessarily Maccabean reference is to be found.

The tradition of the madness of the king, which Rowley connects with the idea of Antiochus "the Mad," deserves extended comment in the light of recent theories.

Central to one of the most telling criticisms of the book of Daniel has been the confusion of the Neo-Babylonian rulers, especially the names of "Nebuchadnezzar" and Belshazzar. Nebuchadnezzar obviously stands out as the Chaldean ruler who was responsible for the Exile itself. Belshazzar, however, was not the son, and thus crown-prince, of Nebuchadnezzar, but rather of Nabonidus (Nabunaid). Suspicion is heightened by the image of Nabonidus given to us by the Neo-Babylonian and Persian sources. Nabonidus is called by Roux "one of the most enigmatic and fascinating figures in the long series of the Mesopotamian monarchs."[9] Not only do we have cuneiform records of the "dreams" of Nabonidus, wherein he defends his religious policies of emphasizing the moon god *Sin,* but his activities clearly incited the Babylonian priesthood of Marduk, whose attitudes toward Nabonidus are well known from such cuneiform documents as "The Verse Account of Nabonidus":

> [. . . law (and)] order are not promulgated by him
> [. . . he made perish the common people through w]-ant,
>   the nobles he killed in war
> [. . . for] the trader he blocked the road. . . .[10]

Throughout this text, Nabonidus was considered a mad and irreligious ruler whom Marduk had rejected by giving to Cyrus the throne of Babylon. Is Nabonidus the original king who figures in the earliest Daniel traditions? Further evidence comes to light on a fragment among the Dead Sea Scrolls called, since J. T. Milik, "The Prayer of Nabonidus."[11] Vermes's translation and suggested emendations are as follows:

> The words of the prayer uttered by Nabunaid king of Babylon [the great] king, [when he was afflicted] with an evil ulcer in Teiman by decree of the [Most High God].
> I was afflicted [with an evil ulcer] for seven years . . . and an exorcist pardoned my sins. He was a Jew among the [children of the exiles of Judah and he said] "Recount this in writing to [glorify and exalt] the name of the [Most High God . . . " and I wrote this . . .]
> "I was afflicted with an [evil] ulcer in Teiman [by decree of the Most High God]. For seven years [I] prayed to the gods of silver and gold [bronze and iron] wood and stone and clay, because [I believed] that they were gods. . . . "[12]

Freedman, in his comments on the Prayer of Nabonidus, suggested that the Qumran community may well have had among its founders some returned exiles (that is, those who came from Babylon more recently than Ezra's time) who maintained earlier traditions of the Daniel-type stories. The similarity between the Daniel stories and the fragment leads one, furthermore, to conclude that Nabonidus was replaced by Nebuchadnezzar in the textual Daniel transmissions, undoubtedly because of the importance of the Chaldean king who was himself responsible for the Exile.

There is one last argument for the replacement of Nabonidus in the Daniel stories as the real basis of the "mad king" tradition. In 1958, C. J. Gadd reported stelae inscriptions found by D. S. Stone in 1956 while examining architecture of a ruined mosque on the site of Harran. The inscriptions are from Nabonidus, who mentions his inclusion of peoples from the West in his armies:

[18]...I let summon
[19]...the peoples of Akkad and of the Hatti-land from
    the border of Egypt
[20]...on the Upper sea as far as the lower sea
    [Nabonidus H2 A Col 2]
[6]...[he]...made the people of the land of Akkad and
    the Hatti-land, whom he had committed
[7]...to my hands [to be] of true mouth and heart with me
[8]...they kept guard for me
[9]...they accomplished my command in the seclusion
    of tracts
[10]...far distant and roads secluded which I travelled.... [13]

Gadd believes that Nabonidus's strained relations with the urban city elite in Babylonia meant that it was "unlikely that the army of Nabonidus, when he withdrew to Arabia, could have been composed mainly of native Babylonians [using the term to describe inhabitants of the ancient cities and country of lower Iraq]." [14] Gadd then noted that the list of places occupied by Nabonidus coincides impressively with lists of Arabian settlements where there was Jewish occupation of some antiquity at the rise of Islam: Taima itself, 'Dedan-al-'Ula, Fadak, Khaybar, Yadi', Medina. While this may be a chronological reach (of some 1000 years), Nabonidus did imply that he planted colonies. Gadd concludes:

> The evidence given by [the inscription] combined with the known situation in later centuries may lead us to infer, with some confidence, that Jews, whether from among the captives in Babylonia or from those remaining in their homeland, were strongly represented among the soldiers and settlers in Arabia. ... Short of actually naming the Jews, its implication could scarcely be stronger. [15]

Finally, "Tema" is specifically referred to in the apocryphal book of Baruch, a text that is given an exilic setting and tradition (Baruch 3:22).

The implications of this were anticipated by Von Soden in 1935, when he said that at least chaps. 2, 3, 4, and 5 of the canonical Daniel are based on stories of Nabonidus in Jewish folk tradition,[16] but the stories may well originate among the diverse ethnic groups in the armies of Nabonidus in his Arabian expeditions, leaving Belshazzar behind in Babylon. All of this serves to suggest strong historical bases for the early origin of the Daniel traditions and argues convincingly against Rowley's evidence for the "madness" of Nebuchadnezzar as inevitably a veiled reference to Antiochus Epiphanes.

Finally, it must be said that Rowley's perspective skips far too lightly over the literary content and form of the stories themselves. Already in 1919, Hölscher concluded that the Maccabean era did not provide the *Gestalt* for the origin of these stories.[17] Ginsberg, I believe, is correct when he stated:

> It would require a really incredible degree of ineptitude to make a writer think of propagandizing against a decree by a wicked king that Jews must worship pagan gods permanently by a story (ch. 6) about a good-natured king who was duped by unscrupulous courtiers into a decree...that prayers to all gods (but not circumcision, or the observance of sabbaths, or dietary laws) be stopped but only for thirty days.[18]

If it is the case that the literary genre and content of the Daniel stories reflects a different basis or experience, how can this be determined? We have already been given a hint above with Davies's comparison of Daniel and Joseph.

Literary Comparisons of Diaspora Stories

In 1895, Ludwig Rosenthal compared the stories of Joseph, Esther, and Daniel. By collating some of the verbal similarities identified by Rosenthal, we can illustrate his approach (although the parallels do not seem as striking in English):

1. *Esther 1:3:* "...in the third year of his reign, he gave a banquet at his court for all his officers-of-state and ministers, Persian and Median army-commanders, nobles and provincial governors."

   Gen. 40:20: "And so it happened; the third day was Pharaoh's birthday and he gave a banquet for all his officials. Of his officials he lifted up the head of the chief cup-bearer and the chief baker." (cf. Dan. 5:1)

2. *Gen. 39:10:* "Although she spoke to Joseph day after day, he would not agree to sleep with her or be with her."

   Esther 3:4a: "Day after day they asked him this, but he took no notice of them."

3. *Esther 1:21:* "This speech pleased the king and the officers-of-state."

   Gen. 41:37: "Pharaoh and all his ministers approved of what he had said." (cf. Dan. 6:2)

Other noted similarities included:

1. Appointment of officials: Dan. 6:2; Est. 2:3; Gen. 40:34, 35.

2. One in whom the Spirit dwells: Gen. 40:38, Dan. 5:11, 14

3. His "spirit was troubled": Dan. 2:1, Gen. 41:8

4. Lack of sleep: Est. 6:1, Dan. 2:1, 6:19

5. Giving of the king's ring: Gen. 41:42, Est. 3:10, 8:2[19]

Although the comparisons made by Rosenthal were uneven, going from form similarities to actual terminological similarities, he concluded that Daniel and Esther were based on Joseph, which he considered the older work.[20]

Rosenthal was on the right track in his comparison of these three stories. More recently, Humphreys has compared Daniel and Esther, which are stories that teach "a lifestyle for the Diaspora."[21] Humphreys began by citing Jeremiah's letter to the exiles, which advised a strategy of living in the diaspora while remaining faithful. This is then related to Nehemiah as a Persian courtier and the Joseph stories, as well as to the version of the Ahiqar story (later "Judaized" in Tobit) found among the Elephantine materials:

These...elements in the cultural setting of the diaspora Jewish communities indicate that in certain circles at least, the possibility of a creative and rewarding interaction with the foreign environment was present and could work for the good of the Jew; and they further indicate that tales of courtiers and court life and intrigue were popular.[22]

Humphreys suggested the elements common to each of these themes:

1. A courtier of outstanding qualities...
2. ...is found in court in recognition of his qualities

3. The courtier's life is endangered
   a. Evil scheme of jealous courtiers
   b. Forgetfulness of ruler
   c. Seemingly impossible task
4. The courtier thwarts problems and wins recognition
5. The courtier is exalted
6. Possible emphasis on low origins of the courtier[23]

Finally, Humphreys cites the Ginsberg/Rowley debate and judges in Ginsberg's favor because the diaspora "advice tale" is likely as a setting for the early Daniel stories:

> One could, as a Jew, overcome adversity and find a life both re-warding and creative within the pagan setting and as a part of this foreign world; one need not cut himself off from that world or seek or hope for its destruction.[24]

Essentially agreeing with Humphreys, Niditch and Doran sought to "tighten up" the literary genre question. They cited Folk Tale type 922 in Aarne and Thompson's massive compilation of folk-tale types, which included the following elements:

1. A lower status person is called before a higher status person to answer difficult question or solve a problem. Sometimes a threat of punishment is involved.

2. The person of high status poses the problem, which no one seems capable of solving.

3. The lower status person solves the problem.

4. The lower status person is rewarded.[25]

Niditch and Doran then compare this folk type to both biblical and some non-biblical sources ("Kunz and His Shepherd"[26]), since the point of such literary analysis, according to Niditch and Doran, is to see where the specific texts differ from the stated "ideal type"; for example, Dan. 2 does not employ the same "economy of expression" as is found in Joseph, Ahiqar, and others. Furthermore, Niditch and Doran, like Davies, doubt the originality of the dream interpretation in Dan. 2, wondering why Nebuchadnezzar would reward a bad omen.

   What is significant in Niditch and Doran's form analysis, I believe, is an aspect of the genre only implied in their work; it was not empha-sized because of their concern with literary, as opposed to sociological, questions. This is the interplay of "low status" and "high status." An emphasis on status would allow the theme of the imprisonment of the hero to emerge as a major social aspect of that relation between the high and low status persons.

In his work on the diaspora novella, Meinhold has not only emphasized the status difference as a key aspect of the stories, but the fact that these stories have a "didactic tendency."[27] The reader is intended to see the central character (Joseph, for example) as a role model. This agrees substantially with the functions of the hero story, as we considered above with Abraham's and Klapp's work on minority hero stories. But what is particularly important in Meinhold's analysis, as with Niditch and Doran's hints, is his realization of the importance of both the status difference in the characters and ethnic differentiation in the authentic diaspora novella.

Meinhold emphasizes the common themes of (1) interaction between foreign populations, (2) the low status of the Jewish hero (always established before the rise in circumstances in the court of the ruler: Gen. 39:1–6a; Est. 2:8–18; Dan. 1:1ff.), (3) the contest with, jealousy of, and threat from members of the foreign population in the court or in the land, and (4) the rise in status after success both for the hero and his or her people.[28]

An Exilic Version of the Joseph Story

Meinhold's work also followed Heaton, who suggested separate strands of the Joseph story, including a late addition.[29] In more recent work, Redford has pursued this in great detail.[30] Redford began his literary analysis with notes about the "wise man as savior" type. But Redford goes far wider in his comparisons, even including Near Eastern stories such as the rise of Marduk:

> The entire pantheon is frustrated by inability to deal with a monster, when along comes a young braggart of a god, a Baal or Marduk, and by his strength and wisdom overcomes the monster albeit at a price. From a mythological setting the motif could have been taken over into stories set on a human plane, e.g., David and Goliath (1 Sam. 17), Daniel and Nebuchadnezzar (Dan. 2), Daniel and Bel (Dan. 5), Amenophis son of Hapu (Menetho); Phritiphantes (Chaeremon); Djoser and Imhotpe (Sehel Famine Inscriptions, 4ff.); Amenophis and the Potter; Si-osir (2 Khamois, ii, 28ff.).[31]

Redford, however, seems to be going too far afield here and loses the main point. This is best seen in a footnote where he denies any polemical character in the Joseph stories:

It seems to us that ... [those who emphasize polemics] ... are laying too great a stress on certain innocent features inherent in the motif itself.... In the Joseph story it is pure coincidence that the latter are Egyptians and Joseph is alien.[32]

By finding only the lowest possible common denominator in all these stories, Redford misses this essential aspect of different status, different ethnic, national, or religious groups, and all the means of conflict in the story that clearly separate Daniel, Esther, and Joseph from other Ancient Near Eastern stories where the ethnic/national element is missing, e.g., the Marduk story. Otherwise, Redford's analysis of the date of Joseph in at least one version is quite convincing.[33]

The Social Function of the Diaspora Hero

It is interesting to note how this type of story is a continued Hebraic form not only in the diaspora of the ancient Israelites, but throughout the common era as a whole. Ausubel, in his collection of Jewish folk tales, suggests a reason for this:

Jewish historic experience has been disturbingly similar in so many ways, in every age and in almost every land of the Diaspora. Jews have never been allowed to sink their roots for long anywhere; they have been forced to be everlasting wanderers on the highways of the world. They have been perpetually faced with the same kind of slanders and persecutions in almost every country in every generation. And their folklore naturally is but a faithful chronicle of these historic experiences. Then, again, we cannot avoid the fact that for three thousand years, the remnants of Israel have maintained their ethnic-cultural identity, which too is an unparalleled historical phenomenon.[34]

To approach the diaspora literary tales of the wise courtier from a sociological perspective is to inquire about the social roots of the literature and the social *function* of the diaspora literature. We have already seen that stories of deliverance are common to our sociological case studies of deported peoples and indeed to minority peoples.

In societies influenced by Christianity, biblical images become natural carriers, as in black spirituals. But we must also compare this with, for example, revivals of stories of the Ninjitsu Swordsmen and "clever fox" stories in the Japanese-American camps, American Indian "messiahs" and hero stories, and the "black Jesus" in the Zionist South African theology.

If we expand the literary image presented to us in Daniel, Esther, and Joseph, we can see how frequently the minority hero motif is detailed with confrontations and proofs of superior cleverness succeeding over the symbols of domination — whether it be rulers, evil advisors, prison, slavery, a lion's den, or other adversaries. The significance of humble Jewish teachers, who overcome adversaries or challenges by their prayerful wisdom alone, are very common. What is especially worthy of further comment is the theme of the minority hero. By hero we mean a deliverer and/or example from among the oppressed or dominated population who rises above (or converses with, or encounters, or debates, or in any way is victorious over) the representatives of the dominant power. Even the stories of Jesus and the Romans (e.g., the centurions) may contain symbolism of "low status confronts high status" (note the centurion who informs Jesus of his great military power, Matt. 8:9, but who must nevertheless come to the humble Galilean to help him despite all the power he represents). In Talmudic traditions as well, stories of wise rabbis in conversation or debate with Romans are common and, whether historical or not, become significant social symbols in themselves.[35]

J. J. Collins states that the polemical purpose of the Daniel stories is significant for understanding the social function of these stories:

> We cannot, of course, claim with any certainty that the tales actually originated among courtiers. However, we cannot doubt that the wisdom of Daniel functioned as a model for the authors and their circle. That circle, then, aspired to be "wise men" who accepted the modes of revelation used by Chaldeans and other Gentile wise men, notably the interpretation of dreams, but affirmed the superior power of the God of the Jews both to reveal secrets and to control events. That affirmation inevitably led to confrontation with the Gentiles.[36]

Collins, among others, considers the diaspora literature specifically to reflect the "resistance literature" of the "wise," those whose God-given wisdom will defeat the wisdom of the dominant power and thus their false gods. The purpose, therefore, according to Collins, is summed up as:

> (1) to remind the Jews that their monotheistic religion is a glorious heritage infinitely superior to the paganism with its gross idol worship; (2) to encourage the Jews to remain loyal to that heritage like the outstanding protagonists of the book who were willing to risk their social, economic, and political status and even their lives by steadfastly refusing to compromise their faith, and (3) to show

dramatically and imaginatively that the God of Israel comes to the rescue and delivers those who believe in him despite even the severest reverses, including death by martyrdom.[37]

If Daniel, Esther, and Joseph are examples of exilic hero stories, designed didactically to advise a "lifestyle for the diaspora," then the hero, as Abrahams, Meinhold, and Collins, emphasized, is a focus for a group: one in whom hopes are placed and one who provides an example as well. It is significant that the result of virtually all the diaspora hero stories is a change of condition, either implied or explicitly stated, for the Jewish people as a whole. Thus, Jewish diaspora hero stories become deliverer stories as well. Furthermore, the rulers themselves form an undeveloped "background" to the story. As Ginsberg noted, they are usually presented as kindhearted but somewhat bumbling monarchs, easily taken in by their advisors *who are always members of the dominant ethnic/racial group of the setting in which the diaspora story takes place*. It is these evil advisors who are the real adversaries of the story, and the emphasis is clearly on the relationship between the Jews, and *them*. The king, almost like God and "the Satan" in Job, appears to move the pieces and may even sympathize with the hero, but does not take a powerful "monarchical" role.

This analysis can be taken a step further. A major element of the hero expectation in Exile is the concept of the "Messiah." With these forms of the "deliverer" an entirely different theological/ethical set of expectations is advanced. In contrast to the "wise man" image of the diaspora novel, largely nonviolent in its piety and power, messianic expectations look to the restoration of Zion and the New David, rather than existence in exile, albeit under better circumstances. The contrast in the stories corresponds to the contrast in the prophetic ideal of Jeremiah on the one hand and Hananiah on the other. The New David represents a possible "second stage" of Abrahams's view of the hero, since in *this* hero tradition, the powerful defeat of the former enemies is a major theme, as is removing exiles from their servitude.

Messiah as Diaspora Hero

The expectation of a future Davidic ruler is a well-worn theme for commentary on exilic literature; it is surveyed by Mowinckel in his comprehensive study *He That Cometh* and thus need not occupy a great deal of comment.[38] Mowinckel, and others of the Scandinavian school, approach the question of messianism from the perspective of "royal ideology." What began with an exilic expectation of the resumption of the throne of David came to have more and more apocalyptic or eschatological connotations, especially when it appeared that the monarchy would not be able to be restored under anything like "normal" conditions.[39]

There is no doubt that hopes for a restored monarchy during the era of return from the Exile were strong, especially centered upon Zerubbabel in Haggai and Zechariah:

> Speak to Zerubbabel, the high commissioner of Judah. Say this, "I am going to shake the heavens and the earth. I will overturn the thrones of kingdoms and destroy the power of the kings of nations. I will overthrow the chariots and their charioteers, horses and their riders will be brought down; they shall fall, each to the sword of his fellow. When that day comes — it is Yahweh Sabaoth who speaks — I will take you Zerubbabel, son of Shealtiel, my servant, it is Yahweh Sabaoth who speaks, — and make you like a signet ring. For I have chosen you — it is Yahweh Sabaoth who speaks...." (Hag. 2:20f.)

> This is the word of Yahweh with regard to Zerubbabel, "Not by might and not by power, but by my spirit, says Yahweh Sabaoth. What are you, you great mountain? Before Zerubbabel, be a plain! He will pull out the keystone to shouts of 'Blessings on it, blessings on it.'... The hands of Zerubbabel have laid the foundation of this Temple, his hands will finish it.... People will rejoice when they see the chosen stone in the hands of Zerubbabel." (Zech. 6ff.)

In his recent and impressive study of Nehemiah, Kellerman believes that Nehemiah was also caught up in the messianic hopes of the restoration of the monarchy.[40]

Nehemiah was originally, according to Kellerman, a messianic figure in the post-exilic community, at least fifty to seventy years after the failure of Zerubbabel.

Among Kellerman's points in support of the messianic nature of Nehemiah's mission: (1) There is mention of "sepulchers of the fathers" in Jerusalem (Neh. 2:3) on the analogy of Persian royal graves, which had already led Galling and others to suggest a Davidic origin for Nehemiah. This would further explain (2) the prayer of Nehemiah, if we could assume Nehemiah's acceptance of "royal" responsibility, which is implied. (3) The warning of rebellion in 6:6 would be further motivated by royal pretensions and unrest in Palestine during Nehemiah's work. (4) We know that Persians used members of indigenous royalty for local administration. Finally Kellerman compares Nehemiah's action in 5:1–13 with Zedekiah's in Jer. 34:8, as that of a monarchical figure who assumes the role of David. Ivry believes that Shemaiah's invitation to

Nehemiah to "close the doors of the Temple" was an invitation to accept publicly the role of king and thus incite a revolution against Persia.[41]

Finally, Nehemiah's work is located by Kellerman in a period of instability in the Persian regime (either during the Libyan-Egyptian rebellions of 463–462 or the rebellion of Maegabyzos, Satrap of Syria in 448.)

The key to the difference in the later redactional traditions about Nehemiah and Zerubbabel, according to Kellerman, was the conflict between a mixed Samaritan-priestly interest and a "Zionist independence group" who looked to the restoration of David.[42]

What the nature of the opposition to the Davidic enthronement and restoration of Nehemiah entailed is an interesting question. Kellerman is inclined to associate it with priests in league with Samaritan-ruling interest, but this would not really explain the priestly interests in isolationism and purity, as evident in Ezra, unless Kellerman is prepared to argue for a *three-way division:* those who stayed in Palestine and became assimilationist under "Samaritan" influence; those who opposed the Davidic model among the exiles in favor of "theocracy" or "ecclesiocracy" (Levites?); and those among the exiles who supported a restoration of David's throne, possibly around Sheshbazzar at first, then certainly Zerubbabel, and finally (most probably) Nehemiah. But these details are uncertain. These examples show that one aspect of the messianic hope of the exilic period was the hope for a "New David." But the most intriguing aspect of messianic expectation must now occupy our attention, that is, the Suffering Servant in Deutero-Isaiah.

Isaiah's Suffering Servant as Diaspora Hero

Sellin's attempt to see Zerubbabel as the Suffering Servant in Deutero-Isaiah was an early insight into the royal features in the description of the Servant.[43] Since Duhm's original separation of the "Servant Songs" from their Isaianic context, debate has raged over the identity of the Servant. North's *The Suffering Servant in Deutero-Isaiah* traced the history of the debate until the late 1940s.[44] Since Mowinckel's work *He that Cometh,* I believe it is fair to say that two rival views are beginning to emerge as related but distinct interpretations of the Servant.

"Individual" Theories

The Scandinavian school, building on the royal ideology interpretations of the Psalms in Engnell and Mowinckel, points out that the Servant is unmistakably described in royal terminology.[45] This view has not necessarily prevented Mowinckel from seeing the Servant as an individual prophet, albeit with royal features.[46] Thus, if an individual is to be insisted upon, then one either follows Sellin in seeing the Servant as one of the actual kings or pretenders to the throne, or another individual, who is otherwise *described* in royal language.

North, like Mowinckel, insists on an individual on the grounds that the Servant is singular in the Servant Songs, which (they agreed) are to be separated from the rest of Deutero-Isaiah. They also see the problem that the Servant is an innocent sufferer and one who "has a mission" to Israel. This has always seemed to rule out a collective interpretation. But North admits that many individuals could fit the requirements, and a "royal" interpretation is only one among many possibilities, such as Isaiah, Uzziah, Hezekiah, Josiah, Jeremiah, Ezekiel, Job, Moses, Jehoiachin, Cyrus, Sheshbazzar, Zerubbabel, Meshullam, Nehemiah, and Eleazar.[47]

A more recent "individual" theory has once again insisted on a royal identity. This has been fully developed recently by Eaton, both in his work on the Psalms and in *Festal Drama in Deutero-Isaiah*[48]; it has its roots in the work on royal ideology by the Scandinavian school, though it was anticipated by Sellin.

Eaton's answer, which is really somewhere between a collective and individual theory, is that the Servant is the *house of David itself.* Although it is not fully "individual," Eaton's view is decidedly anti-collective and is an ingenious variation of the "individual-with-royal-traits" view of Mowinckel and others.

"Collective" and "Minority" Theories

While it is true that the problems of the "mission to Israel" and "innocent suffering" are significant for a *total collective theory,* they are quite adequately accounted for if we consider the work that has been done on what North called the "righteous, or pious minority theory," or if we agree simply that the Servant is a collective representative of the *exiles* who returned. The older approach to defending the minority theory still accepted the thesis of the difference between Duhm's separated songs with their context and the rest of Deutero-Isaiah. Kaiser also apparently accepted the difference between the songs, but went a long way toward insisting on the relevance of the context for interpreting the song passages. Recently, however, an essay by Mettinger has cast serious doubt on the continued belief in separate songs. We shall consider briefly the older collective/minority view before looking more closely at Mettinger's contribution.

König's 1899 work on Isaiah is one of the most important studies by the early protagonists of the collective/minority theory. Already in 1872, Knobel had suggested that Isa. 57:3–10 revealed a sharp antagonism between groups within the Israelite population. The language of

Isa. 57:1–2 about the "upright person" who is put to death, the "faithful" who are "taken away," and the second use of "taken away" leads us to speculate about the Exile as a factor in the divisions suggested. König also saw references to the Exile in the language of 52:2–6 and believed this imagery related to 53:2ff., which is, of course, one of the songs.

König anticipated in a slightly different way the argument of Anthony Phillips[49] by suggesting that the "innocence" of the sufferers of Exile did not come from an original state of sinlessness, but from that fact that Babylon had overstepped its role as God's rod of anger and thus Israel was paying more than was due as punishment (Isa. 47; Zech. 1:15; Ps. 44:18; Isa. 51:19, 52:2–4; Jer. 16:18).[50]

König also saw a return from death, or near death, as a powerful image of the return from the Exile. He compared the Servant's experience with language about, and from, the period of Exile in texts such as Jer. 51:34, 44, Jonah, the famous valley of Dry Bones in Ezek. 37:11 and 19:2ff., esp. 19:6ff.; and Ezek. 33:10, 39:25 (cf. the release of prisoners in Isa. 42:7, 49:9, and the "new birth" of Isa. 66:8).

It is essential for the minority theories to establish the existence of conflict between the Israelites themselves.[51] König believed that Mic. 3:1ff. and Isa. 65:13ff. pointed to an internal conflict. One of the issues was a change in attitude toward other nations, a change reminiscent of the opposing theological opinions of Jeremiah and Hananiah.[52] This change in attitude also carried with it changes in the depiction of the Servant. Perhaps most significant in this ethical/theological vacillation in attitude was the belief of the exiles that Cyrus was the Lord's "messiah" who conquered Babylon without the predicted destruction (Cyrus boasted that Babylon fell without his soldiers even having to draw their swords).[53]

Finally, the theme of the righteousness of *one* sparing the *whole nation* was common and should remind readers of this same motif in the diaspora hero stories.

In sum, the older minority theory tried to identify the Servant as a representation of the collective suffering of the exiles or another minority among the people. It is important to note here that the minority theory always led to a certain breaking down of any hard separation between the Servant Songs and the rest of Isaiah.[54]

But the most significant modern proponent of reading the songs as an integral part of Isaiah is Mettinger in his polemically entitled essay, "A Farewell to the Servant Songs."[55] The strength of Mettinger's argument is that all the imagery of Deutero-Isaiah, including all the instances of the term "servant" or "slave," must be taken together to determine the identity of the Servant symbol in Deutero-Isaiah. Other Deutero-Isaiah Servant passages that must be taken into consideration include 41:8, 9, 19; 43:10; 44:1, 21, 26; 45:4; 48:20; 54:17. The idea of a servant people is furthermore found in 1 Kings 8:30; Jer. 30:10; 46:27, 28; Ezek. 28:25; 37:25, among other instances.

By means of this line of argument, Mettinger points out that the textual evidence — such as the oscillation between plural and singular imagery in Isa. 55:3–5, the similarity between 50:9 and 51:8, mistreatment of 50:6 compared with 51:23, and finally the term "formed," used of Israel in 43:1, 7, and 21, and of the Servant as well — all strengthen the case for treating the book as a coherent whole.

Mettinger's solution to the problem of the identity of the Servant is a collective minority theory:

> It would be... difficult to imagine an historical individual whose ignominy and humiliation would have been capable of making the sort of impression on the Gentiles as that represented by Is. 53:1–6. Strictly considered, it is difficult to understand how scholars have been able to operate with such diverse alternatives as leprous rabbi, the prophet himself, or another (however imposing) individual personality.[56]

The main differences between Eaton and Mettinger are represented not only in a disagreement about individual vs. collective representation, but also about the continued viability of the separation of the songs from their context (although Eaton never totally discounts the interpretive significance of the context). But perhaps most significant is the difference in the hope for the exiles as conceived by Eaton on the one hand and Mettinger and Kaiser on the other. Eaton sees the exiles as a people who expect a king like David. Mettinger and Kaiser think that the expectation for the future centered on the hope for a "king-like" *era* when all Israel is again ruled spiritually by God as king, an era led by a righteous minority who serve as a remnant of the truth and hope for the future.

Because of the *social* significance of the hero stories, both in the trials the hero must undergo and his God-given success for himself and his people, it becomes clear that the Suffering Servant can take on an individual image as well as a social image and still remain a meaningful theme for the exilic period. In the same way, Daniel, Joseph, Mordecai, and Esther became social heroes. Seen in this manner, the urgency of separating individual from collective theories is overcome, and the entire context of the message of Deutero-Isaiah is allowed to teach us the meaning and significance of the Servant. We can therefore agree with Mettinger's emphasis on the context of the Servant in the text and consider König's work on the minority to make the most sense of the greatest amount of textual material.

The Diaspora Hero as Social Symbol

There are three different types delineated in our analysis of the diaspora hero. The first is the righteous individual, wise man, or courtier who saves the entire people by divinely inspired, clever wisdom or by pious practice. The second is the conquering king, who is restored to the throne. The third is the community of the righteous, refined by the fires of Exile and oppression and thus the new "innocent" foundation for the restoration of Israel. But even this third can be collectively represented in an individual.

The confusion of the identity of the Suffering Servant is a direct result of the fact that the Servant concept itself is a literary/theological product of the Exile, as is the expectation of a new king and the literary motif of the wise courtier. *All* these are variations of the diaspora hero, the deliverer, the hoped-for end to the conditions of Exile, separation, and powerlessness. From a sociological perspective, the specific identity of the Servant is actually not as important as the social function of the Servant as hero, which inevitably relates it both to the diaspora stories and to messianic expectations of the New David.

Even if the Servant was an individual, then Abrahams's analysis of the hero as social symbol has given us an interpretative sociological concept that leads to a less exotic understanding of the social significance of the Servant than Robinson's concept of a Hebraic notion of "corporate personality."[57] The "righteous minority" view comes the closest to explaining not only the identity, but more important, the social function and socio-psychological context of the Servant, the diaspora stories, and the expectations of the New David.

Each of the three options involves a rise from present adversity to God-inspired salvation or redemption. We have pointed out the major significance of the low and high status elements of the diaspora story and already made clear reference to the suffering-to-redemption theme of the Servant motif in Deutero-Isaiah. But a further key to the Davidic expectations and themes of Deutero-Isaiah, which led Eaton to his views, is the theme of humiliation and restoration.

The social importance of this theme, whichever of these three herotypes it is associated with, is not properly understood apart from its exilic roots in a captive, powerless, "low status" minority and the hope and resistance that the existence of the hero as social type persistently encourages. We have seen the forms of messiahs, heroes, and saviors that occurred in our case studies of deportation, and it remains only to refer back to some of these examples for analogies to guide biblical study.

"Prison" as a Literary Symbol of Exile

If we are correct, then the form, and perhaps even some of the details, of the hero type in the exilic texts may clearly reflect social conditions in the Babylonian Exile itself. As we have stated, a major theme in these texts is captivity and imprisonment, overcoming adversity and "low status," and/or facing the threat of death.

There are a number of Old Testament terms that are rendered in English as "prison." Gen. 39:20–40:3 frequently uses the term *bēt Hasohar,* which Brown, Driver, and Briggs in their *Hebrew Lexicon* consider an Egyptian loan word. Also, the Joseph stories use a *bēt HāMišmarkem,* "house of those under guard" (Gen. 42:19), where the context suggests a man held as security. A more unusual use is David's seclusion of ten concubines kept totally separated from David. This does not imply "prison" in the strict sense, since no punishment is implied.

Samson, when he was rendered powerless, worked at a mill in the *bēt Ha'āšyrîm* (Judg. 16:21)

In the commentaries I consulted on the Samson sagas, there is very little comment on the significance of this term in Judg. 16. Did the Philistines have an institution like a "house of bondage" or "prison"? Judg. 16 is usually considered a later addition to the Samson saga, dated to the Deuteronomic Historian at the latest.[58] The presence of this term, however, should raise questions about the date of this material.

'Āsîr is a common term for "prisoners," from the verb to "tie," "bind," or "imprison," *'asar,*[59] which is frequently used again in the late Joseph stories (Gen. 39:20, 40:3, 5). It appears in Isa. 42:7; 49:9; 61:1; and Ps. 146:7c–8a (cf. Ps. 107:10). It is interesting to note that in Isa. 49:9 and Ps. 146:7c–8a, the combination of release from prison, with "opening eyes" or "sight to the blind" is common (cf. Zech. 9:12). A "Surpu Hymn" (incantation to Marduk of Babylon) contains the same association:

[beginning "It rests with you, Marduk . . . "]
[31] to set free the prisoner, to show (him) daylight
[32] him who has been taken captive, to rescue him
[33] him whose city is distant, whose road is far away
[34] let him go safely to his city
[35] to return the prisoner of war and the captive to his people
. . .
[73] may the sick get well, the fallen get up
[74] the fettered go free, the captive go free
[75] the prisoner see the light (of day)[60]

The Verse Account of Nabonidus celebrates the end of his reign with the following passage:

[to the inhabitants of] Babylon, a joyful heart is given,
[like prisoners] when the prisons are opened
[Liberty is restored] to those who were surrounded by oppression.[61]

The most common term is *bit kilih* (in Hebrew *bēt kele'*), an Akkadian loan word found in Neo-Assyrian texts but more commonly in Neo-Babylonian texts. It obviously relates to the use of the verb *kālā'*, "restrain," "hold back" (cf. Jer. 32:2, 3; 1 Sam. 25:33; Gen. 23:6; Ps. 119:101; Ps. 88; Num. 11:28; and, in reference to exiles, Isa. 43:6). The *bēt kele'* is found in the Deuteronomic Historian, 1 Kings 22:27; 2 Kings 17:4 (in direct reference to the Assyrians); and in the account of Jehoiachin's internment and release in 2 Kings 25:27.

One of the most interesting passages is Jer. 37, especially vv. 4, 15, and 16, where three different terms for prison are used.

Bēt Hābur is a curious construction, found in Exod. 12:29, but otherwise exclusively in exilic sources. Of particular interest is that the recurring phrase about a pit "where there is no water" occurs three times: the first in Joseph (Gen. 37); the second in Jeremiah (38:6); and finally, in direct reference to exiles, in Zech. 9:11. This brings them in close proximity to each other, as we have already determined above for the Joseph story.

The image of the pit is associated with death in Ps. 88, and Gedaliah and his followers were thrown into a pit after they were murdered (Jer. 41:7–9). In Lam. 3:53 and 55 the catastrophe of the Exile is compared to being thrown into a pit, from which the people call on God's name.

The well-known image of the Egyptian captivity is the Deuteronomic term, *bēt 'bᵉdîm*, which is translated "house of bondage" but is probably better rendered "house of slavery." It is almost always found in the stereotypical phrase about God's liberation of the Jews from Egypt (cf. Exod. 13:3, 14; 20:2; Deut. 5:6; 6:12; 7:8; 8:14; 13:6, 11; Josh. 24:17; Judg. 6:8; Jer. 34:13; and, interestingly, Mic. 6:4). This concept is in the latest stratum of the Deuteronomic history. Redford doubts that the tradition of the Jews working on the cities of Pithom and Raamses is any older than 525 B.C.E. Redford's questions about the tradition of forced labor in Egypt also raise questions about the Exodus traditions and their date, but these would take us far afield.[62]

The frequency of the image of imprisonment may be significant, especially when liberation (cf. Isa. 49 and 61) is seen in terms of release from prison, and the *bēt hābur* obviously has an exilic use. The vast majority of instances of terms for prisons and imprisonment are cases of *unjust imprisonment of the righteous,* whether individual prophets or a people (the sole exception is 2 Sam. 20:3). Furthermore, most examples, apart from the imprisonment of prophets, are cases of *foreign prisons;* indeed, even the instances of prophets in prison usually occur during the Exile or as a result of a foreign threat. Third, we must recall that prisons are *not* an indigenous form of judiciary institution in Israel. They are never mentioned in the legal corpus of the Pentateuch, and (with the exception of 2 Sam. 20:3, which is obviously not much of an exception), prisons as an institution are not even hinted at during the monarchical era. Finally, it is significant that most hero types of the exilic period — Joseph, Jehoiachin, Daniel, *and the Servant* — suffer imprisonment "innocently" and are eventually delivered. This deliverance from prison has great significance in all the other instances, and significance is attached to Jehoiachin's release from prison recorded at the end of 2 Kings. His release may have stirred messianic speculation that is no longer a part of the Deuteronomic history. Otherwise, its casual mention in the form we have it seems pointless.

In his recent work on the Suffering Servant in Isa. 53, Whybray has made some interesting remarks on the Servant and imprisonment. Whybray believes that the Servant in Isa. 53 was a real individual, most likely Deutero-Isaiah himself, who suffered "ill-treatment by the Babylonian authorities" for preaching God's sure deliverance of the Jews from Babylon.[63] Whybray speculates that the text referred to imprisonment because that was what happened to Deutero-Isaiah, but the text of Isa. 53, a "thanksgiving for a liberated prophet," was preserved because of its meaning for the exiles as a whole. On the symbolic significance of imprisonment, then, we agree essentially with Whybray. Although we do not agree with his identification of the Servant, it is the symbolic significance of this Servant and his experience that was the important factor in preserving the text.

Imprisonment in the Ancient Near East

Some interesting studies can here be briefly noted. In an important article exploring the subject, San Nicolo states, "A prison-punishment in the formal sense is essentially unknown in Near Eastern jurisprudence."[64]

So if we are not talking about prison as punishment, then we conclude that the images in the biblical material, and those of the Ancient Near Eastern texts cited, more likely refer to confinement, especially confinement as a result of superior military power. We know from the Bible, and tentatively from the Weidner Tablets, that Jehoiachin was in some kind of confinement. His imprisonment may support Eaton's case that most exilic "imprisonment" images are inspired by the fate of the royalty, but our discussion of the social significance of a general hero-type leads us to conclude that confinement *became an established symbol for the exiles who reflected on their fate in Babylon.* The metaphor of imprisonment, and references to places of imprisonment, do not grow more plentiful during the exilic period by pure chance, especially noting its foreignness to the Israelite judicial system. The experience of exile was compared to prison, and liberation was seen as release from that prison, "opening the eyes of the imprisoned." Thus the diaspora hero types, whether king, courtier, or collective remnant, had to overcome this social reality. If this imagery was so powerfully a part of exilic writing and memory, does it significantly matter what the details of the actual social situation were? All we need to establish for the mechanisms for survival to be operative is a condition of threat for minorities who faced a crisis. The diaspora hero stories were maintained by a people who compared their social existence to imprisonment. It is only in the context of this symbolism that the function of the diaspora hero stories as resistance literature of a deported, landless minority make sense.

NOTES

1. Neusner has written helpfully on the variety of referents that "messianism" can have in rabbinic materials, which is suggestive for the variety of ideas that it can connote in biblical materials. I am using the term somewhat more generally to refer to an expected person, sent by God, to deliver the Jews from bad circumstances. See "Messianic Themes in Formative Judaism," *Journal of the American Academy of Religion,* 52 (1984).

2. See H. H. Rowley, "The Unity of the Book of Daniel," reprinted in *The Servant of the Lord and Other Essays* (London, 1952).

3. See H. L. Ginsberg, "The Composition of the Book of Daniel," *Vetus Testamentum,* 4 (1954).

4. Rowley, "The Unity of the Book of Daniel," p. 247.

5. Ibid., p. 270.

6. Ibid., p. 271.

7. P. R. Davies, "Daniel Chapter Two," *Journal of Theological Studies,* NS 27 (1976), p. 400.

8. Ginsberg, "The Composition of the Book of Daniel," p. 255.

9. G. Roux, *Ancient Iraq* (London, 1964), p. 352.

10. J. B. Pritchard, ed., *Ancient Near Eastern Texts,* 2nd ed. (Princeton, 1955), p. 313.

11. J. T. Milik, in *Revue Biblique,* 63 (1956); see also D. Freedman, "The Prayer of Nabonidus," *BASOR,* 145 (1957).

12. G. Vermes, ed., *The Dead Sea Scrolls in English,* 2nd ed. (London, 1975), p. 229.

13. C. J. Gadd, "The Harran Inscriptions of Nabonidus," *Anatolian Studies,* 8 (1958).

14. Ibid., p. 85.

15. Ibid., p. 86.

16. W. von Soden, "Eine babylonische Volksüberlieferung von Nabonid in den Daniels-erzählungen," *Zeitschrift für die Alttestamentliche Wissenschaft* (Berlin), NF 12 (1935).

17. G. Hölscher, "Die Entstehung des Buches Daniel," *Theologische Studien und Kritiken,* 92 (1919).

18. Ginsberg, "The Composition of the Book of Daniel," p. 255.

19. L. Rosenthal, "Die Josephsgeschichte mit den Büchern Ester und Daniel verglichen," *Zeitschrift für die Alttestamentliche Wissenschaft* (Berlin), 15 (1895); see also *Zeitschrift für die Alttestamentliche Wissenschaft,* 17 (1897).

20. Ibid., p. 284.

21. W. Lee Humphreys, "A Lifestyle for Diaspora: A Study of the Tales of Esther and Daniel," *Journal of Biblical Literature,* 92 (1973).

22. Ibid., p. 213.

23. Ibid., p. 217.

24. Ibid., p. 223.

25. Susan Niditch and Robert Doran, "The Success Story of the Wise Courtier: A Formal Approach," *Journal of Biblical Literature,* 96 (1977), p. 179.

26. N. Ausubel, ed., *A Treasury of Jewish Folklore* (New York, 1955), pp. 101–103.

27. A. Meinhold, "Die Diasporanovelle: Eine alttestamentliche Gattung," dissertation, Greifswald, 1969, p. 59.

28. Ibid., p. 134.

29. E. W. Heaton, "The Joseph Saga," *Expository Times,* 59 (1947).

30. Donald Redford, *A Study of the Biblical Story of Joseph (Gen 37–50)* (Leiden, 1970).

31. Ibid., pp. 96ff.

32. Ibid., p. 96, note 6.

33. "Central to chapters 40 and 41, which deal with Joseph's rise to power, is the theme of the wiseman, who comes forward when the king is at his wits' end and saves the monarch and the kingdom from a terrible fate. Stories of wisemen and magicians possessed of miraculous powers were very popular in Ancient Egypt, especially in the Middle Kingdom (2100–1700 BCE). But in these tales, far from acting the part of deliverer of the land, the wiseman is nothing more than an entertainer. The closest parallels to Joseph's role as saviour comes from Demotic, and from the contemporary literatures of Western Asia. For the motif of the wiseman wrongfully imprisoned and subsequently re-instated, parallels are again forthcoming only from the second third of the first millennium BCE....

"One can only conclude that the reason why the historical books and the Prophets say nothing of the Joseph romance is that the narrative was not yet in existence when they were written; in other words, the chronological limits assigned above to the background of the story, c. 650–425 BCE, are quite probably valid for the date of the composition as well. This time span puts us into the period when the Diaspora with all its consequences was a reality. Do we hear a faint echo of Exile in the story of a boy, sold as a slave, into a foreign land, whither shortly his clan journeys to join him themselves to enter into a state of servitude to a foreign crown?" (ibid., pp. 241, 250).

34. Ausubel, *A Treasury of Jewish Folklore,* p. xvii.

35. For an opinion that these are not particularly significant, see M. D. Herr, "The Historical Significance of the Dialogues between Jewish Sages and Roman Dignitaries," *Scripta Hierosolymitana,* 22 (1971).

36. John J. Collins, "The Court Tales in Daniel and the Development of Apocalyptic," *Journal of Biblical Literature,* 94 (1975).

37. J. J. Collins, *The Apocalyptic Visions of the Book of Daniel* (Chico, Calif., 1976), pp. 84–85.

38. S. Mowinckel, *He That Cometh* (Oxford, 1956).

39. Ibid., pp. 5–7, 155. Mowinckel's central point is that most, if not all, of the prophetic passages about the "messiah" or future king, are to be seen as exilic expectation of the restoration of monarchy: Isa. 4:2; 7:10–17; 8:8b, 10b; 9:1–6; 10:21; 11:1–9, 12; 16:5, 32:1–8; 55:3; Jer. 17:25; 23:5–33:17; 30:9, 21; Ezek. 17:22–24; 24:23f.; 37:22–25; Hos. 3:4f.; Amos 9:11; Mic. 4:8; 5:1–3; Zech. 9:9f. ; As Mowinckel states: "The characteristic Jewish future hope did not exist as a hope of restoration until there was a restoration to be accomplished. It originated and was developed after the fall of the state. Accordingly, the Messianic hope in the strict sense arose at the same time as the hope of restoration and as an integral part of it" (p. 155).

40. U. Kellermann, *Nehemia: Quellen Überlieferung und Geschichte* (Berlin, 1967).

41. A. Ivry, "Nehemiah 6, 10: Politics and the Temple," *JSJ,* 3 (1972). But if Nehemiah's role was "messianic," it seems to be similar to the role suggested in Ezekiel's

restoration program. If Gese is correct in thinking that the Ezekiel program was constructed largely with Zerubbabel in mind, then perhaps Kellerman is right in suggesting that Nehemiah appeared as the last representative of the *Nasiim* before the final rise of the high priest. The messianic themes that Nehemiah contains, according to Kellerman's thesis, are the following (many of which are reminiscent of Sellin's list): (1) rebuilding of city and Temple despite enemies; (2) rebuilding of social justice in the land; (3) rebuilding of state independence; (4) re-establishment of Torah, especially the Sabbath observance. See H. Gese, "Der Verfassungsentwurf des Ezechiel Kap. 40–48," *Beiträge zur historischen Theologie*, 25 (Tübingen, 1955); E. Hammerscheib, "Ezekiel's View of the Monarchy," *Studia Orientalia Ioanni Pedersen* (1953); Kellerman, *Nehemia: Quellen Überlieferung und Geschichte*, p. 179.

42. Kellerman, *Nehemia: Quellen Überlieferung und Geschichte*, pp. 174ff.

43. E. Sellin, *Serubbabel: Ein Beitrag zur Geschichte der Messianischen Erwartung und der Entstehung des Judentums* (Leipzig, 1898). It is interesting to note that Sellin's attempt to relate the Servant to Zerubbabel was not unreasonable, whether his identification was correct or not. Sellin believed that, by tracing the five basic elements in pre-exilic(!) prophecies of restoration, he could associate the prophetic language with the events surrounding Zerubbabel's arrival in Palestine. These events included the expectations that as soon as the temple was rebuilt: (1) God would once again dwell with the people, (2) Israel would be gathered from all lands, (3) "the peoples" would bring their treasures to God, serve God, and join in worshipping this God, (4) Judah would once again be a fruitful, powerful land with Zerubbabel at its head, and (5) the "shoot" of the House of David had already been chosen, and on his head the crown would rest (p. 27).

It was Sellin's idea, however, that the expectation of a future, personal messianic king contrasted sharply with the priestly expectations during and after the Exile: "The influence of the Priestly codex therefore means an official break with the hope of a personal Messiah" (p. 62). In any case, Sellin's main contribution was not merely the presentation of expectations surrounding Zerubbabel, but a theory about his defeat and possible martyrdom. Not only does this explain, for Sellin, why Nehemiah had to begin with a destroyed city wall when Haggai and Zechariah assume rebuilding, but a setback represented by Zerubbabel's defeat seems to fit the spirit of mourning and defeat in Mic. 4:10–13, Lam. 4:17–5:22, and Isa. 63–66. Isa. 63:18, for example, speaks of possessing the Temple "a little while" (p. 86). But Sellin's evidence for a martyred Zerubbabel is scanty. Lam. 4:17–5:22 could well be referring to the Exile itself rather than some later tragedy; Mic. 4:10–13 specifically refers to Babylon. Sellin's attempt to connect Zerubbabel with Deutero-Isaiah's Servant is dependent on establishing such a martyrdom for Zerubbabel, as is his theory about a murdered Moses (which impressed Freud but few others). He also holds for a late redaction of Deutero-Isaiah, which included the individual Servant Songs only after the failed attempt to revive the monarchy. Despite the failure of his central thesis, Sellin was among the earliest commentators, to note the royal imagery of Isaiah, which he used to defend his identification of the Servant with Zerubbabel.

44. C. R. North, *The Suffering Servant in Deutero-Isaiah* (Oxford, 1948).

45. I. Engnell, *Divine Kingship in the Ancient Near East* (Uppsala, 1943); Mowinckel, *He That Cometh*, p. 143.

46. Mowinckel, ibid., p. 228.

47. North, *The Suffering Servant in Deutero-Isaiah*, p. 192.

48. J. H. Eaton, *Festal Drama in Deutero-Isaiah* (London, 1979). We can take issue, however, with Eaton's insistence that the Servant is consistently an individualized figure *in contrast to other collective symbols for Israel.* For example, Eaton explains away Isa. 49:3, where Israel is called Servant, as merely a collective-ancestor representation by citing Eissfeldt (whose theories Eaton had earlier dismissed); he then says that three of the four songs occur in Isa. 49–55, a "subcycle" wherein the nation is "generally individualized as female Zion" but otherwise as a plurality — except for 51:13–16, which is "patchy," according to Eaton (pp. 63–64). Thus, the Servant in these songs, individual and male, is

something *other than* the individualizations of a female Zion, "patchy bits," and references outside the boundaries of the "subcycle" under consideration.

This view is curious. According to Eaton's own work, God's "romance" with the female-represented *place* of Zion is a theme found in the royal ideology mythos. (See Eaton's own category of "Zion as Mother, wife and Queen," Ps. 47, 51, 132 [pp. 20–21], but note Ps. 132, where the people are called sons of Zion, implying something other than the female Zion itself.) Only once, in the "patchy" 51:16, is Zion specifically equated with people, and in all other instances it appears that Zion means the geographical place because the people are called her "sons." So we cannot be at all certain of Eaton's claims. Second, however, the distinction between "subcycles" 40–48 and 49–55 must not be taken to mean separate books where meanings, connotations, and cross-references are considered to be completely different. Surely such a division is as artificial as the original separation of the "songs" from their context. Thus the people of Israel are "individualized" in many ways throughout Deutero-Isaiah. Our disagreement with Eaton is that these individualized names can only be separated from each other in the text by artificial divisions of the text into "songs" and "cycles" in such a way that even the vocabulary is treated as unique to each "section." Isaiah, like other prophets, freely used symbolic terms and individualized groups *throughout his work.* This rules out the suggestion that the Servant cannot be yet another symbolic representation of more than a single individual — especially in the light of 49:3 and other "non-song" passages where Israel is specifically named as "Servant." We would question the basis upon which Eaton dismisses the collective interpretation by differentiating the context of "individual" and "group" terms. This leaves the two objections, shared by many others, about the innocence of the Servant and his mission to Israel.

49. Anthony Phillips, "Double for All Her Sins," *Zeitschrift für die Alttestamentliche Wissenschaft* (Berlin), 94 (1982).

50. E. König, *The Exiles Book of Consolation Contained in Isaiah 40–66,* (Edinburgh, 1899), p. 27. "...to the nation...or to a portion of the people..." (A. Kuenen, *The Prophets and Prophecy in Israel: A Historical and Critical Enquiry,* trans. Milroy [London, 1877], pp. 221, 224). See also O. C. Whitehouse, *The Century Bible, Isaiah XL–LXVI* (Edinburgh, 1908), and A. Knobel, *Der Prophet Jesaia Erklärt von Dr. August Knobel* (Leipzig, 1872), p. 433.

51. König, *The Exiles Book of Consolation Contained in Isaiah 40–66,* p. 183.

52. Ibid., p. 54.

53. *Ancient Near Eastern Texts,* ed. J. Pritchard (Princeton, 1968), p. 306.

54. In 1908 Whitehouse, too, wondered whether the exiles themselves were the collective source for the idea of the Servant. See A. Kapelrud, "The Identity of the Suffering Servant," *Ancient Near Eastern Studies in Honor of Albright* ed. H. Goedicke (Baltimore, 1971). More recently, Kapelrud has added his voice to the "minority theory."

55. Mettinger begins his analysis with a spirited refutation of the literary unity of the four songs themselves, followed by a detailed literary theory of the unity of Deutero-Isaiah itself which argues against the separation of the Servant Songs. Mettinger argues for a symmetrical structure composed of strategically placed "hymns" (42:10–13; 44:23; 45:8; 48:20–21; 49:13; 51:3 [fragmentary]; 52:9–10; and 54:1–3) and what he calls "gemstone passages" (44:24–45:7 and 52:13–53:12, with 49:1–2 as the center between the two). Mettinger furthermore suggests a planned document from which the songs cannot be credibly separated (note that some of the hymns are included in songs). It must be said, however, that just as with Eaton's "cycles," Mettinger's literary divisions, somewhat inspired by Westermann's work on "hymns," are the weakest link in the argument, as Eaton's alternative plan reveals. Until such literary units are certain, it is hard to "identify" them as parts of a consistent, and symmetric, whole literary work. See Tryggve N. D. Mettinger, *A Farewell to the Servant Songs: A Critical Examination of an Exegetical Axiom,* Scripta Minora, 1982–83 (Lund, 1983).

56. Ibid., p. 38.

57. H. W. Robinson, "The Hebrew Conception of Corporate Personality," in *Werden und Wesen des Alten Testaments,* Volz, Stummer, Hempel, eds. (Berlin, 1936).

58. J. Crenshaw, *Samson* (Atlanta, 1978), p. 64; J. A. Soggin, *Judges,* Old Testament Library (London, 1981). Gray mentions the thematic similarity with the descent into the Underworld of Ceracles, *Joshua, Judges and Ruth,* The Century Bible (London, 1967), pp. 235ff. R. Boling dates Samson to the eighth century: *Judges,* The Anchor Bible (Garden City, N.Y., 1975), p. 30. A full commentary on the alleged mythic associations of the Samson saga is in C. F. Burney, *The Book of Judges* (New York, 1970), pp. 391ff.

59. Brown, Driver, and Briggs, *Hebrew Lexicon,* p. 63.

60. Erica Reiner, *Surpu Sumerian and Akkadian Incantations* (London, 1958).

61. *Ancient Near Eastern Texts,* ed. J. Pritchard (Princeton, 1968), p. 306.

62. See on Raamses and Pithom, D. Redford, "Exodus 1:11," *Vetus Testamentum,* 13 (1963).

63. R. N. Whybray, *Thanksgiving for a Liberated Prophet: An Interpretation of Isaiah Chapter 53,* JSOT Supplement Series (Sheffield, 1978), p. 59.

64. San Nicolo, "Eine kleine Gefängnismeuterei in Eanna zur Zeit des Kambyses," *Münchener Beiträge zur Papyrusforschung und antiken Rechtsgeschichte,* 2 (1945), p. 1. For an earlier period, see also J. Renger, "Wrongdoing and Its Sanctions: On 'Criminal' and 'Civil' Law in the Old Babylonian Period," *Journal of Economic and Social History of the Orient* (Leiden), 20 (1977).

Chapter 8

The Sociology of the Return

In the chapter on sociological paradigms, we considered the social impact of exile in relation to the phenomenon of a return from exile, a rejoining of populations that had been separated by crisis and/or deportation. If our thesis about social adaptation during the Exile is valid, and if that adaptation was unique to those who were in exile, then we should expect to find a conflict at the return from exile, a sort of "culture shock" created by the mixing of two populations that have developed for almost a century along different lines and in different ecological and cultural circumstances. It is the purpose of this final chapter to investigate the debates about social divisions and conflict in the post-exilic community, taking into consideration the models of "return" that we have suggested from the sociological data. We will therefore consider those passages that provide evidence of social conflict. As a starting point, we will consider Hag. 2:10–14. The debate surrounding this passage reveals many related issues, some of which are important in this context. For example, the issue of economic injustice between those who were in an advantaged position at the restoration and those who were disadvantaged, the issue of the "Samaritans," and the conflict about the rebuilding of the Temple all relate to the debate regarding this passage. The logic of beginning with Haggai as a way into the related material should become obvious as we proceed.

Haggai's Question

The most important prophetic sources for the post-exilic community of Israel are Haggai and Zechariah. If there is a "Trito-Isaiah" consisting of Isa. 56–66, then there is a good deal of evidence to suggest that it was composed and appended to the Isaianic corpus after the return to Palestine.[1] Outside the prophetic sources, attention should also be given to Ezra-Nehemiah as the only narrative source of information about

179

events after the return.[2] But Haggai is one of the *earliest* sources of information after the return, and is therefore of primary importance.

For a discussion of social/religious conflict in the post-exilic community, Hag. 2:10–14(–19) provides an appropriately controversial starting point. Haggai's oracles are usually dated with confidence according to the internal chronology given, that is, ca. 520 B.C.E. Of particular concern is the final phrase:

> Haggai then spoke out, "It is the same with this people," he said, "the same with this nation as I see it — it is Yahweh who speaks — the same with everything they turn their hands to, and what they offer there is unclean."

The LXX adds the following curious phrase, part of which echoes Amos 5:10:

> ... because of their quickly won gains, they will suffer for their labors and you hated those dispensing justice at the city gate.

The context in Amos 5 is an oracle against economic injustice that is detrimental to the poor. Could this be placed here because of an early interpretation of this passage as referring to those repressing the poor of the return?

In 1908, Rothstein argued that this passage represents yet another example of the break between the post-exilic Judaic community and the Samaritans, i.e., those who began their syncretistic religion because of the exchange of populations by the Assyrian conquerors, as particularly reported in the Annals of Sargon.[3] This view has many current supporters, as John Bowman, for example, believed that the trouble started only with the return. While Bowman is suggesting that the differences had to do with the return, he finds the root of the trouble in the religious differences of the North and South.[4] As Rothstein's views continue to be influential, it is important to repeat some of the most important points he raised, now conveniently and recently summarized in Koch's discussion of this passage:

1. Haggai cannot possibly be denouncing the Judaic community of exiles as impure in the ninth month, when he had just three months earlier proclaimed them to be pure and seemed satisfied that a good beginning was accomplished.

2. The terms used, that is, *Ha'ām* and *Hagôy,* signify "the people" and "nation" outside Israel, especially in the unique combination used here. These terms are likened to the use of "nation" and "people" in (what are now called) "Oracles against the Nations."[5]

3. Hag. 2:5 states that God dwelt with the people, and thus they cannot have been "impure" at the same time.

4. Rothstein held that Ezra 4:1–6 referred to the same event as Hag. 2:10–14, but this involved contradicting Ezra's dating of the event in 538 and placing it in 520 to agree with Haggai. Since Galling's work, however, this rearrangement of the events of the return to 520, has gained widespread acceptance.[6] This finds support in Haggai's statement that the Temple *still* lay in ruins.

5. Lastly, Rothstein held that this section ended with v. 14, and thus had no original contact with what followed. Rothstein dated the following passage, that is, 2:15–19, with the date given in 1:15, which otherwise does not seem to have a passage to correlate with it.[7]

This series of points has led many scholars to accept a very early origin for the Samaritan schism by associating it with the Assyrian repopulation policy in the Northern kingdom and the resulting religious mixture as reported in 2 Kings 17 (a passage used specifically by Josephus in his condemnation of the Samaritans[8]). Once this was accepted, then many of the "biblical theologies" have had to deal with a perceived "problem" of the exclusive nature of the post-exilic community.

Both Wolff[9] and Elliger[10] have attempted to deal with the theological problem by associating it with the importance of preserving the pure faith of Israel in rebuilding true religion, and with it, the Temple.[11] There is here also the suggestion that Haggai wishes to avoid the political confrontation threatened by the Samaritans, but it is clearly the problem of exclusivity that troubles both Wolff and Elliger.

Rothstein's original assumption that Hag. 2:10–14 refers to the Samaritan split is open to question. Another scholarly tradition, seen especially in the work of Mitchell (1912),[12] Bloomhardt (1928),[13] Welch (1935),[14] Ackroyd (1968),[15] and May (1968),[16] sees Hag. 2:10–14 as a condemnation of the returning Jewish community itself, in the same vein as the first chapter and for the same reason: the building of the Temple. Bloomhardt, for example, considered the Temple to have been of absolute significance in both the religious and social reconstruction of Israel and indeed offers the most "political" view of the Temple as of revolutionary importance, as a symbol of restoration during the instability of Darius's early reign.[17] Bloomhardt then related this to the question of purity and the question regarding the object of 2:10–14. The Jews had to rebuild the Temple in order to regain purity.[18]

This perspective is shared largely by Ackroyd, both in an early series of articles on Haggai and in his study *Exile and Restoration*. As Ackroyd states, "If their offerings are unclean — that is, unacceptable — then so is their whole life and condition."[19] Perhaps Welch was correct when he stated that it was a previous altar that was being objected to, suggesting a social/religious conflict between those who returned and those who had their own altar already set up. Furthermore, Bloomhardt and Ackroyd (inasmuch as he follows Bloomhardt) must posit a foreign impure element nearby as a source of pollution, thus suggesting that social interaction is involved with the Haggai passage. This seems to contradict, or at least qualify, their refusal to see a second group in the terms *ha'-ām* and *ha-gôy*. But it remains to consider two more significant objections to the presence of a second group in Hag. 2:10–14.

Klaus Koch believes that a form-critical analysis of this passage reveals that, in fact, Hag. 2:10–14 should *not* be separated from what follows, i.e., 2:15–19. Haggai's oracles are constructed, according to Koch, in a tri-partite structure. Similarly, Koch divides the first oracles, 1:2–8, into the following sequence:

  1:2–4: The past
  1:5–6: The present as the division between past and future
  1:7–8: The future[20]

In the final section, 2:15–19, the promise for the future is based on the previous verses 10–14. Koch reasons that if the promise for the future is for the Israelites, so must the warning of 10–14 also be for this same community. Koch believes, as do the scholars mentioned before, that this passage makes no mention of intergroup tensions, much less the Samaritan schism.

Lastly, and perhaps most significantly, May has argued that there are many prophetic analogies both to the arguments of the prophets that the people can be unclean and to the double use of the reference "nation" and "people."[21] May must first, however, separate the sayings of Haggai from the work of a redactor's hand. May does not believe that Haggai himself made any references to the separation of communities in Palestine, using the term "remnant" (which he would say belongs to a "later redactor" under the influence of the Chronicler[22]).

May's linguistic arguments are, at first, impressive. He states that "the burden of proof lies on those who presume [the reference to another people in 2:14] and would therefore make a distinction between 'the people' in 2:14 and 'this people' in 1:2 [the latter of] ... which refers to the Judean community."[23] But the separation of a redactor's words from the prophetic words of Haggai may be a stumbling block for May's analysis. Is the use of "this people" in 1:2 a word from Haggai, or is the hypothetical redactor simply *quoting* the use of 2:14? Do the actual words of Haggai begin with v. 4, after: "And these were the words of the Lord spoken by Haggai the prophet"? Further, May attempts to deal with the use together of *Ha'ām* and *Hagôy.* For this, he cites other examples from Isa. 1:4; 10:6; Exod. 33:13; and also Ps. 33:12. None of these cases, however, has the same construction as Haggai. There is a problem here in trying to argue against a "technical" use of *'ām* and *gôy.* Either they are technical, in which case other references such as those that May cites are valid indicators, or they are not technical terms, in which case May's other references are pointless, since non-technical, common terms must surely be determined by the context in which they are used.[24] Because these terms are quite common, however, May's arguments from the other sources on the dual use of *'ām* and *gôy* are not particularly convincing.

May believes, further, that the charge of Israelites being "unclean" in Haggai's speech is comparable with Isa. 64:56, "We have all become like the one who is unclean." But then May *contrasts* this with Isa. 52:1f., where the threat of pollution is from foreigners, specifically the Babylonians.[25] But why cannot this point be reversed? I believe that Isa. 52:1f. is comparable with Hag. 2:10–14, but *contrasts* with Isa. 64:56 for the simple reason that the metaphorical language is about contact *between two entities* in Isa. 52 and about a state of being in Isa. 64. Hag. 2:10–14, too, involves a comparison of entities (and peoples) and not a state of being. Thus May's arguments do not seem to counter the force of the analogy in Hag. 2:10–13, and his choice of "contrasting" and "comparative" passages appears arbitrary. The argument must proceed to other evidence. But there is yet another problem.

Samaritanism in Recent Debate

As we have seen, a significant assumption of Rothstein is the idea that the "others" Haggai is referring to are the Samaritans, already in existence in the late sixth century. References to Samaritans are assumed to be in both 2 Kings 17 and Ezra 4. We can now refer to the recent fine study of the whole problem of Samaritanism by R. J. Coggins, *Samaritans and Jews.*[26] A consideration of Coggins's conclusions is of importance to our view of Haggai 2:10–14 and indeed to our view of social conflict.

Coggins began his survey with a consideration of the Old Testament passages that supposedly refer to the Samaritan schism. 2 Kings 17:34b–40, for example, uses the term "Samaritans," but this only means "residents of Samaria." Furthermore, the Chronicler makes no use of this passage, which would have served his purpose if such a schism were a social reality of his time. Indeed, the first use of the 2 Kings 17 passage as an "anti-Samaritan" passage is in Josephus (*Ant.,* IX, 277–291). 2 Kings 17:24–41, as 2 Chron. 30, appear to talk about heathenism in the Northern kingdom, it is true, but is this Samaritanism? Or is this a typically Deuteronomic sermon explaining the fall of the Northern kingdom by referring to religious impropriety? As Coggins comments:

> If the Deuteronomic movement had its origins in the North, and if the former prophets in their completed form are essentially the product of the Deuteronomic group, why should there be such hostility toward the North? Part of the answer might be that there is here a kind of converts' zeal against old associations, and an anxiety to uphold the claims of Jerusalem as the place which Yahweh had chosen. But whatever the cause of this hostility, it was essentially aimed against the alleged evils of the old Northern Kingdom; it cannot be construed as an attack upon Samaritanism.[27]

In the prophetic corpus, Duhm had already suggested in 1898 that Isa. 56:9–57:13 contained a polemic against the Samaritans. But Coggins objects that all that is discussed in the Isaiah passage is possible conflict within the Jewish community itself, especially regarding "foreigners" who join the community. There is no explicit reference to Samaritans.[28]

The internal dating of Haggai *is* sufficiently questionable in Coggins's view to render one of Rothstein's arguments very unstable, namely, whether a community called pure can, a few months later, be called impure. If the chronology of the book as a whole is questioned, Rothstein's point vanishes, as the oracles of purity could be attributed to the same period of Haggai's ministry, and thus no contradiction would exist. Lastly, Coggins has convincingly shown that the identification of the group theoretically opposed to the Jerusalem Temple community as Samaritans involves a significant assumption about the Samaritan community itself. That is, Samaritanism could hardly be considered "heathen" or "syncretistic" if its main trait came to be *precisely its conservatism.*[29] Still, commentators such as Morton Smith maintain that such an evolution is possible,[30] although Coggins has given good reason to believe that this is unlikely.

Although we agree that the "other group" are not Samaritans, Coggins has overstated the case when he says that there is no evidence for any kind of group conflict, or any "dramatic schism." Indeed, the Exile itself is surely the most dramatic schism of the period, and any resulting social conflict must surely be seen in the context of this event. In short, while it is unlikely that the Samaritans are being referred to in Haggai (or Trito-Isaiah or Zechariah), Haggai is talking about internecine conflict. As we said above, even those who rejected the Samaritan schism, such as Welch, did posit a conflict or schism of some sort. Welch had suggested that Haggai is preaching against an old altar that was rejected as impure by the returning exiles. This depends on Welch's view that Deuteronomic cultic observances were continued on the Temple site (see above, chapter 2). Welch offers the alternative view that the conflict of groups in Haggai is between the returned exiles and those that remained, and not necessarily the "Northern" peoples only. Welch's view has the added attraction of combining a debate about an altar with the involvement of the priests and questions of purity. But does this do justice to the nature of purity as a symbolic metaphor? We shall consider this further below.

Rudolph is also not convinced by those who see no intergroup conflict in Hag. 2:10–14 (though it should be noted that his work antedates that of Coggins). He believes that Rothstein's criticisms are still largely ignored or remain unanswered. For example, Rudolph maintains that the stylistic use of *Ha'ām* and *Hagôy* recalls certain aspects of previous references to Northern people and to those who mixed with them.[31]

Koch's form-critical view, as we noted, does not deal directly with Rothstein's points, but tries to overrule them according to his form-critical analysis of the same material. Rudolph is willing to concede that 2:15–19 belongs with the previous material, but more subtly argues that the chronological sequence must be carefully determined within the passage itself.

According to Rudolph, Haggai wants to say that life has been good since the laying of the foundation or the resumption of work, and therefore Haggai does not want the work and the growing good fortune to be endangered by impurity from outside sources. Thus, the continuation of 2:10–14 in 2:15–19 is a reminder about the present time, *not a promise about the future.*

Essential to Rudolph's view, of course, is his belief that the date in 2:18 is a gloss inconsistent with the passage in which it stands, which assumes that the foundation has already been laid. That this date is generally considered inaccurate is widely accepted (see the Jerusalem Bible, where a note questioning the authenticity of this date appears in the edition intended for the general reader). The original oracle, then, picks up again with the words "today and henceforth." Thus, the questions whether "seed is in the barn" and "plants still yield little" are rhetorical questions requiring a positive answer, that is, "yes, the seed is in the barn now," and, "yes, plants are bearing fruit." Otherwise, mentioning the fate of the people since the resumption of work is pointless. Rudolph therefore removes the force of Koch's argument by accepting the larger context but questioning the exact meaning of the time frame within this larger context. Implicit in this argument is Rudolph's acceptance of the order of the oracles, as Hag. 1 assumes the work is not yet begun, while the present passage assumes the work has begun and is in progress.

Rudolph continues to argue for the acceptance of Rothstein's views and makes it clear that an absolute conclusion is not possible on internal, linguistic evidence alone. Can this impasse be broken by another approach?

Pollution and Social Interaction

First of all, we want to know *who* is being addressed by Haggai. From a formal point of view, we find that Haggai's oracles fit what Westermann, in his work on prophetic speech, has called the "messenger formula," beginning with "Thus says...."[32] Hence the prophet is acting as the deliverer of God's message to the people.

Second, and most important, the symbolic logic of the metaphor is important and requires close attention. The metaphor does not deal with a single entity that is in a particular "state of being," whether "pure" or "impure" (as is the case in Isa. 64:56, quoted by May). We would have expected a single substance or people in the metaphor if one body of people were meant by Haggai. The prophet, however, refers to two substances *in relation to each other, transferring purity or impurity from one to the other*. The metaphor refers to groups of actual people, for the text plainly makes the transition from 2:14, "So it is with this people...." There would be a strain in the logic of Haggai's argument if we did not make this transition from "relations between substances" to "relations between peoples." A separation between pure and impure groups (food or bodies) implies a schism between those that are addressed by Haggai and those referred to as *Ha'ām* and *Hagôy*.

We have already made reference in another section to the work of Mary Douglas in relation to purity, especially her important work *Purity and Danger*.[33] Her argument is relevant here also, especially her assertion that purity fears (particularly in relation to body excretions) relate to ritualistic anxiety about classification and protection of boundaries: "When rituals express anxiety about the body's orifices, the sociological counterpart of this anxiety is a care to protect the political and cultural unity of a minority group."[34]

Douglas's theory that pollution fears are related to societal strains is strikingly confirmed by the passage we are considering, where the two themes of purity and group integrity are explicitly integrated. Thus, the arguments of Rudolph, which provide a plausible answer to the linguistic debate, along with our criticism of May's rather arbitrary lexical comparisons, are further supported by a more careful symbolic analysis of the logic of the metaphor.

This is further supported by our work on the priestly material in chapter 5 above, but also by a consideration of another term, *tāmē,* "to make impure" (also used adjectively). The vast majority of the cases of this root in various forms is in Leviticus, as one might expect (some 167 of 296 instances) followed by Ezekiel (43) and Numbers (36). All other instances of this term (some fifty occurrences, including the use of the term three or four times in Haggai) are spread over material where it is not the main or common theme of the text.

As the priestly material of Leviticus is most concerned with purity and pollution, it important to refer to the fact that interspersed with long discussions of purity laws are exhortations not to mix with the *pagans* in the land. This is especially evident in Lev. 18:24ff. and 20:22–26. Indeed, Lev. 18:24 is itself a significant passage, coming as it does at the end of a long discussion of sexual mores. The implication is that such sexual practices are indicative of surrounding peoples, i.e., *Hāgôy*, "nations" and "defiled themselves" in the same context.

In Num. 19, the use of *tāmē* coincides with a clear concern with the uncleanness as if it were "infectious," and thus the overriding concern is with the preservation of the community of faith.

Lev. 20:22–26 makes the explicit connection between the maintenance of purity laws and the maintenance of isolation from impure people.

Lastly, we must recall that the Exile itself was frequently considered by Ezekiel to be the result of the pure Jewish people allowing themselves to be defiled by "pagans," thus again emphasizing the dangers of social intercourse (often comparing it to sexual intercourse in Ezekiel's graphic language, Ezek. 23). In Ezek. 20, the famous chapter with the theme of God's action "for the sake of my name," defilement was a result of contact with enemy nations. The theme of exile as punishment for defilement is found in Ezek. 22 as well, all of these passages employing the technical term *tāmē*.

The grounds for arguing that Hag. 2:10–14 reflects social conflict are strong, for whenever defilement was discussed in the context of defilement by inanimate and living things and enemy nations, *all discussions are exilic or post-exilic.* But even if Haggai is referring to the Jewish community themselves as those who are defiled, surely the reason is not because the Temple was not yet built (which would have meant that pollution was unalterably universal at the destruction of the Temple). In Lev. 18 and 20, clear references to the Exile are contained in the post-exilic punishment clauses, which again repeat warnings against defilement (Lev. 18:28; 20:22). Such warnings seem to be foreign to the subjects of the chapters themselves, dealing as they do with familial relations, but make sense in the context of social interaction.

In Ezekiel, the defilement that brought the punishment of God by means of exile was precisely *contact with foreign peoples.* Thus, it is reasonable to assume that if Haggai is reviving the exilic worry about "pollution" of the people, then he is referring to defilement because of contact with impure people, not merely the lack of a Temple. So even if "this people" and "this nation" are the community of Jews, and not outsiders, we are still faced with the strong probability that the defilement was a result of mixing with impure people in the land.

To summarize the discussion thus far, attention has been focused on the debate over who the "other group" in question is. Many Scholars have been led to a false conclusion that if this "other group" is not the Samaritans, then there is no group interaction being referred to at all. To reject the idea that the passage refers to *some* kind of group conflict, however, is to reject out of hand the evidence of Ezra 4, Ezekiel, and Jeremiah, as we have seen. Further consideration of the restoration events reveals that there are many candidates for conflict other than the Samaritans.

Conflict of "Religious Ideology"

Some interesting ideas about sources of post-exilic conflict come from those scholars who are a part of what E. W. Nicholson has referred to as the "Back-to-Wellhausen" movement. This tendency is seen in Morton Smith's work, *Palestinian Parties and Politics that Shaped the Old Testament,* and Bernhard Lang's work, *Der Einzige Gott,* translated as *Monotheism and the Prophetic Minority.*[35]

Smith and Lang both begin with the amorphous and frequently syncretistic character of pre-exilic Israel.[36] 1 Kings 11:5 clearly has Solomon building Temples to other gods, and Lang cites the belief in local and national gods (Deut. 11:39; Mic. 4:5; 2 Kings 17:30f.).

Smith believes (what he calls) the "Yahweh Alone Movement" to have begun in the early ninth century, encouraged by the Reforms of Asa. Jehoshaphat was the first king to bear a Yahwist name and was a contemporary of Elijah, of whose violent exploits against Ba'al worship we need little reminding. As Smith states, "Evidently, from this period on there was a newly important element in the situation: the demand that all Israel worship Yahweh and Yahweh alone."[37]

Lang and Smith believe that Hosea is the most significant early exponent of a theology of the Yahweh Alone movement. Smith relates the marriage themes of Hosea to the Canaanite fertility religions of Ba'al, but Hosea clearly excludes any co-worship, and Yahweh usurps the function of Ba'al as possessor of land and people. Lang furthermore suggests that Hosea 13:4 may even be the earliest source for the later composition of the Ten Commandments.

The significance of this background becomes clear when both Smith and Lang refer to the continued conflict between the "parties." The Yahweh Alone movement continued as a minority that struggled against the continued syncretism all around, and among, the Jewish people. Citing the constant anti-idolatry messages of the prophets (Jer. 44:15ff.) through the Exile (Ezek. 14:1dff.) and even into the Persian period (Zech. 10:2, 13:2). Smith points out that it was a constant struggle in all periods.[38] Lang, largely agreeing with this reading of "monolatry" arising from a "Yahweh Alone" sect, uses more direct sociological terms in describing it: "Yahweh Alone worship can be understood as a crisis cult which continued beyond the actual crisis situation. Or, rather, the crisis situation is perceived as permanent."[39]

After the fall of the Northern kingdom, the Yahweh Alone movement moved South and continued its campaign during Hezekiah's reforms and then, especially, in the Josianic reforms. The final breakthrough to monotheism was achieved during the Exile: in Deuteronomic historical works that are seen as the historical account of the negative consequences of syncretism; in Ezekiel; and, most famously, in Deutero-Isaiah. Thus, the birth of Judaism has its roots in theological reflection on the theodicy of the Exile: "The Yahweh-Alone movement contributes to the foundation of Judaism through four major issues which stand in this literature: education, the sabbath, control of orthodoxy, and national restoration."[40]

Interestingly, Lang even believes that the Deuteronomic exhortation to watch other members of the family has its roots in the social pressure of a new religious movement that is potentially divisive of even family bonds (Deut. 13:2–9, cf. Luke 8:19–21!)

Thus, one can talk about a conflict between "Yahweh Alonists" and "syncretists." But does this line follow the division between exiles and those left in Palestine during the Exile? Smith does not think it is quite so simple.

Syncretists were clearly among the exiles, if one interprets intermarriage of the priests in Exod. 10:18–28 as motivated by such a syncretistic mood (or at least not prevented by a monotheistic one!). That economic interests were involved between the exiles as former landlords and the *dallat ha-'areṣ* left behind is specifically indicated by Smith.[41] But the religious conflict remains uppermost in Smith's analysis. If there were religious conflicts among the exiles, their common economic plight would have led to alliances in the struggle to regain territory and power. Thus, Smith believes that he finds evidence for an "uneasy alliance" between priests and Yahweh Alonists. This is seen by the compromise hammered out between Zerubbabel and those who promoted him as the Yahweh Alonists' messiah, and Jeshua, the high priest. Zech. 3 indicates that Jeshua was made pure and thus acceptable, and Haggai and Zechariah speak of both Jeshua and Zerubbabel as leaders of the exile community, against, Smith presumes, the syncretists. Referring specifically to Hag. 2:10–19, Smith agrees that what is objected to in this passage was a cultic altar and religious community of those left in the land. If Janssen's thesis that a large population remained in Palestine is correct, we have no reason to doubt the presence of a large number of people who represent the kind of syncretistic worship that so horrified Ezekiel in his vision of his return to the Temple (Ezek. 8:1ff.). (But note that Janssen believed many of these community members to be among those responsible for Deuteronomy itself.)

Class Conflict in the Restoration: Paul Hanson and Hugo Mantel

Obviously, justice cannot be done to Smith and Lang's theories in such a brief review. What we are specifically interested in, however, is the suggested lines of conflict. The main conflict, of course, is that between the Yahweh Alonists and the syncretists, which Smith traces straight on into the New Testament and rabbinic period. But the second conflict, which Smith alone develops, is the possible social and economic effects on the exiles who were powerless against those still in the land at the return from their exile. We shall see that a more careful view of the economic situation would lead to another explanation of the intermarriage problems of the priests and "chief men."

Paul Hanson's *The Dawn of Apocalyptic* approaches the problems of the beginning of Apocalyptic literature in our period by positing social tensions between two groups during and after the Exile.

Early in Hanson's work, we see that he is drawing a distinction between those who "dream and have visions" and those who face the pragmatic decisions of power and control, especially with regard to the cult.[42] This opposition, Hanson believes, continues from even earlier struggles between Zadokites and Levites, and thus Levites find support from the Isaianic version of the restoration. The latter might use terms such as "servants" to designate themselves, and Isa. 63:18 suggests that this conflict was "internal" and therefore between rivals within the community of Israelites, not between Israelites and non-Israelites or "syncretists."[43]

The visionary group is pro-Levite. The visionary group ethos is a continuation of the prophetic condemnation of the Temple and its practices (Amos 5:21–24, Mic. 3:12, Isa. 1:10–11; Jer. 7:1ff.; 11:14ff.; 13:13; and 26:1). This is a key to the most important conflict that Hanson uses to strengthen his case, the conflict between Zadokite priesthood and the Levites (undoubtedly an element in Jeremiah's attitude, as he comes from the Levitical stronghold of Anathoth[44]).

Ezekiel's restoration program certainly has Zadokites in a prominent role, and there does appear to be an anti-Levite bias in Ezek. 44; 40:46b; and 48:11. This is the group that Hanson calls "pragmatic" and thus "ideological."

But there is a complication when writings of a "visionary" nature are also used to justify the building of the Temple with Persian support, such as in Zech. 6:8–14. Hanson then comments: "This text...[indicates]...that the specific genres used are incidental, interchangeable, and adopted only insofar as they are suitable carriers of the propagandistic message of the hierocracy."[45]

The Zadokites, apparently, dream dreams only when they don't have a Temple (that is, when they are "disenfranchised" in some way also). Surely this is a strained explanation for the fact that the literature does not easily line up along the lines of "Zadokite" vs. "Levite-Visionary" quite so easily — and the fact that apocalyptic genres are always different and changing. What would a "pure" apocalyptic be? Ultimately, apocalyptic literature aims at the message of God's sovereignty over history, but not using any one metaphor or image in the process.

As far as the conflict between Zadokites and Levites is concerned, there is little doubt that the two groups fell out. But the evidence, especially the chronological evidence, can be interpreted in different ways. In his recent history of the priesthood, for example, Cody points out that (contrary to Hanson) Ezekiel's restoration program represents an important compromise between the two groups, with Levites gaining some advantages they did not previously have.[46]

Contrary to supporting exclusive claims of either Levite or Zadokite, Trito-Isaiah shows signs of a profound generalization of the priesthood in Isa. 61:6, where *all Israelites are priests to the rest of the world.* Moreover, Isa. 66:21 states that even some from foreign nations will be taken to be priests and Levites. Cody notes that by the time of Ezek. 8:2, both groups are called the "sons of Aaron."

Finally, however, what is most perplexing in Hanson's analysis is the apparently minor role played by the Exile itself in the conflicts he has identified. Surely one who otherwise connects literary developments with social circumstances cannot fail to see the singular significance of this event; yet we are left with the impression that the quarrels between the "ideologists" and the "visionaries" take place in exile as if on a stage, with the return simply a change of scenery. Hanson's use of the adjectives "oppressed" and "disenfranchised" combined with "minority" beg the question of whether more than religious conflicts and access to religious power is involved. Hanson only briefly alludes to Isaianic passages regarding social justice as possible keys to understanding social conflict, and he does not probe the social circumstances of this time.[47]

A reading along similar lines, but with more attention to the formative nature of the Exile itself, is provided by Hugo Mantel in a 1973 article, "The Dichotomy of Judaism During the Second Temple."[48]

Mantel believes that the conflicts of the Hellenistic era between the Pharisees and Sadducees can be traced to sixth- and fifth-century conflicts along similar socio-political lines; thus he works backward into the time we are concerned with. Mantel's main sources are Ezra and Nehemiah.

Mantel first wonders whether the Persian king would really commission a direct interference with internal religious disputes in Palestine,

thus casting some doubt on the Artaxerxes "rescript." More significantly, however, Mantel wonders why Ezra had no contact with the
existing high priest or other Temple personnel in Jerusalem; as we have
seen in Haggai-Zechariah, such personnel were a reality soon after the
dedication of the Temple in 515 B.C.E. Furthermore, there is no hint
that the separation from others called for by Ezra is a separation from
"syncretism." Lastly, Ezra 7:25–26 interestingly implies that the law
that Ezra metes out applies only to those who "know the law" (having
been taught?), and punishment also only applies to them. Who, then,
are those to whom Ezra speaks? Precisely to that community, states
Mantel, which called itself again and again the "sons of the Golah":

> Ezra's mission was not concerned either with Persian governmental
> affairs or with official, cultic religion in Judah. It was concerned
> with the Community of the Exiles, the "Sons of the Exile" which
> was within the Judean state, . . . the autonomous community of the
> Jews who had returned from Babylonian Exile.[49]

Mantel believes that this community had its own elders and autocracy
(the $z^{\varepsilon}q\varepsilon n\hat{\imath}m$) according to Ezra 9:1 and 10:5. He furthermore notes the
very exclusivist language used by Ezra and Nehemiah, exemplified by
the assembly of Ezra 10, and the fact that 10:5 implies that "Israel" is the
term only for those who belong to the community in question. Does Ezra
7:25 imply, along with Jeremiah 40:11, that there are other communities
of "true Israelites" in other places, which Ezra will organize according
to "his ideology'?

Mantel thus develops the very interesting theory that the returned
exiles formed an autonomous community on the strength of the social
bonds created during the Exile.[50]

The Exile community were exhorted to support the Levites, and only
the Exile community celebrated the festival of "booths" (Sukkot). This
separation of Ezra and the absence of the priests led Mantel to suggest
that Ezra may be the first of what eventually became the position of an
"Exilarch," as reported in Talmudic literature:

> Whether the office of the Exilarch stems from an early period or
> not, we have seen the Jews in Babylonia — the Golah — consti-
> tuted a unit. The reading of the Torah by trained "explainers"
> seems to have been an established custom.[51]

In conclusion, Mantel believes that the religion of the "sons of the Golah" was different from the Temple religion of the high priests. What
was the nature of this "separate religion"? Mantel lists his suggested
outline: (1) obligation for all to study Torah; (2) authorities for inter-

pretation not priests; (3) the beginnings of Midrash (the Torah had to be "interpreted" and translated); (4) prohibition of intermarriage, not just the priestly prohibitions of Exod. 34:16, Deut. 7:4; (5) prohibition of even transport of goods on the Sabbath; (6) celebration of booths, transferring the piety of believing into the individual home; (7) rules that were not from the law of Moses (Neh. 10:55); (8) the institution of Nehemiah's reforms and debt remissions.[52]

We have thus considered three variations on the theme of religious-social conflict in exilic and especially post-exilic Palestine, all three of which to a greater (Mantel, Smith, Lang) or lesser (Hanson) extent consider the social implications of the Exile. But there remains the provocative suggestion made by both Smith and Janssen that the Exile also created the potential for and evidence of a conflict on economic, as well as religious, grounds.[53] An interesting body of literature has recently gathered around this theme, which until now has received only limited attention, particularly among Western scholars.

Class Conflict: Materialist Theories

An important aspect of this argument is the potential conflict between the large population that remained behind and the returning old "aristocracy." This provides the material for a "class"-aligned conflict, as suggested by Janssen in his section "Die Bevorzugung der Dallath Ha'Aretz durch die Babylonier." Janssen points to the cordial relationships between Jeremiah and the Babylonians, the latter apparently well aware of Jeremiah's implicitly "pro-Babylonian" stand.[54] The possibility of a Jerusalemite "fifth column" within the late pre-exilic community may have had some influence on the redistribution of the land among those left behind on the land (Jer. 40), although as "workers" and not owners, according to both Alt and Janssen.[55] Janssen makes the interesting point that the threat of "foreigners" possessing the lands and fields of Israelites was a common warning used by the prophets (Amos 5:11; Mic. 6:15; Jer. 5:17). In the Exile we might imagine the foreigners to be Babylonians, but Janssen refers to the internal conflict of Trito-Isaiah to suggest that the "foreigners" were other Israelites, the *new 'ām ha-'arεṣ,* since they now possessed the land and enjoyed its fruit, placed in power by their Babylonian benefactors.[56] This replacement policy is reflected in passages such as 1 Kings 8:33 and Deut. 28:43 (which warns of others "in your land"). Thus Hag. 2:10-14(-19), with its impure people, and the mention of robbers in Zech. 4:1-5, 5-11, all reflect the problem of loss of land by those in exile.

In the following important passages, we see what a significant issue land possession was for the exiles:

The word of Yahweh was then addressed to me as follows, "Son of
man, your brothers, your kinsmen, the whole House of Israel, these
are told by the citizens of Jerusalem, 'You have been sent away
from Yahweh; it is to us that the land was given as our domain.'
Say therefore, 'The Lord Yahweh says this — Yes, I have sent them
far away among the nations and I have dispersed them to foreign
countries; and for a while I have been a sanctuary for them in the
country to which they have gone.' Then say, 'The Lord Yahweh
says this: I will gather you together from the peoples. I will bring
you all back from the countries where you have been scattered and
I will give you the land of Israel. They will come and will purge it
of all the horrors and filthy practices.'" (Ezek. 11:14–18)

The Word of Yahweh was then addressed to me as follows, "Son of
man, the people living in those ruins in the land of Israel say, 'Abraham was alone when he was given possession of this land. Now
we are many and we hold the country as our domain.'" "Very
well, then, tell them, 'The Lord Yahweh says this: You eat blood
[or "you eat on the mountains"], you raise your eyes to your idols,
you shed blood, are you likely to keep possession of the land? You
rely on your swords, you engage in filthy practices, you each commit adultery with your neighbors' wives: are you likely to retain
possession of the land?'" (Ezek. 33:23–27)

These passages should be seen in the context of Jeremiah's redemption of family lands, after which he states, "Fields and vineyards will
once again be bought in this land" (Jer. 32:6–15). On the basis of these
texts, and the reported redistribution of lands of the people among the
"poorest of the land," it is obvious that we must consider the possible
implications of land dispossession in relation to the return of the exiles.

The most important theorists of class conflict who work on this period are Joel Weinberg and Heinz Kreissig.[57]

Their orientation is explicitly materialist, but their attention to the
social and economic basis of possible conflicts in the restoration community is intriguing and provocative; and thus their political orientation
should not prejudice a serious reading of their work. Such prejudice is
unfortunately all too frequent among Western readers of Eastern European and Soviet authors.[58]

Kreissig's monograph is more concerned with the Achaeminid period, but his ideas about the formation and struggle in the Jewish community depend on his analysis of the pre-exilic period, specifically in
relation to the monarchy. Kreissig's view is that monarchy in Israel ap-
proached a kind of despotic control by the king over massive proportions
of the land, which was previously held in the ownership of the clan-

units.[59] If this was the case, then it is clear what an important change had come about in Judea as a result of the Neo-Babylonian conquest, a rural land redistribution that radically altered the royal landholdings.[60]

Alt had already noted the significant difference between the Assyrian practice of creating a new aristocratic level beholden to the Assyrians alone for power and position as opposed to the Neo-Babylonian practice of simply deporting the old aristocracy to a central area.[61] In their place, they simply divided the land among those who undoubtedly served as supervisors of the new king's property. In Alt's view the result of this was that the land of Judah was not made into an independent province, but was simply annexed to Samaria. Thus, the Samarian aristocracy were able to extend their influence into the southern area. On this basis, Alt explained the interest of the Samarian governor in the later building programs of Zerubbabel and Nehemiah. Alt supported this view by citing Jer. 41, the pilgrimage of northern Yahwists to the Jerusalem altar, a pilgrimage assumed to be impossible before the fall of the southern state and the disappearance of the border that separated them.

So, on the one hand, the population of Judah may have struggled on as best they could after the conquest, in small settlements other than the destroyed cities, as suggested by archaeological evidence, and others may have formed new main population centers, as implied by the movement of Gedaliah to Mizpah (Jer. 40). One could easily assume that many of these people did very well, creating a new "upper class" on its own terms. Nehemiah's later efforts to repopulate Jerusalem as a center of power may well reflect the diversified settlement pattern as a result of the destruction of Exile. The rise of a new upper class answerable to the Babylonians is furthermore proved by the Neo-Babylonian involvement in Gedaliah's resettlement and Zedekiah's earlier appointment. Indeed, Gedaliah is referred to as a "governor." If Alt is wrong, Gedaliah was the first of many "governors" whom the Persians presumably continued to appoint (Neh. 5:15, the "former governors," Nehemiah's predecessors) or perhaps *began* to appoint. Nehemiah suggested that some of these previous governors "laid heavy burdens on the people," thus constituting an aristocracy or a centralized economic power. But it need not be the Samarian aristocracy that is referred to; it could be one from among those that stayed behind during the Exile. Against Alt, there does not seem to be a need to posit a foreign aristocracy in order for an "upper class" to exist in the area of Palestine after the Exile.

The strong tendency in Ezra to discuss the foreigners in the immediate area with terms such as "impurity," which echo the complaints in Ezekiel cited above, does suggest the possibility of religious mixing, a syncretism that could arise as a result of the northern influence.

We must contend with two points raised by Kreissig in his analysis. One is that an internal aristocracy within Palestine, and possibly even within the Golah community itself as indicated by Ezra-Nehemiah, was present during the restoration. The other is that there is also a presence of an external aristocracy, indicated not only by the "Samarians" and their interest in Judean affairs, but also implied by the intermarriage of the "chief men and priests" (Ezra 9:1–3). Kreissig supposes that material motivation to regain land was high among the returning Jews from Mesopotamia, particularly among the sons of former landowners.[62]

There may be further hints about the economic domination of an internal hierarchy or aristocracy. Kippenberg suggests that the Darian innovation of silver currency throughout the Persian empire, as reported by Herodotus (*Hist.*, 111, 89) may have encouraged the growing impoverishment of farmers who had to produce more surplus to exchange for silver (explicitly mentioned in Neh. 5) to pay taxes. It would also have thus encouraged a breakdown of families into smaller units, which were then able to produce more surplus.[63] The failure of some families would then lead to debt-bondage, also reported in Neh. 5. Nehemiah's reforms thus sought to deal with this growing economic problem among the Golah community. This is a significant suggestion for one main reason: if the economic conditions described by Nehemiah came about entirely after the restoration, then the continued use of a term like "sons of the Golah" to refer to the community of the Exile was at best sentimental and at worst a distortion of the historical facts.

Summary

The sons of the Golah returned to Palestine only to find their land in the hands of a new *'ām ha-'areṣ*, which may have included some of the Samarian upper class, or the "fifth column" previously supported by Jeremiah and Gedaliah, or former debtors and even slaves. Some of the families were able to re-establish themselves quickly, by intermarriage or by independent means, e.g., those whom Haggai scolds for building their own homes before attending to the Temple. But the majority of the returned exiles created a separate community with an independent ethos and, if Mantel is correct, some unique religious ideas as well. This community also found itself engaged in a largely class-oriented conflict with both the aristocracy from the return and those who were able to intermarry and regain their former status. Attention to social mechanisms for survival, however, cautions against a predominantly materialist basis for post-exilic conflict. Although the separate religious, social, and structural development of the exiles (apart from those that stayed behind) was antagonized by the arguments over property and finances, nonetheless such conflicts had many other causes as well. All the evidence, as we have seen, does not lead to an exclusively socio-economic religious explanation.

But there is little doubt that Ezra's constant use of exclusive terms regarding these "sons of the Golah," the frequent exhortations against intermarriage with the impure of the land, thus possibly corrupting the "pure seed," the priestly reforms of Lev. 25 and Neh. 5, all add up to a self-conscious community that is occupied with self-preservation, both as a pure community in a religious sense and also preservation in a material sense; this self-consciousness continued at least two generations after the return of 520 B.C.E. Haggai's use of "remnant of the people" has its sociological/theological parallel in Ezra's use of the "sons of the Exile," which is a salient term not only for those it includes, but also for those it excludes.

To return to the beginning with Hag. 2:10–14(–19), we recall that according to our analysis of the impact of disaster, deportation en masse, domination, and minority existence, biblical exegesis about the realities of Exile must begin with the assumption that such social conflicts are likely. It is sociologically unrealistic to assume that the norm is no conflict (a "null hypothesis") until conflict is undeniably proved.

Social boundaries erected as a mechanism for survival during the Exile led to conflicts after the return to Palestine. The exiles formed a self-consciously defined community, a *Hibakusha* community, a community of "survivors" who returned to Palestine with a theology of acquired innocence and purity as opposed to the defilement of those who remained behind. Such a theological hubris on the part of the exile community must have created havoc and sparked the other fuel for conflicts, such as economic abuse and religious infidelity.

To be troubled by what appears to be "exclusivism" on the part of Haggai or to feel a need to put an acceptable face on the separation of the marriages in Ezra-Nehemiah is to profoundly misunderstand the nature of group solidarity and survival of minorities. Sociological literature, as we have seen, trains the biblical exegete to see in these mechanisms a creative response to the threat of domination and minority existence. We are invited to look at Ezra-Nehemiah, Haggai, and others from an "exilic consciousness," from the perspective of their worries and experiences, rather than our own supposedly liberal, twentieth-century humanism that is offended by such protectionism on the part of minority groups. To theologize from the perspective of the exiles, however, is to start from a radically different assumption about the nature of the people of God, an assumption perhaps foreign to modern Christian theologians outside the minority traditions. From the perspective of the "Fourth World," such conflicts between the "world" (and its threat of impurity) and the "true fellowship," or the "remnant," are *necessary* for continued survival.

NOTES

1. For date of Joel as fourth or even third century, see O. Eissfeldt, *The Old Testament: An Introduction* (Oxford, 1965), pp. 392ff.; Otto Kaiser, in his *Introduction to the Old Testament* (Oxford, 1975), dates Haggai to 520 B.C.E.; Joel to post-400; Malachi to 400–350, and Zech. 1–8 to the last quarter of the sixth century (see pp. 230ff.).

2. See Sara Japhet, "The Supposed Common Authorship of Chronicles and Ezra-Nehemiah Investigated Anew," *Vetus Testamentum*, (1968). I follow Japhet's work and treat these sources separately.

3. J. Rothstein, *Juden und Samaritaner* (Leipzig, 1908); see *Ancient Near Eastern Texts*, p. 284).

4. John Bowman, *Samaritanische Probleme: Studien zum Verhältnis von Samaritanertum, Judentum and Urchristentum* (Stuttgart, 1967), p. 12.

5. "Oracles against foreign nations" is not Rothstein's phrase.

6. K. Galling, *Studien zur Geschichte Israels im Persischen Zeitalter* (Tübingen, 1964).

7. On these points, see K. Koch, "Haggais unreines Volk," *Zeitschrift für die Alttestamentliche Wissenschaft* (Berlin), 79 (1967).

8. Josephus, *Ant.,* IX, 277ff. (Loeb ed.).

9. H. W. Wolff, *Dodekapropheten,* Biblischer Kommentar (Neukirchen, 1961).

10. K. Elliger, *Die Propheten: Nahum, Habakuk, Zephanja, Haggai, Sacharja, Maleachi,* Das Alte Testament Deutsche (Göttingen, 1967).

11. Ibid., p. 95.

12. H. G. Mitchell, *A Critical and Exegetical Commentary on Haggai, Zechariah, Malachi and Jonah,* International Critical Commentary (Edinburgh, 1912).

13. Paul F. Bloomhardt, "The Poems of Haggai," *Annual of the Hebrew Union College* (Cincinnati), 5 (1928).

14. A. Welch, *Post-Exilic Judaism* (Edinburgh, 1935).

15. P. Ackroyd, *Exile and Restoration* (London, 1968).

16. H. G. May, "'This People' and 'This Nation' in Haggai," *Vetus Testamentum,* 18 (1968).

17. Bloomhardt, "The Poems of Haggai," p. 155.

18. Ibid., p. 172.

19. Ackroyd, *Exile and Restoration,* p. 168. As we shall see, the claim that Israel was not yet holy without its Temple is an assumption based largely on Haggai, but even Haggai's earlier warning about the absence of the Temple was based on bad events (e.g., drought) and not fear of unatoned "impurity." Where, then, is this idea corroborated?

20. Koch, "Haggais unreines Volk," p. 60.

21. May, "'This People' and 'This Nation' in Haggai."

22. Ibid., p. 192.

23. Ibid., pp. 192f.

24. This was E. W. Nicholson's argument in his article on the *'ām ha-'areṣ:* "The Meaning of the Expression, 'Am Ha'Aretz' in the Old Testament," *Journal of Semitic Studies* (Manchester), 10 (1965). Once the idea of a technical term is rejected, it is clear that context largely determined the use of this phrase.

25. May, "'This People' and 'This Nation' in Haggai," pp. 194ff. This would appear to be a case against our question in note 19 above, but in neither Isaiah passage is the context one of cult and the need for sacrifice to make the unclean people clean again. Indeed, in Isaiah, the point is that uncleanness comes from injustice, and thus the metaphor is yet another example of a prophetic anti-Temple polemic.

26. R. J. Coggins, *Samaritans and Jews: The Origins of Samaritanism Reconsidered* (Oxford, 1975).

27. Ibid., p. 28.

28. Ibid., p. 43.

29. Ibid., p. 138.

30. "The Samaritan cult on Mt. Gerizim is probably a survival of one practiced during the Israelite monarchy..." (Morton Smith, *Palestinian Parties and Politics that Shaped the Old Testament* [New York, 1971], p. 92).

31. W. Rudolph, *Haggai — Sacharja 1–8 — Sacharja 9–14 — Maleachi* (Göttingen, 1976), p. 49. Considering the other uses of the specific phrase reveals that in one instance, Exod. 33:13, when it is included in the prayer of Moses, the term is "Israel." In Judg. 2:20 and 1 Kings 18:10, it refers to foreign nations — the same as in Jer. 12:17, 18:8, 25:12, 27:8, etc. One obviously could not argue for a technical term. Rudolph argues for its stylistic use in combination with 'am, but this is also a weak argument.

32. C. Westermann, *Basic Forms of Prophetic Speech* (London, 1967).

33. Mary Douglas, *Purity and Danger* (London, 1966).

34. Ibid., p. 124.

35. Bernard Lang, *Monotheism and the Prophetic Minority: An Essay in Biblical History and Sociology* (Sheffield, 1983).

36. Smith, *Palestinian Parties and Politics that Shaped the Old Testament*, p. 18.

37. Ibid., p. 22.

38. Ibid., p. 23.

39. Lang, *Monotheism and the Prophetic Minority*, p. 2.

40. Ibid., p. 55.

41. Ibid.

42. P. Hanson, *The Dawn of Apocalyptic* (Philadelphia, 1975), pp. 14ff.

43. Ibid., p. 71.

44. On this point, see the remarks by Aelred Cody in *A History of the Old Testament Priesthood* (Rome, 1969).

45. Hanson, *The Dawn of Apocalyptic*, p. 256.

46. Cody, *A History of the Old Testament Priesthood*, p. 166.

47. Hanson, *The Dawn of Apocalyptic*, pp. 120–121.

48. Hugo Mantel, "The Dichotomy of Judaism during the Second Temple" *Annual of the Hebrew Union College* (Cincinnati), 44 (1973).

49. Ibid., p. 63.

50. Ibid., p. 66.

51. Ibid., p. 73.

52. Ibid., p. 75.

53. See Janssen's discussion of *Dallet Ha'Aretz* in *Juda in der Exilszeit* (Göttingen, 1956).

54. Ibid.

55. A. Alt, "Die Rolle Samarias bei der Entstehung des Judentums," *Kleine Schriften zur Geschichte des Volkes Israel,* 2, (Munich, 1953).

56. Janssen, *Juda in der Exilszeit*, p. 54.

57. J. Weinberg, "Probleme der sozialökonomischen Struktur Judäas vom 6. Jahrhundert v.u.z. bis zum 1. Jahrhundert u.z.," Zu einigen wirtschaftshistorischen Untersuchungen von Heinz Kreissig, *Jahrbuch für Wirtschaftsgeschichte,* 1 (1973); see bibliography for further references to Weinberg; B. Funck, "Zur Bürger-Tempel-Gemeinde im nachexilischen Juda" (review of Kreissig), *KLIO,* 59 (1977), pp. 491–496; Hans G. Kippenberg, *Religion und Klassenbildung im antiken Judäa: Eine religionssoziologische Studie zum Verhältnis von Tradition und gesellschaftlicher Entwicklung* (Göttingen, 1978); Heinz Kreissig, *Die sozialökonomische Situation in Juda zur Achamenidenzeit,* Schriften zur Geschichte und Kultur des Alten Orients 7 (Berlin, 1973).

58. In a recent article comparing the reforms of Solon to Nehemiah, Yamauchi claims that this comparison was "to his knowledge" suggested by Morton Smith. In fact, these three, Weinberg, Kippenberg, and Kreissig, as well as Eisenstadt, have considered such a comparison. See Edwin Yamauchi, "Two Reformers Compared: Solon of Athens and Nehemiah of Jerusalem," *The Bible World,* Festschrift for Cyrus Gordon, ed. Rendsburg, Adler, Arfa, Winter (New York, 1980).

59. See Gottwald's helpful analysis of social structure and function in *The Tribes of Yahweh* (Maryknoll, N.Y., 1979).

60. Kreissig, *Die sozialökonomische Situation in Juda zur Achamenidenzeit,* pp. 26–32.

61. Alt, "Die Rolle Samarias bei der Entstehung des Judentums," p. 327.

62. Kreissig, *Die sozialökonomische Situation in Juda zur Achamenidenzeit,* p. 37.

63. H. Kippenberg, *Religion und Klassenbildung im antiken Judäa.*

Chapter 9

Conclusions

After establishing the facts of the exile and gathering the evidence typically cited for the conditions of exile, I argued that the Ancient Near Eastern empires, and especially both the Neo-Assyrian and the Neo-Babylonian empires, were very concerned with the overt symbols of empire and conquest. Payment of tribute, threat of armies, internally and externally directed propaganda both written and pictorial, and finally deportation itself, must be seen in their sociological context as symbols of power and empire. These symbols are best understood as symbols of colonialism and domination.

The martial tactic of deportation is not unique to the first millennium B.C.E., and a more wholistic understanding of behavioral responses to mass deportation can be achieved by a careful consideration of analogous situations where observation of social and religious response is available. Since the biblical material we have today is the product of the successful maintenance of social and religious identity, it follows that the most important analogies will be cases of successful resistance by ethnic groups to the social and ideological threats of a conquering or dominant authority.

After a detailed examination of sociological research in the areas of group crisis, minority behavior, and contact between ethnic groups in situations of unequal distribution of power, we focused on four "cases" to provide analogies for group responses; these cases were the Japanese-American internment in World War II in the United States; black slavery societies and religious responses in the New World; South African Bantustans and the Zionist religious responses to segregated living; and the movement of the residents of Bikini Island (the Marshall Islands) by the United States.

A careful examination of recent research in the behavioral patterns of these cases suggested certain common features. We selected four behavioral patterns, mechanisms for survival, which we illustrated from the cases (and some relevant material in other cases as well).

201

The first mechanism for survival was structural adaptation. In this mechanism, the basic social organization of the group under stress combines traditional structures with innovations and new leadership to provide a combination of continuity and flexibility. The Japanese-Americans began to expand traditional familial authority structures to take in the physical realities of the barrack dwellings where numbers of nuclear families were housed. The Bikini Islanders reformed their societal structures when the traditional land-based hierarchy was totally removed. The Zionist churches reflected Zulu tribal structure, yet incorporated innovations. In the biblical material the rise of elders reflected *continuity* with pre-exilic social authority structures, while the demographic changes of the *Bēt 'Āb/Bēt 'Ābôt* (with the *roš* as the communal leader) represented a structural adaptation. Although we are not able to detail *why* these changes were functional in exile, there is circumstantial evidence to suggest that the *Bēt 'Ābôt* reflected settlement response patterns of the exiles and the leadership structure. The continued use of terminology from this social division suggests the significance of this change even two generations after the restoration.

The second mechanism is related to structural adaptation, namely, the rise of new leadership in crisis and the typical split in strategic theories expressed by leaders in dominated situations. The split is between those leaders who argue for total, often violent, resistance and those who call for social and nonviolent resistance, with more of an ideological and cultural strategy of group boundary maintenance. The struggle of the elders in the Japanese-American camps to assert their traditional authority in the face of an Americanization program that encouraged a less traditional, and younger, leadership more familiar with English and American traditions has been well documented. The role of black preachers as a new elite in slave societal relations was considered by Raboteau's study of slave religion, and the fall of traditional leadership to new leaders with new plans was documented by Kiste in his study of the Bikini Islanders.

The obvious place to look for crisis leaders in Israel is in the prophets. The conflict between Jeremiah and Hananiah illustrates a conflict not only about "true and false prophecy" but is an example of conflicting strategies of resistance and survival for groups under stress. The issue of the appropriate strategy of resistance toward Babylon reveals that the letter of Jeremiah, far from indicating "easy conditions" in exile, was in fact a call to abandon plans for a "holy war" against the Babylonians inspired by a false promise that God would crush Babylon and bring home the exiles in a short time. The context of the letter, namely, a debate with Hananiah and other prophets over the future of the Exile (and the Neo-Babylonian execution of prophets mentioned in the same chapter), confirms this interpretation, as does Jeremiah's otherwise somewhat enigmatic advice to seek the *shalom* of the city in which they lived.

Third, the role of ritual behavior is well documented in studies of colonized peoples (Fanon, Memmi, Mannoni) but has often been written of as a pathological and escapist retreat into cult by powerless people. The theories of Mary Douglas, however, lead to the important suggestion that ritual is a means of protecting social boundaries, and thus a creative mechanism. "Boundary rituals" were traced in the cases (and other related material) to suggest that purity regulations, especially, may be a significant source of boundary maintenance rituals. A consideration of Lev. 11 in the context of recent work on the elaboration of law leads to the conclusion that, while Israelite laws of the pure and impure are arguably older than the Exile, the exilic and post-exilic *strata* of legal debate and *elaboration* of these laws reveal a prevailing concern for maintenance of separation from the unclean; this is related to worries about the *transfer* of pollution from foreigners. This is most dramatically illustrated in the dissolution of mixed marriages in the restoration period (Ezra and Nehemiah).

Fourth, folklore innovations can be illustrated in the rise of new hero stories to illustrate models of behavior. Klapp and Abraham's work on the clever hero motif helped us to recognize the significance of stories of this kind in the folklore of our cases, especially the folklore of black slavery, the legends in the Japanese-American camps, and the images of the "black Jesus" in Zionist Bantu theology.

In the Bible, the diaspora novella illustrates the pious, clever hero who overcomes *physically more powerful* members of the dominant ethnic group and is favored by the king, whose role is always a passive, almost God-like character. There is also the key element that the hero faces imprisonment. Messiah figures and the Suffering Servant are also types of the diaspora hero, who faces a task of rising from low status to success. Imprisonment, specifically alluded to in the Suffering Servant material and the diaspora novella, was considered a key motif because the Exile itself was described as prison. Imprisonment and the eventual success of the diaspora hero became a powerful image of the life in exile, and a consideration of all forms of and terms for "imprisonment" reveal it to be a dominant exilic metaphor and image.

Finally, consistent with the social development of a group under stress, there is textual evidence for conflict between the returning exiles and those still in the land. The unique development of the exilic structure and ideology led to a permanent separation and separate ("sectarian") consciousness of the exile community, which continued to emphasize purity boundaries and use delimiting identification markers like "remnant," "holy seed," and most importantly "sons of the Exile." The economic conflicts between the exiles and those who remained behind were considered to exacerbate, but not cause, this conflict.

Several related studies suggest themselves from this work. First, we have not investigated the socio-linguistic aspects of the Exile, especially the possible lexical influences of "imperial Aramaic" on Hebrew. Very interesting studies (by Peter Suzuki, for example[1]) have documented the linguistic impact of the camp experience on the spoken Japanese of the residents, who constructed a Japanese-English terminology for aspects of camp life. Perhaps a similar approach could be taken to the Aramaic portions of the Hebrew Bible.

Second, there is the Lament literature. Most of the cases studied revealed examples of new forms of poetry and artwork of the type that could be called "lament" and "mourning" literature as reflections of social crisis. Such a study might suggest new approaches to the book of Lamentations and its innovations.

Finally, on a human level, it is a sad commentary that literature about exiles, about struggles of minorities, and about group crisis is all too plentiful from ancient to modern time. This is perhaps most ironic in the case of those whose exile began so long ago and first led them to ask the question that continues to echo throughout history: "How can we sing the Lord's song in a foreign land?"

Postscript:
Toward a Contemporary Theology of Exile

There is obvious resistance to the construction of a contemporary "theology of exile." For many Jews, Zionism and the modern state of Israel represent the fulfillment of a long anticipated end to exile, or what Fackenheim called a re-entry "into history." For most Christians, since the time of Constantine and the "Christianization of Rome" in the fourth century of the Common Era, Christian theology has been a theology of power, its modern apologists referring to this as "accepting responsibility" — echoing a theme that is discernible from St. Augustine to Reinhold Niebuhr. For most Protestant Americans, the exercise of worldly power is not rejected, although it may occasionally be tempered by an ethic of a "just war" derived more from Rome than Nazareth. This is represented pre-eminently in the willingness of Christians to accept the death of the "enemies" of the political system for which they have "accepted responsibility." To summarize such a contemporary perspective, John Howard Yoder has used the phrase "Neo-Constantinianism."[2]

History also reveals that under a red flag, the ethics of power change very little. For both capitalist and Marxist, Exodus leads to King David. Let one example stand for the dozens that could be cited on this point:

> The Exodus is the key event that models the faith of Israel. Unless we begin from this central event, neither Israel's faith nor the formation of its religious traditions and sacred books are understandable.... The Exodus is established as a radical datum, exceedingly profound, in which both Israel and we ourselves must interpret God and ourselves. The Exodus becomes an inexhaustible "reservoir-of-meaning"... whence its unique hermeneutical possibilities for Latin American theology.[3]

Niebuhr's more conservative defense of American values represented an acceptance of the moral "ambiguity" that is required for power politics: "Let those who are revolted by such ambiguities have the decency and courtesy to retire to the monastery where medieval perfectionists found their asylum."[4] Such is the power of Exodus as a compelling biblical image in modern theological discourse. But it is our thesis that there is another biblical paradigm that presents the world with a far more radically subversive theology of action than Exodus.

Exodus is the road to nationalism and power. But there is another biblical paradigm. It is a warning against Exodus theology. In the place of Joshua the revolutionary conqueror, it points to Jeremiah the prophet of subversive righteousness and Ezra the priest of a radically alternative community. In the place of David the emperor, it points to Daniel the wise. In the place of Solomon's great Temple, it points to the perseverance of singing the Lord's song in a foreign land. It is a religion of the landless, the faith of those who dwell in Babylon.

The God of War

To construct a theology of exile, we must begin with the basic antagonism between the Semitic God as creator over against that which is created. Among the ancient Semitic myths, out of whose raw materials came the Hebraic refinement, there is the image of God as a warrior against chaos, historicized as the God of liberation against Egypt (Exod. 15). Thus the Hebraic view presents us with God over against creation. Between these two irreconcilable poles stands humanity, cursed with the "image of God" that casts it adrift between divinity and creation. Attempts to circumvent this state of being only result in the anger of God, who constantly calls humanity to rise above that which was not created in God's image, yet also demands that we remove our shoes when standing on holy ground. Attempts to identify too closely with creation — the constant temptation of pagan, agricultural religiosity (the attempt to find our home in creation) — leads to identification with a place, and thus to all the trappings of pagan nationalism, e.g., monarch, army, empire. All these ancient symbols have contemporary significance. But to worship the "God of War" is to worship in the context of a basic conflict, a basic antagonism between Creator (the call to what could be) and creation (that which merely is). If monarch, army, and empire are associated with a nation/creation ethos, worshipping the "God of War" is paradoxically an act of anti-militarism and anti-nationalism, because we do not identify too closely with any created place! For the faithful, this is a call to the "alienation" of the believer's hope over against an insipid reality. It is a call to a state of existential exile. As the modern Palestinian exile Edward Said has written:

> The exile knows that in a secular and contingent world, homes are always provisional. Borders and barriers, which enclose us within the safety of familiar territory, can also become prisons, and are often defended beyond reason or necessity. Exiles cross borders, break barriers of thought and experience.[5]

So the first image for a contemporary theology of exile is the realization that we are not "home," we live in Babylon. And the one who would be faithful to the creator God must resist the temptation to slip back into a modern "Ba'al" worship of a graven image: the nation-state, power over other humans, power from nature and creation.

> Now in Babylon you will see gods made of silver, of gold, of wood, being carried shoulder-high, and filling the gentiles with fear. Be on your guard! Do not imitate the foreigners, do not have any fear of their gods, as you see their worshippers prostrating themselves before and behind them. Instead, say in your hearts, "Master, it is you that we must worship." For my angel is with you; your lives will be in his care. (Baruch 6:3–6)

"Yet Awhile Longer . . .": Exile as Temporary

In writing about exile, Said quoted the view that national identities that are secure and grounded create the literature of epic, the affirmation of life as it is. The alienation of exile, however, creates the novel, the fictional dream world of what could be. Thus we become familiar with the archetype of the exile artist, who sees with a disenfranchised vision. Yet,

> to think of exile as beneficial, as a spur to humanism, or to creativity, is to belittle its mutilations. Modern exile is irremediably secular and unbearably historical. It is produced by human beings for other human beings; it has torn millions of people from the nourishment of tradition, family and geography.[6]

Similarly, to say that the *theological* state of the modern Christian is exile is not the same as saying that exile is good. To be exiled is to be away from home, but home does exist; for the Christian "home" is the promised Reign of God that was initiated, "planted," during Jesus' ministry. The temptation is to artificially end exile before God ends our exile. The temptation is to engage in the idolatry of Hananiah's false promise and to "re-enter history" with a share of worldly power. But whether Marxist or capitalist, the step into power is a step backward into paganism and its rituals. As we can easily see, this has its Jewish and Christian (as well as Islamic) versions. For this reason, the dissenters from Hananiah's nationalism — those who constantly see Babylon when commanded by their comrades to see the New Jerusalem — speak a language that in profound ways is a subversive "lingua franca." This can be illustrated very well by comparing the visions of two such dissenters. The first is Simon Dubnow, whom we have had occasion to cite earlier in this work.

Dubnow was a prominent Yiddishist and Jewish historian who inveighed against a militant Zionism (during its early theoretical formulations in Eastern Europe) that dreamed of power and political/military strength. In its place, Dubnow articulated a vision of Jewish "minority" existence that was redemptive, yet consciously rejecting the power of destruction. Dubnow's vision of autonomous minority existence was a call to live with integrity according to his profound spiritual vision of unity for a people. Although Dubnow's social and political views have not gained a large following in Jewish circles (nor is it my purpose to suggest that it should be embraced by modern Jews), his vision can provide significant and creative resources for the construction of a Christian theology of exile because of its roots in an "exilic" reading of ancient Jewish history:

> At the very moment when the strength and fertility of the Jewish mind reached the culminating point occurred a political revolution — the period of homeless wandering began. It seemed as though, before scattering the Jewish people to all ends of the earth, the providence of history desired to teach it a final lesson, to take with it on its way. It seemed to say, "Now you may go forth. Your character has been sufficiently tempered; you can bear the bitterest of hardships. You are equipped with an inexhaustible store of energy, and you can live for centuries, yea, for thousands of years, under conditions that would prove the bane of other nations in less than a single century. State, territory, army, the external attributes of national power, are for you superfluous luxury. Go out into the world to prove that a people can continue to live without these attributes, solely and alone through

strength of spirit welding its widely scattered particles into one firm organism" — and the Jewish people went out and proved it....

In its second half, the originality of Jewish history consists, indeed, in the circumstance that it is the only history stripped of every active political element. There are no diplomatic artifices, no wars, no campaigns, no unwarranted encroachments backed by armed force upon the rights of other nations, nothing of all that constitutes the chief content — the monotonous and for the most part idea-less content — of many other chapters in the history of the world.[7]

The second voice is John Howard Yoder, Mennonite theologian and social ethicist, who perhaps has most successfully given voice to the "minority," non-national Christian traditions otherwise known by a variety of names: the "Radical Reformation," the "Free Churches," or "Believers Churches" — Quakers, Mennonites, Church of the Brethren, Waldensians, Moravians, Molokans, etc. Yoder has given articulate voice to the meaning of a "dissenting theology." In writing about the "kingdom as a social ethic," Yoder emphasizes the power inherent in a minority community:

The believing community as an empirical social entity is a power for change. To band together in common dissidence provides a kind of social leverage which is not provided by any other social form. The subordinate community with its own internal covenants is able to provide economic and social as well as moral support to individuals standing with it against the stream who could not stand alone....

Dissenters support one another in opposition in such a way that their combined power of resistance is far more than the sum of the resistance potential of each member taken separately....

Popular education, institutionalized medicine, and the very concept of dialogical democracy in the Anglo-Saxon world generalize patterns which were first of all experimented with and made sense in a free-church Christianity....

The credibility and comprehensibility of an alternative vision which does not always convince on the part of an individual original or "prophetic" person, is enormously more credible and comprehensible if it is tested, confirmed, and practiced by a community....

It is the function of minority communities to remember and to create utopian visions. There is no hope for society without an awareness of transcendence.[8]

It does not require sophisticated analysis to see that the views of Dubnow and Yoder are rooted in the experience of faithful minorities and represent what we have called "Fourth World" perspectives. It is thus not surprising that many of the social mechanisms for survival that we saw in the exilic biblical literature can be expressed as positive theological values that are essential for the understanding of a contemporary theology of exile.

Violence and Nonviolence: Jeremiah vs. Hananiah

My kingdom is not of this world. If my kingdom were of this world, my men would have fought to prevent my being surrendered ... As it is, my kingdom does not belong here. (John 18:36–37)

For many of the early Christians, the refusal to commit murder was couched not so much in the language of "sacredness of human life" or an ancient "pacifism," but rather from a disengagement from an allegiance to the rule of "Babylon" — that is, any authority but Jesus.[9] This exilic ethic is echoed in the witness of eighteenth-century Church of the Brethren member John Naas, which can be compared to the third-century witness of Marcellus in Tangiers:

The king of Prussia to John Naas:
  "Why will you not enlist with me?"
  "Because," said he, "I have already, long ago, enlisted into one of the noblest and best of enrollments, and I would not, and indeed could not, become a traitor to him. . . . "
  "Why, to whom, then? Who is your captain?"
  "My captain," said, he, "Is the great Prince Immanuel, our Lord Jesus Christ. I have espoused his cause and therefore cannot, and will not, forsake him."[10]

Marcellus (298, Tangiers):
  After throwing down his soldier's belt in front of the legionary standards which were there at the time, he bore witness in a loud voice, "I am a soldier of Jesus Christ, the eternal king. From now I cease to serve your emperors and I despise the worship of your gods of wood and stone. . . . It is not fitting that a Christian, who fights for Christ his lord, should be a soldier according to the brutalities of this world."[11]

Dubnow, too, clearly saw the implication of his Jewish exilic ethics for the issue of violence:

There is absolutely no doubt that Jewish nationalism in essence has nothing in common with any tendency toward violence. As a spiritual or historical-cultural nation, deprived of any possibility of aspiring to political triumphs, of seizing territory by force or of subjecting other nations to cultural domination, it is concerned with only one thing: protecting its national individuality and safeguarding its autonomous development in all states everywhere in the Diaspora. It has no aggressive national aspirations even of the kind found among other peoples that lack political independence but live on their own soil and show the tendency to wipe out the national minorities living in their midst.... The Jewish nationality is an outstanding example of a collective individuality which protects itself against attacks from the outside but never stops to attack on its own and is not able to do so. A nationality of this kind manifests the highest sense of social justice, which demands that the equality of all nations be recognized as an equal right of all to defend themselves and their internal autonomous life.[12]

For Christians to reject the artificial Exodus, whether proclaimed by a new Moses or Marx, is to submit ourselves to living the true Reign that Jesus proclaimed — a Reign not yet fully arrived, yet beginning to be present and promised in its fulfillment.

To live as exiles, therefore, is to renounce violence. Indeed, nonviolence is an ethical value that has its roots in the Hebrew Scriptures, as illustrated in the exilic ethic preached by Jeremiah over against Hananiah, or Ezra's rejection of armed guards in favor of the protection of God (Ezra 8:21–23). But Hebraic nonviolence is not "passive-ism." Jeremiah was an activist who preached activism: Survive! Flourish! Do not decrease there! To be exiled from the future means to live with the promise, not the sword. But it still means to live and be effective — to be the constantly present, living critique. This is why the early Christians, though nonviolent, were otherwise decidedly "militaristic" in language, in social persistence, and in the realization that living in exile meant a kind of constant state of "mobilization" and identification with the cause of those who suffer.

Put on the full armor of God, so as to be able to resist the devil's tactics. For it is not against human enemies that we have to struggle, but against the principalities and the ruling forces who are masters of the darkness of this world, the spirits of evil in the heavens. That is why you must take up God's armor, or you will not be able to put up any resistance on the evil day, or stand your ground even though you exert yourselves to the full.

So stand your ground, with truth a belt around your waist, and uprightness a breastplate, wearing for shoes on your feet the eagerness to spread the gospel of peace, and always carrying the shield of faith so that you can use it to quench the burning arrows of the Evil One. And then you must take salvation as your helmet and the sword of the Spirit, that is, the word of God. (Eph. 6:14ff.)

This dialectic between an aggressive ethic and the refusal to use weapons is perhaps best expressed in the early Quaker image taken from Revelation: "the lamb's war." A modern theology of exile that incorporates "the lamb's war" would banish from Christian theological debate the notion that a nonviolent ethic is somehow "passive resignation." The German revolutionary theorist Kurt Hiller once wrote that at the moment he ejected the money changers from the Temple, Jesus exemplified true Hebraic nonviolence because "we don't have a pacifist harp to pluck, we instead have a pacifist hammer to swing"!

At its root, violence is a form of idolatry because it is an attempt to make Babylon into the New Jerusalem by means of our own strength. To worship a place, to give it our allegiance and reverence, when that place is not the Reign of God, is idolatry, and what passes for contemporary fundamentalist Americanism is simply one version.

Separation from the World: The Politics of Ezra

You know that among the gentiles those they call their rulers lord it over them, and their great men make their authority felt. Among you this is not to happen. No, anyone who wants to become great among you must be your servant, and anyone who wants to be first among you must be slave to all.... For the Son of man himself came not to be served but to serve, and to give his life as a ransom for many. (Mark 10:43ff.)

To be the church in Babylon will also involve an understanding of rituals of separation.

Do not model your behavior on the contemporary world, but let the renewing of your minds transform you, so that you may discern for yourselves what is the will of God. (Rom. 12:2)

Most contemporary Christians in the United States do not observe rituals of separation. The church's sacraments are rarely understood to be ritualized reminders of the difference between the Reign of Christ and the surrounding world.

There are traditions, however, that can remind modern Christians of separation. The Amish observance of simplicity, for example, can be seen either as nonsense in a materialist society where religiosity "sells" according to its promise of financial success, or as intentional resistance to such an ideology:

> In the type of technology they utilize and in the organizational innovations they have selectively introduced, the Amish have demonstrated a remarkable sensitivity to and control over the process of change.... The use of horses, kerosene lamps, and one-room schoolhouses cannot be explained as a repudiation of modernity. Nor does the use of unsophisticated technology indicate an absence of self-consciousness or an uncritical approach to existing social institutions. In fact, in the context of contemporary United States, its use represents the very essence of self-conscious choice.[13]

Observance of Kosher dietary laws in the Jewish Orthodox and Conservative traditions of Judaism, as well as Islamic laws of diet, can teach Christians something of living in Babylon. As the New Testament frequently indicates, the early Christian *partial* rejection of dietary laws (but only partial! see Acts 15:22ff.) did not immediately result in a breakdown of the consciousness of separation because of the nature of pre-Constantinian Roman society. Today our very inability to understand the purity worries of Ezra during the Exile reveals that we no longer live in a consciousness of Babylon. For minority Christian traditions, however, many of whom still have worries about "corruption from outside," "marrying outside the faith," etc., Ezra's concern is far more understandable. The conformist influence of homogenizing umbrella organizations like the National Association of Evangelicals on formerly prophetic, courageous movements like the Quakers and Mennonites is one of the saddest examples that we can cite in American church history. The cautious, sometimes even annoying, defensiveness of minority traditions has its understandable aspects. The challenge facing a theology of exile is to preserve integrity and unity without turning back the clock in a forced historicism on the one hand, or, on the other hand, allowing a kind of cultural/theological decimation from the majority culture. The theology of exile should embolden an intentional defensiveness, first by affirming the defensive instinct as appropriate theologically, then translating that defensive instinct into terms appropriate for modern Babylon and for the commands of the gospel to live an expression of God's love for the world. As Yoder states: "The reference to the 'radicals' of the early centuries is not made with a view to undoing the passage of time but with a view to properly reorienting our present movement forward in light of what we now know was wrong with the way we had been doing before."[14]

The prayer of Jesus was not that his followers would be removed from the world, but that they might be a faithful presence within it. For this, we need to regain a consciousness of being a people apart and will probably need to rethink our worship rituals in order to incorporate some consciousness of "difference" and "separation," or to put it more succinctly, nonconformity to the world. The maintenance of traditional rituals or cultural practices can be translated by means of a theology of exile so that their purpose is not confused. The purpose is not to separate the "pure" people from the "impure" people, but rather to maintain a nonconformity to the world *as the basis from which to work for change.* To be the presence of the Reign of Christ in the world requires that the Reign of Christ be clearly modelled and unique, or it offers nothing but a chaplaincy to the mundane. Theologically, this does not mean the maintenance of "quaint cultural traits" to entertain the tourists, but rather to maintain those profound insights into the nature of being exiles in Babylon that many of the minority non-state churches share. An excellent example is the Mennonite emphasis on the Eucharist as a communal reaffirmation of a unique life together, rather than a Protestant, individualized remembrance of Jesus in history — detached from contemporary significance.

The point of rituals of separation is that they must at the same time be rituals of preservation. At this point, then, the understanding of the minority "exile" churches provides a theological practice that has profound meaning for "Fourth World" peoples who live in similar sociological circumstances, e.g., American Indians, Vietnamese, Laotian and Cambodian immigrant societies.

The theology of exile affirms the separation from conformity, the preservation of culture in a minority, the unique needs of exiled or refugee peoples, in a manner that Exodus theology cannot understand.

The Rev. Lawrence Hart, who is both a Cheyenne peace chief and a Mennonite minister, is a modern example of one who understands this unity of purpose. It was the purpose of the Cheyenne "peace chief" to be the "Advocate" of peace and survival, often in defiance of more militant members of the warrior castes among the Cheyenne. Although their leadership in attempting to live at peace with the white settlers was often rewarded with martyrdom, Lawrence Hart repeats the creed of the Peace Chief to this day with great emotion and conviction:

If you see your mother or sister being harmed by someone, or if your son is killed in front of your tipi, you do not go and seek revenge; go and smoke the pipe, for you are a Cheyenne chief.[15]

To understand this as passivity, as "doing nothing," is to completely miss the point: "The entire focus of Cheyenne spiritual beliefs centers on the survival of the people as one unified whole."[16] The peace chief's creed was based on an ethic of survival and resistance to an ethic of militaristic bravado. Their role was to seek the end to any and all conflicts. In short, the Cheyenne peace chief's creed is the same as that of Jeremiah preaching to the exiles: Survive! Do not decrease!

The point is clear: A theology of Exodus has little meaning to Fourth World peoples who have no "promised land" to dwell in after escaping "pharaoh." What does Exodus mean for the Cheyenne, the Navajo, the Hopi, the Blackfoot...? But Babylon is an image understood only too well.

The Hope for an End: Living under the Altar

To live according to a theology of exile is to live "under the altar."

I saw underneath the altar the souls of all the people who had been killed on account of the word of God, for witnessing to it. They shouted in a loud voice, "Holy true Master, how much longer will you wait before you pass sentence and take vengeance for our death on the inhabitants of the earth? Each of them was given a white robe, and they were told to be patient for a little longer."
(Rev. 6:9–11)

The exiles in Babylon told the stories of heroes who eventually conquered, who lived through prison and the darkness to point the way for living in exile (Daniel did not conquer Babylon and reign himself; Joseph ruled under Pharaoh, similarly Mordecai; Esther became queen, but did not return to Palestine). So we too live with our "hero story" — the Resurrection of Jesus. Resurrection is the promise that we live "under the altar" — but that Babylon will fall. There is a clear similarity between the themes of the exile hero stories — Esther, Daniel and the Three, and Joseph — and the image of Jesus as the conquering "lamb" in Revelation. The notion of a sacrificial lamb as the conqueror contains precisely the same elements of identification, sociologically, with the condition of the readers, as the exile stories provided for the exiled Judeans.

The entire New Testament is written from the perspective of exile. As Knibb has written, the notion that the exile did not end as predicted (the "seventy years" of Jeremiah) persisted as a theological and sociological theme long after the conquest of the Western empire by the Persians and the subsequent return of the "sons of the Exile."[17] The symbol of exile remained a powerful image throughout the early New Testament era and provided the central image in the exile writings of the political prisoner on Patmos known to us only as "John."[18] Because of this, it can be argued that a "Fourth World" perspective is the one that provides the clearest insights into the conditions under which our Christian sacred writings were first written.

Structural Nonconformity

The theology of exile, finally, comes to terms with the actual form of being the people of God as itself of great significance. This can be exemplified in the early Quaker movement, where decision making was based on "seeking God's will through the sense of the meeting" as a whole, and not voting. The Quaker method, read sociologically, is based on the realization that "truth" can come from minorities of one or more, who otherwise would not have a voice against the majority will: "Let it not be so among you!..." So, too, with the leadership of women. Quakers recognized women as ministers of equal calling with men, based again on their community as a model of the nonconformed Reign of Christ wherein there is no "Jew or Greek, slave or free, male or female" (Gal. 3:28).

The church in Babylon needs to organize itself according to its vision and not according to models of patriarchal, majority, powerful domination. It will often seek communitarian models that facilitate its life together. Most such experiments evolved from the experimentation of the "exile" churches. As we have seen in our textual analysis, the "Citizen-Temple-Community" (Weinberg) that developed from the "sons of the Golah" was just such an alternative community.

To end where we began, it is clear that a theology of exile will be resisted by both the traditional Christian apologetics of power and the liberation theologians. What is not clear, however, is that these views have a monopoly on biblical paradigms for their theological formulations. Until we deal with the ethical/theological challenge that living in Babylon presents modern followers of Jesus, the biblical message in its entirety will not be represented in contemporary theological debate. For those whose liberation ethic is only *partially* derived from the gospel, the challenge remains — would a "Sermon on the Mount" politics inevitably require a minority existence? Does the gospel place us in the Fourth World?

Exodus is not the model for faithful obedience in the context of modern America with its appropriately pentagonal manifestations of power. Radical discipleship requires a more subversive theology for living in Babylon.

NOTES

1. See Suzuki's "The Ethnolinguistics of Japanese Americans in the Wartime Camps," *Anthropological Linguistics,* 18, no. 9 (December 1976).

2. See John Howard Yoder, "The Constantinian Sources of Western Social Ethics" and "The Kingdom as Social Ethic," *The Priestly Kingdom: Social Ethics as Gospel* (Notre Dame, 1984).

3. J. Severino Croatto, *Exodus: A Hermeneutics of Freedom* (Maryknoll, N.Y., 1981), pp. 12–13.

4. Quoted in Guenter Lewy, *Peace and Revolution* (Grand Rapids, 1988).

5. See Edward Said, "The Mind of Winter: Reflections on Life in Exile," *Harpers,* September 1984, pp. 49ff.

6. Ibid.

7. Simon Dubnow, *Nationalism and History,* ed. K. Pinson (New York, 1958, 1961), pp. 262–263.

8. Yoder, *The Priestly Kingdom,* pp. 91ff.

9. A frequently heard rejoinder to early Christian pacifism is that the early Christians did not reject military service because of "pacifism," but rather because of their resistance to idolatry and homage to Caesar; this reflects the inability to see these issues as integrally connected from the perspective of a theology of exile. This is typically an issue in the interpretation of Tertullian's viewpoint.

10. Rufus D. Bowman, *The Church of the Brethren and War, 1708–1941* (New York, 1971), p. 45.

11. Jean Michel Hornus, *It Is Not Lawful for Me to "Fight"* (Scottdale, Pa., 1980), p. 138.

12. Dubnow, *Nationalism and History,*, p. 97.

13. Marc Olson, "Modernity, the Folk Society and the Old Order Amish," *Rural Sociology,* 46, no. 2 (1981), p. 306.

14. Yoder, *The Priestly Kingdom,* p. 87.

15. Lawrence Hart et al., "The Cheyenne Way of Peace," photocopied manuscript from the author, Clinton, Okla.

16. Ibid. But see also Stan Hoig, *The Peace Chiefs of the Cheyenne* (Norman, Okla., 1980).

17. Michael Knibb, "The Exile in the Literature of the Intertestamental Period," *Heythrop Journal,* 27 (1976).

18. The comparison of the phrase "... on account of the Word of God ... " in Rev. 1:9, and again in 6:9, combined with the evidence of Roman exiling of political prisoners to Mediterranean islands (Tacitus, *Annals,* 3:68) leads me to agree with the tradition that "John" was a political prisoner on Patmos.

Bibliography

Aberle, D. "The Prophet Dance and Reaction to White Contact," *Southwestern Journal of Anthropology*, 15 (1959).

Abrahams, R. "Some Varieties of Heroes in America," *Journal of the Folklore Institute* (U.S.A.), 3 (1966).

Abu-Lughod, J. "Migrant Adjustment to City Life: The Egyptian Case," *American Journal of Sociology*, 67 (1962).

Ackroyd, P. "Studies in the Book of Haggai," *Journal of Jewish Studies* (Oxford), 2 (1951), and 3 (1952).

———. "Two Old Testament Historical Problems of the Early Persian Period," *Journal of Near Eastern Studies*, 17 (1958).

———. *Exile and Restoration*. London, 1968.

Adam, Barry. *The Survival of Domination*. New York, 1978.

Adams, Robert McC. "Strategies of Maximization, Stability, and Resilience in Mesopotamian Society, Settlement, and Agriculture," *Proceedings of the American Philosophical Society*, 122 (1978).

———. *Heartland of Cities: Surveys of Ancient Settlement and Land Use on the Central Floodplain of the Euphrates*. Chicago, 1981.

Aharoni, Y. *Excavations at Ramat Rahel*. Rome, 1962.

Albrecktson, B. "Studies in the Theology of the Book of Lamentations," *Studia Theologica Lundensia*, 21 (1963).

Albright, W. F. "The Ration Lists," *Biblical Archaeologist*, 5 (1942).

———. "The Nebuchadnezzar and Neriglissar Chronicles," *BASOR*, 143 (1956).

Alt, A. *Essays in Old Testament History and Religion*. Oxford, 1966 (from *Kleine Schriften zur Geschichte des Volkes Israel*. Munich, 1953).

Alt, A., Christensen, Götze, Grohmann, Kees, and Landsberger, eds. *Kulturgeschichte des Alten Orients*. Munich, 1933.

Armstrong, John. "Mobilized and Proletarian Diasporas," *American Political Science Review*, 70 (1976).

Auerbach, E. "Die Babylonische Datierung im Pentateuch und das Alter des Priester-Kodex," *Vetus Testamentum*, 2 (1952).

———. "Der Aufsteig der Priesterschaft zur Macht im Alten Israel," *Vetus Testamentum Congress Volume*. Bonn, 1962.

Ausubel, N., ed. *A Treasury of Jewish Folklore*. London, 1948.

Avigad, N. "A New Class of YEHUD Stamp," *Israel Exploration Journal*, 7 (1957).

————. "Bullae and Seals from a Post-Exilic Judean Archive," *Monographs of the Institute of Archaeology* (Jerusalem), 4 (1976).

Bach, R. "Bauen und Pflanzen," in R. Rendtorff and K. Koch, eds. *Studien zur Theologie der Alttestamentlichen Überlieferungen.* Berlin, 1961.

Baentsch, B. *Leviticus.* Handkommentar zum Alten Testament. Nowack, ed. Göttingen, 1903.

Balandier, G. "The Colonial Situation: A Theoretical Approach," in Wallerstein, ed. *Social Change and the Colonial Situation.* New York, London, 1951.

Baltzer, K. "Das Ende des Staates Juda und die Messias-Frage," in R. Rendtorff and K. Koch, eds. *Studien zur Theologie der Alttestamentlichen Überlieferungen.* Berlin, 1961.

Barkun, M. *Disaster and the Millennium.* New Haven, 1974.

Barth, Frederick. *Ethnic Groups and Boundaries: The Social Organization of Culture Difference.* Bergen, London, Oslo, 1969.

Baskauskas, Liucija. "The Lithuanian Refugee Experience and Grief," *International Migration Review,* 15 (1981).

Batton, L. *Ezra and Nehemiah.* International Critical Commentary. Edinburgh, 1913.

Bea, A. "König Jojachin in Keilschrifttexten," *Biblica,* 23 (1942).

Begrich, J. "Die priesterliche Tora," in Volz, Stummer, and Hempel, eds. *Werden und Wesen des Alten Testaments.* Beihefte zur Zeitschrift für die Alttestamentliche Wissenschaft, 66. Berlin, 1936.

Bendix, Richard. *Max Weber: An Intellectual Portrait.* London, 1962.

Bendor, Zvi. "The Israelite Bet 'Ab from the Settlement to the End of the Monarchy." English summary of Hebrew dissertation at Hebrew University. Jerusalem, 1982.

Benzinger, I. *Die Bücher der Könige.* Kurzer HandKommentar zum Alten Testament. Marti, ed. Freiburg, 1899.

Ben-Zvi, I. *The Exiled and the Redeemed.* London, 1958.

Berger, Peter, and Thomas Luckmann. *The Social Construction of Reality.* London, 1967.

Berry, G. R. "Was Ezekiel in the Exile?" *Journal of Biblical Literature,* 49 (1930).

————. "The Unrealistic Attitude of Post-Exilic Judaism," *Journal of Biblical Literature,* 64 (1945).

Beyse, K. M. *Serubbabel und die Königserwartungen der Propheten Haggai und Sacharja.* Stuttgart, 1972.

Bickerman, E. "The Edict of Cyrus in Ezra," in *Studies in Jewish and Christian History.* Part 1. Leiden, 1976.

Bleicher, Josef. *Contemporary Hermeneutics: Hermeneutics as Method, Philosophy and Critique.* London, 1980.

Bloomhardt, Paul F. "The Poems of Haggai," *Annual of the Hebrew Union College* (Cincinnati), 5 (1928).

Bogaert, P.-M., ed. *Le Livre de Jeremie.* Leuven, 1981.

Bonnell, V. "The Uses of Theory, Concepts, and Comparison in Historical Sociology," *Comparative Studies in Society and History,* 22 (1980).

Boskoff, A., and W. Cahnman. *Sociology and History.* New York, 1964.

Bowman, J. *Samaritanische Probleme Studien zum Verhältnis von Samaritanser-tum, Judentum and Urchristentum.* Stuttgart, 1967.

Brass, P. R. "Ethnicity and Nationality Formation," *Ethnicity*, 3 (1976).

Brenner, E. "To Pray or to Be Prey: That is the Question — Strategies for Cultural Autonomy of Massachusetts Praying Town Indians," *Ethnohistory*, 27 (1980).

Bretan, R. "Institutional Completeness of Ethnic Communities and the Personal Relations of Immigrants," *American Journal of Sociology*, 70 (1965).

———. "Impelled Group Migration: Minority Struggle to Maintain Institutional Completeness," *International Migration Review*, 23 (1973).

Bright, John. *A History of Israel.* 3rd ed. Philadelphia, 1981.

———. *Jeremiah.* The Anchor Bible. New York, 1981.

Brinkman, J. A. *A Political History of Post-Kassite Babylonia, 1158–722 B.C.* Analecta Orientalia 43, Rome.

———. "Merodach Baladan II," in *Studies Presented to Leo Oppenheim.* Chicago, 1964.

Brockington, L. H. *Ezra, Nehemiah and Esther.* Century Bible. London, 1969.

Brody, Eugene, ed. *Behaviour in New Environments: Adaptation of Migrant Populations.* Newbury Park, Calif., 1969–70.

Brown, P. "Enemies and Affines," *Ethnology*, 3 (1964).

Brownlee, W. H. "Ezekiel's Poetic Indictment of the Shepherds," *Harvard Theological Review*, 51 (1958).

———"The Aftermath of the Fall of Judah According to Ezekiel," *Journal of Biblical Literature*, 89 (1970).

Brueggemann, W. "The Kerygma of the Priestly Writers," *Zeitschrift für die Alttestamentliche Wissenschaft* (Berlin), 84 (1972).

———. "Jeremiah's Use of Rhetorical Questions," *Journal of Biblical Literature*, 92 (1973).

Carmichael, C. *The Laws of Deuteronomy.* Los Angeles, 1974.

Carroll, R. P. *When Prophecy Failed.* New York, 1979.

———. *From Chaos to Covenant: Uses of Prophecy in the Book of Jeremiah.* London, 1981.

Caulfield, M. D. "Culture and Imperialism: Proposing a New Dialectic," in Dell Hymes, ed. *Reinventing Anthropology,* New York, 1974.

Claburn, W. E. "The Fiscal Basis of Josiah's Reforms," *Journal of Biblical Literature*, 92 (1973).

Clastres, Pierre. *Society against the State.* New York, 1974.

Clements, R. E. "The Prophecies of Isaiah and the Fall of Jerusalem," *Vetus Testamentum*, 30 (1980).

Clemmer, R. O. "Truth, Duty and Revitalization of Anthropologists: A New Perspective on Cultural Change and Resistance," in Dell Hymes, ed. *Reinventing Anthropology.* New York, 1974.

Cody, A. *A History of Old Testament Priesthood.* Analecta Biblica, 35. Rome, 1969.

Cogan, M. *Imperialism and Religion.* Chico, Calif., 1974.

———. "Israel in Exile: The View of a Josianic Historian," *Journal of Biblical Literature*, 97 (1978).

Coggins, R. J. *Samaritans and Jews: The Origins of Samaritanism Reconsidered.* Oxford, 1975.

Cohen, A. *Urban Ethnicity.* London, 1974.

Cohen, E. "Expatriate Communities," *Current Sociology,* 24 (1977).

Cohen, Naomi. "Jewish Names as Cultural Indicators in Antiquity," *Journal for the Study of Judaism,* 7 (1976–77).

Cohen, R. "Ethnicity: Problem and Focus in Anthropology," *Annual Review of Anthropology,* 7 (1978).

Collins, J. J. "The Court-Tales in Daniel and the Development of Apocalyptic," *Journal of Biblical Literature,* 94 (1975).

——. *The Apocalyptic Visions of the Book of Daniel.* Chico, Calif., 1977.

Coogan, M. D. "Life in the Diaspora," *Biblical Archaeologist,* 37 (1974).

——. *West Semitic Personal Names in the Murashu Documents.* Chico, Calif., 1976.

Cook, J. M. *The Persian Empire.* London, 1983.

Cornell, J. B. "Ainu Assimilation and Cultural Extinction: Acculturation Policy in Hokkaido," *Ethnology,* 3 (1964).

Coser, Lewis. "The Alien as a Servant of Power: Court Jews and Christian Renegades," *American Sociological Review,* 37 (1972).

Crenshaw, J. *Prophetic Conflict: Its Effect upon Israelite Religion.* Beihefte zur Zeitschrift für die Alttestamentliche Wissenschaft. Berlin, 1971.

Cross, F. M. "A Reconstruction of the Judean Restoration," *Journal of Biblical Literature,* 94 (1975).

Curtiss, Samuel Ives. *Primitive Semitic Religion Today.* Chicago, 1902.

Daiches, S. *The Jews in Babylonia in the Time of Ezra and Nehemiah according to Babylonian Inscriptions.* London, 1912.

Dandamayev, M. A. "Social Stratification in Babylonia (7th–4th Centuries B.C.)," in Harmatta and Komoroczy, eds. *Wirtschaft und Gesellschaft im Alten Vorderasien.* Budapest, 1976.

——. "State and Temple in Babylonia in the First Millennium B.C.," *State and Temple Economy in the Ancient Near East,* ed. E. Lipinski, Orientalia Lovaniensia Analecta 6 (1979).

——. "The Neo-Babylonian Citizens," *KLIO,* 63 (1981).

——. "The Neo-Babylonian Elders," in *Societies and Languages of the Ancient Near East.* Wiltshire, 1982.

Daniels, Roger. *Concentration Camps USA: Japanese Americans in World War II.* New York, 1971.

Davidson, R. "Orthodoxy and the Prophetic Word," *Vetus Testamentum,* 14 (1964).

Davies, P. R. "Daniel Chapter Two," *Journal of Theological Studies* (Oxford, London), 27 (1976).

Davies, W. D., and L. Finkelstein, eds. *The Cambridge History of Judaism,* vol. 1, *The Persian Period.* Cambridge, 1984.

Day, John. "The Daniel of Ugarit and Ezekiel and the Hero of the Book of Daniel," *Vetus Testamentum,* 30 (1980).

Demsky, A. "Pelekh in Nehemiah 2," *Israel Exploration Journal,* 33 (1983).

Despres, Leo, ed. *Ethnicity and Resource Competition in Plural Societies.* Paris, The Hague, 1975.

Douglas, Mary. *Purity and Danger.* London, 1966.

──── . *Implicit Meanings.* London, 1975.

Driver, S. R. *Introduction to the Literature of the Old Testament.* Edinburgh, 1891.

──── . *The Book of the Prophet Jeremiah.* London, 1906.

Dubnow, S. *History of the Jews: From the Beginning to Early Christianity.* New York, 1967.

Duhm, B. *Das Buch Jeremia.* Kurzer Handkommentar zum Alten Testament. Tübingen, 1901.

Eaton, J. H. *Festal Drama in Deutero-Isaiah.* London, 1979.

Eichenbaum, J. "A Matrix of Human Movement," *International Migration,* 13 (1975).

Einzig, P. *Primitive Money in Its Ethnological, Historical and Economic Aspects.* London, 1949.

Eisenstadt, S. "Paralleleinblicke in das jüdische und römische Familien und Erbrecht," *KLIO,* 40 (1962).

──── . "The Format of Jewish History: Some Reflections on Weber's Ancient Judaism," *Modern Judaism,* 1 (1981).

Eissfeldt, O. *Introduction to the Old Testament.* Oxford, 1965.

Elat, M. "The Monarchy and the Development of Trade in Ancient Israel," in *State and Temple Economy in the Ancient Near East,* E. Lipinski, ed. Orientalia Lovaniensia Analecta 6 (1979).

Elliger, K. *Leviticus Handbuch zum Alten Testament,* vol. 4. Tübingen, 1966.

──── . "Sinn und Ursprung der Priesterlichen Geschichtserzählung," *Kleine Schriften zum Alten Testament.* Munich, 1966.

──── . *Die Propheten Nahum, Habakuk, Zephanja, Haggai, Sacharja, Maleachi.* Alte Testament Deutsch. Göttingen, 1967.

Elliot-Binns, L. E. "Some Problems of the Holiness Code," *Zeitschrift für die Alttestamentliche Wissenschaft* (Berlin), 67 (1955).

Eph'al, I. "The Western Minorities in Babylonia in the 6th–5th Centuries BC: Maintenance and Cohesion," *Orientalia,* NS, 47 (1978).

──── . "On Warfare and Military Control in the Ancient Near Eastern Empires: A Research Outline," in C. Tadmor and M. Weinfeld, eds. *History, Historiography, and Interpretation: Studies in Biblical and Cuneiform Literatures.* Jerusalem, 1983.

Epstein, A. L. *Ethos and Identity: Three Studies in Ethnicity.* London, 1978.

Evans, C. D. "Judah's Foreign Policy from Hezekiah to Josiah," *Scripture in Context.* W. W. Hallo et al., eds. Pittsburgh, 1980.

Evans, G. "Ancient Mesopotamian Assemblies," *Journal of the American Oriental Society* (New Haven), 78 (1958).

──── . " 'Gates' and 'Streets': Urban Institutions in Old Testament Times," *Journal of Religious History,* 2 (1962–63).

Fernea, R. A., and James Malarkey. "Anthropology of the Middle East and North Africa," *Annual Review of Anthropology,* 4 (1975).

Feucht, Christian. *Untersuchungen zum Heiligkeitsgesetz.* Berlin, 1964.

Flaschberger, E. "The Marginal Man and His Marginal Attitude," *Research Group for European Migration Problems*, 10 (1962).

Foerster, W. *From the Exile to Christ.* Philadelphia, 1964.

Fohrer, G. *Introduction to the Old Testament.* London, 1970.

———. *History of Israelite Religion.* London, 1973.

Forster, P. "Empiricism and Imperialism: A Review of the New Left Critique of Social Anthropology," *Anthropology and the Colonial Encounter.* Talal Asad, ed. London, 1973.

Foster, B., and G. White. "Ethnic Identity and Perceived Distance between Ethnic Categories," *Human Organization*, 41 (1981).

Francis, E. K. *Interethnic Relations: An Essay in Sociological Theory.* Oxford and Amsterdam, 1976.

Franklin, J. H. *From Slavery to Freedom: A History of Negro Americans.* New York, 1969.

Freedman, D. N. "The Prayer of Nabonidus," *BASOR*, 145 (1957).

———. "The Chronicler's Purpose," *Catholic Biblical Quarterly*, 23 (1961).

———. "Son of Man, Can These Bones Live?" *Interpretation*, 29 (1975).

Fretheim, T. "The Priestly Document: Anti-Temple?" *Vetus Testamentum*, 18 (1968).

Freydank, H. "Die Rolle der Deportierten im Mittelassyrischen Staat," in J. Hermann and I. Sellnow, eds. *Die Rolle der Volksmassen in der Geschichte der Vorkapitalistischen Gesellschaftsformation.* Berlin, 1975.

Frost, S. B. "The Death of Josiah: A Conspiracy of Silence," *Journal of Biblical Literature*, 87 (1968).

Frymer-Kensky, T. "Pollution, Purification and Purgation in Biblical Israel," *The Word of the Lord Shall Go Forth.* Winona Lake, 1983.

Funck, B. "Zur Burger-Tempel-Gemeinde im nachexilischen Juda" (review of Kreissig), *KLIO*, 59 (1977).

Gadd, C. J. "The Harran Inscriptions of Nabonidus," *Anatolian Studies*, 8 (1958).

Galling, K. *Studien zur Geschichte Israels im Persischen Zeitalter.* Tübingen, 1964.

———. "The 'Gola-List' According to Ezra 2 ‖ Neh. 7," *Journal of Biblical Literature*, 70 (1971).

Gammie, John G. "On the Intention and Sources of Daniel 1–6," *Vetus Testamentum*, 31 (1981).

Geertz, C., ed. *Old Societies and New States.* New York, 1963.

Gese, Hermut. "Der Verfassungsentwurf des Ezechiel Kap. 40–48," *Beiträge zur historischen Theologie*, 25. Tübingen, 1957.

Giesebrecht, F. *Das Buch Jeremia*, 2nd ed. Handkommentar zum Alten Testament. Göttingen, 1907.

Ginsberg, H. L. *Studies in Daniel.* New York, 1948

———. "The Composition of the Book of Daniel," *Vetus Testamentum*, 4 (1954).

Gispen, W. H. "The Distinction between Clean and Unclean," *Oudtestamentische Studien*, 5 (1948).

Glazer, N., and D. Moynihan, *Ethnicity.* New Haven, 1975.

Goiten, S. *In the Land of Sheba.* New York, 1947.

Goldberg, H. "The Mimuna and the Minority Status of Moroccan Jews" *Ethnology,* vol. 17 (1978).

Gordis, R. "Democratic Origins in Ancient Israel: The Biblical 'Edah,' " *Alexander Marx Jubilee Volume,* JTS. New York, 1950.

Gordon, C. *Ugaritic Literature.* Rome, 1949.

———. "The Origin of the Jews in Elephantine" *Journal of Near Eastern Studies,* 14 (1955).

———. *The World of the Old Testament.* London, 1960.

Gordon, Cyrus. "Colonies and Enclaves," *Studi Orientalistici in onore di Giorgio Levi Della Vida.* Rome, 1956.

Gottwald, Norman K. *Studies in the Book of Lamentations.* London, 1954.

———. " 'Holy War' in Deuteronomy: Analysis and Critique," *Review and Expositor,* 56 (1964).

———. *The Tribes of Yahweh,* Maryknoll, N.Y., 1979.

———, ed. *The Bible and Liberation.* Maryknoll, N.Y., 1983.

Gould, R. "Indian and White Versions of the 'Burnt Ranch Massacre,' " *Journal of the Folklore Institute* (U.S.A.), 3 (1966).

Gowan, D. "The Beginnings of Exile Theology and the Root GLH," *Zeitschrift für die Alttestamentliche Wissenschaft* (Berlin), 87 (1975).

Graburn, N.H.H. *Ethnic and Tourist Arts: Cultural Expressions from the Fourth World.* Los Angeles, 1976.

Graham, J. N. "Vinedressers and Plowmen," *Biblical Archaeologist,* March 1984.

Grayson, A. K. *Assyrian and Babylonian Chronicles.* New York, 1975.

Grintz, Jehoshua. "Do Not Eat on the Blood," *Annual of the Swedish Theological Institute,* 13 (1970–71).

Gunneweg, A.H.J. "Am H'Aretz: A Semantic Revolution," *Zeitschrift für die Alttestamentliche Wissenschaft* (Berlin), 95 (1983).

Gurewicz, S. B. "The Deuteronomic Provisions for Exemption from Military Service," *Australian Biblical Review,* 6 (1958).

Hammerscheib, E. "Ezekiel's View of the Monarchy," *Studia Orientalia Ioanni Pedersen.* 1953.

Handleman, D. "The Organization of Ethnicity," *Ethnic Groups,* 1 (1976).

Hansen, Holgar. *Ethnicity and Military Rule in Uganda.* Scandinavian Institute of African Studies, Report no. 43. Upsalla, 1977.

Hanson, Paul. *The Dawn of Apocalyptic.* Philadelphia, 1975.

Haran, M. " 'Shiloh and Jerusalem': The Origin of the Priestly Tradition in the Pentateuch," *Journal of Biblical Literature,* 81 (1962).

———. "The Law Code of Ezekiel 40–48 and Its Relation to the Priestly School," *Annual of the Hebrew Union College* (Cincinnati), 50 (1979).

Harmatta, J. "The Literary Patterns of the Babylonian Edict of Cyrus," *Acta Antiqua,* 19 (1971).

———. "The Rise of the Old Persian Empire: Cyrus the Great," *Acta Antiqua,* 19 (1971).

Hasel, G. *"The Remnant": The History and Theology of the Remnant Idea from Genesis to Isaiah.* Berrien Springs, Mich., 1972.

Hayes, J. H. "The Tradition of Zion's Inviolability," *Journal of Biblical Literature,* 82 (1963).

Hechter, M. *Internal Colonialism: The Celtic Fringe in British National Development, 1536–1966.* Los Angeles and Berkeley, 1975.

Helm, H. *Essays on the Problem of Tribe.* Proceedings of the 1967 Annual Spring Meetings of the American Ethnological Society. Seattle, 1968.

Herr, M. D. "The Historical Significance of the Dialogues between Jewish Sages and Roman Dignitaries," *Scripta Hierosolymitana,* 22 (1971).

Herrmann, S. *A History of Israel in Old Testament Times.* 2nd ed. London, 1975.

Hill, Ch. R. *Bantustans: The Fragmentation of South Africa.* London, 1964.

Holladay, W. L. "A Fresh Look at 'Source B' and 'Source C' in Jeremiah," *Vetus Testamentum,* 25 (1974).

———. "God Writes a Rude Letter (Jeremiah 29:1–23)," *Biblical Archaeologist,* 1983.

Hölscher, G. "Die Entstehung des Buches Daniel," *Theologische Studien und Kritiken,* 92 (1919).

Humphreys, W. L. "A Lifestyle for Diaspora: A Study of the Tales of Esther and Daniel," *Journal of Biblical Literature,* 92 (1973).

Hurvitz, Avi. "The Evidence of Language in Dating the Priestly Code," *Revue Biblique,* 81 (1974).

Hyatt, J. P. "Jeremiah and Deuteronomy," *Journal of Near Eastern Studies,* 1 (1942).

———. "Jeremiah and War," *Crozer Quarterly,* 20 (1943).

Hymes, Dell, ed. *Reinventing Anthropolgy.* New York, 1974.

Irwin, William. "Ezekiel Research since 1943," *Vetus Testamentum,* 3 (1953).

Ishida, Tomoo. "The People of the Land and the Political Crisis in Judah," *The Annual of the Japanese Biblical Institute.* Sekine and Satake, ed. Tokyo, 1975.

Ivry, Alfred. "Nehemiah 6,10: Politics and the Temple," *Journal for the Study of Judaism,* 3 (1972).

Jacobsen, T. "Primitive Democracy in Ancient Mesopotamia," *Journal of Near Eastern Studies,* 11 (1943).

James, E.O. *The Old Testament in the Light of Anthropology.* London, 1935.

Janssen, Enno. *Juda in der Exilszeit.* Göttingen, 1956.

Japhet, Sara. "The Supposed Common Authorship of Chronicles and Ezra-Nehemiah Investigated Anew," *Vetus Testamentum,* 18 (1968).

———. "People and Land in the Restoration Period," in *Das Land Israel in biblischer Zeit.* Göttingen, 1981.

———. "Sheshbazzar and Zerubbabel," *Zeitschrift für die Alttestamentliche Wissenschaft* (Berlin), 94 (1982), and 95 (1983).

Jones, D. R. "The Cessation of Sacrifice after the Destruction of the Temple in 586 B.C.," *Journal of Theological Studies* (Oxford, London), 14 (1963).

Jorgenson, J. G. *The Sun Dance Religion: Power for the Powerless.* Chicago and London, 1972.

Kaiser, O. *Der königliche Knecht.* Göttingen, 1959.

———. *Introduction to the Old Testament.* Oxford, 1975.

Kapelrud, A. "The Date of the Priestly Code (P)," *Annual of the Swedish Theological Institute,* 3 (1964).

———. "The Identity of the Suffering Servant," *Near Eastern Studies in Honor of W. F. Albright*. Goedicke, ed. Baltimore, 1971.

Kashima, Tetsuden. "Japanese-American Internees Return, 1945–1955: Readjustment and Social Amnesia," *Phylon*, 41 (1980).

Katzir, Y. "Preservation of Jewish Identity in Yemen: Segregation and Integration as Boundary Maintenance Mechanisms," *Comparative Studies in Society and History*, 24 (1982).

Kaufmann, Y. *The Religion of Israel from Its Beginning to the Babylonian Exile*. Chicago, 1949.

Kayal, Philip. "Religion and Assimilation: Catholic Syrians in America," *International Migration Review*, 7 (1973).

Kehnscherper, G. "Der 'Sklave Gottes' bei Deuterojesaja," *Forschungen und Fortschritte*, 40. Berlin, 1966.

Kellerman, Ulrich. *Nehemia: Quellen, Überlieferung, und Geschichte*. Beihefte zur Zeitschrift für die Alttestamentliche Wissenschaft, 102. Berlin, 1967.

Keyes, Charles. "Towards a New Formulation of the Concept of Ethnic Group," *Ethnicity*, 3 (1976).

———, ed. *Ethnic Adaptation and Identity*. New York, 1979.

Kiernan, J. P. "Where Zionists Draw the Line: A Study of Religious Exclusiveness in an African Township," *African Studies*, 33 (1974).

Kilian, R. *Literarkritische und Formgeschichtliche Untersuchungen des Heiligkeitsgesetzes*. Bonner Biblische Beitrag. Bonn, 1963.

———. "Die Priesterschrift Hoffnung auf Heimkehr," *Wort und Botschaft*. J. Schreiner, ed. Würzburg, 1967.

Kippenberg, H. G. *Religion und Klassenbildung im antiken Judäa: Eine religionssoziologische Studie zum Verhältnis von Tradition und gesellschaftlicher Entwicklung*. Göttingen, 1978.

Kitagawa, Daisuke. *Issei and Nisei: The Internment Years*. New York, 1967.

Kitano, H. L. *Japanese-Americans: The Evolution of a Sub-Culture*. New York, 1969.

Klapp, Orrin E. "The Clever Hero," *JAF*, 67 (1954).

Klausner, J. *The Messianic Idea in Israel*. London, 1956.

Klein, R. "Old Readings in 1 Esdras: The List of Returnees from Babylon," *Harvard Theological Review*, 62 (1969).

Knibb, Michael. "The Exile in the Literature of the Intertestamental Period," *Heythrop Journal*, 27 (1976).

Knobel, A. *Der Prophet Jesaia Erklärt*. Diestal, ed. Leipzig, 1872.

Koch, K. "Haggais unreines Volk," *Zeitschrift für die Alttestamentliche Wissenschaft* (Berlin), 79 (1967).

———. "Ezra and the Origins of Judaism," *Journal of Semitic Studies* (Manchester), 19 (1974).

———. *Die Priesterschrift von Ex. 25 bis Lev. 16: Eine Überleiferungsgeschichtliche und literarkritische Untersuchung*. Göttingen, 1959.

König, R. *The Exiles Book of Consolation contained in Isaiah 40–66*. Edinburgh, 1899.

Kopytoff, Igor. "Slavery," in *Annual Review of Anthropology*. Beals, Speigal, Tyler, eds. Palo Alto, Calif., 1982.

Kornfeld, W. *Studien zum Heiligkeitsgesetz Lev. 17–26.* Vienna, 1952.

Kraeling, E. *The Brooklyn Museum Aramaic Papyri.* New Haven, 1953.

Kreissig, H. *Die Sozialen Zusammenhänge des Judaischen Krieges.* Berlin, 1970.

———. "Problem der Sozialökonomischen Struktur Judas vom 6. Jahrhundert v.u.z. bis zum 1. Jahrhundert v.u.z.," *Jahrbuch für Wirtschaftsgeschichte,* 1 (1973).

———. *Die Sozialökonomische Situation in Juda zur Achamenidenzeit.* Schriften zur Geschichte und Kultur des Alten Orients 7. Berlin, 1973.

Kuenen, A. *The Prophets and Prophecy in Israel: A Historical and Critical Enquiry.* London, 1877.

———. "Die Chronologie des persischen Zeitalters der jüdischen Geschichte," *Gesammelte Abhandlungen zur Biblischen Wissenschaft von Dr. Abraham Kuenen.* Freiburg, 1894.

Külling, S. *Zur Datierung der "Genesis P Stücke."* Kampen, 1964.

Kunz, E. "The Refugee in Flight: Kinetic Models and Forms of Displacement," *International Migration Review,* 7 (1973).

———. "Exile and Resettlement: Refugee Theory," *International Migration Review,* 15 (1981).

Kuschke, A. "Arm und Reich im Alten Testament mit besonderer Berücksichtigung der nachexilischen Zeit," *Zeitschrift für die Alttestamentliche Wissenschaft* (Berlin), 57 (1939–40).

———. "Die Lagervorstellung der priesterschriftlichen Erzählung," *Zeitschrift für die Alttestamentliche Wissenschaft* (Berlin), 63 (1951).

———, ed. *Verbannung und Heimkehr: Beiträge zur Geschichte und Theologie Israels im 6. und 5. Jahrhundert v. Chr.* Tübingen, 1961.

Kutsch, E. "Das Jahr der Katastrophe: 587 v. Chr.," *Biblica,* 55 (1974).

LaBarre, W. *The Ghost Dance.* London, 1972.

Lambert, W. G. "The Reign of Nebuchadnezzar I: A Turning Point in the History of Ancient Mesopotamian Religion." *The Seed of Wisdom.* McCullough, ed. Toronto, 1964.

———. "Nebuchadnezzar, King of Justice," *Iraq,* 27 (1965).

Lang, B. *Kein Aufstand in Jerusalem Die Politik des Propheten Ezechiel.* Stuttgart, 1981.

———. *Monotheism and the Prophetic Minority: An Essay in Biblical History and Sociology.* Sheffield, 1983.

Langdon, S. *Building Inscriptions of the Neo-Babylonian Empire.* Paris, 1905.

Lanternari, V. *The Religions of the Oppressed.* New York, 1963.

———. "Nativistic and Socio-Religious Movements: A Reconsideration," *Comparative Studies in Society and History,* 16 (1974).

Larsen, Mogens Trolle. "Power and Propaganda: A Symposium on Ancient Empires," *Mesopotamia,* Copenhagen Studies in Assyriology, vol. 7 (1979).

Lee, Russell D., and Donald E. Gelfand. *Ethnic Conflicts and Power.* New York, 1973.

Leuze, O. *Die Satrapieneinteilung in Syrien und in Zweistromlande von 520–320.* Halle, 1935.

Levenson, J. D. *Theology of the Program of Restoration of Ezekiel 40–48.* Chico, Calif., 1976.

Levine, Baruch. "The Netinim," *Journal of Biblical Literature*, 82 (1963).

Lewis, B. *The Sargon Legend.* Cambridge, Mass., 1980.

Lewy, G. "The Late Assyro-Babylonian Cult of the Moon and Its Culmination at the Time of Nabonidus," *Annual of the Hebrew Union College* (Cincinnati), 19 (1949).

Lieberson, S. "A Societal Theory of Race and Ethnic Relations," *American Sociological Review*, 26 (1961).

Lifton, R. J. *Death in Life: The Survivors of Hiroshima.* London, 1967.

Linton, R. "Nativistic Movements," *American Anthropologist*, 45 (1943).

Loader, J. "The Exilic Period in Abraham Kuenen's Account of Israelite Religion," *Zeitschrift für die Alttestamentliche Wissenschaft* (Berlin), 96 (1984).

Lombardi, Luigi. "Folklore as Culture of Contestation," *Journal of the Folklore Institute* (U.S.A.), 11 (1974).

McClellan, G. S. ed. *Southern Africa.* Portland, Ore., n.d.

Macdonald, J. S. "Chain Migration, Ethnic Neighborhood Formation, and Social Networks," *The Milbank Memorial Fund Quarterly*, 92 (1964).

McEvenue, S. E. "The Political Structure in Judah from Cyrus to Nehemiah," *Catholic Biblical Quarterly*, 43 (1981).

McKay, John. *Religion in Judah under the Assyrians.* SBT 26. London, 1973.

McKenzie, J. L. "The Elders in the Old Testament," *Analecta Biblica*, 10 (1959).

Macleod, W. C. "The Origin of Servile Labor Camps," *American Anthropologist*, 31 (1929).

MacWhite, E. "On the Interpretation of Archaeological Evidence in Historical and Sociological Terms," *American Anthropologist*, 58 (1956).

Makabe, Tomoko. "Canadian Evacuation and Nisei Identity," *Phylon*, 41 (1980).

Malamat, A. "The Last Wars of the Kingdom of Judah," *Journal of Near Eastern Studies*, 9 (1950).

———. "Jeremiah and the Last Two Kings of Judah," *Palestine Exploration Quarterly* (London), (1951).

———. "Megiddo, 609 B.C.: The Conflict Re-Examined," *Acta Antiqua*, 22 (1974).

———. "The Twilight of Judah," *Vetus Testamentum Congress Volume*, 28 (1974).

Mannoni, Dominique O. *Prospero and Caliban: The Psychology of Colonization.* London, 1964.

Mantel, Hugo D. "The Dichotomy of Judaism During the Second Temple," *Annual of the Hebrew Union College* (Cincinnati), 44 (1973).

Margaliot, M. "Jeremiah 10:1–16: A Re-Examination," *Vetus Testamentum*, 30 (1980).

Mason, R. "The Relation of Zechariah 9:14 to Proto-Zechariah," *Zeitschrift für die Alttestamentliche Wissenschaft* (Berlin), 88 (1976).

Maunier, R. *The Sociology of Colonies: An Introduction to the Study of Race Contact.* London, 1949.

May, H. G. " 'This People' and 'This Nation' in Haggai," *Vetus Testamentum*, 18 (1968).

Meinhold, A. "Die Diasporanovelle: Eine Alttestamentliche Gattung." Unpublished doctoral dissertation. Greifswald, 1969 (see *Zeitschrift für die Alttestamentliche Wissenschaft* (Berlin), 1975–1976).

Memmi, A. *The Colonizer and the Colonized*. London, 1969.

Mendels, D. "Hecataeus of Abdera and a Jewish 'patrios politeia' of the Persian Period," *Zeitschrift für die Alttestamentliche Wissenschaft* (Berlin), 95 (1983).

Mendelsohn, I. "Samuel's Denunciation of Kingship in the Light of the Akkadian Documents from Ugarit," *BASOR*, 143 (1956).

Merton, R. K. *Social Theory and Social Structure*. New York, London, 1978.

Meshorer, Ya'Akov. *Ancient Jewish Coinage*. New York, 1982.

Mettinger, T.N.D. "A Farewell to the Servant Songs: A Critical Examination of an Exegetical Axiom," *Scripta Minora*. Lund, 1983

Meyer, E. *Die Entstehung des Judentums: Eine Historische Untersuchung*. Halle, 1896.

———. *Der Papyrusfund von Elephantine*. Leipzig, 1912.

Mildenberg, Leo. "YEHUD: A Preliminary Study of the Provincial Coinage of Judea," in *Greek Numismatics and Archaeology*. Morkholm, ed. 1979.

Milik, J. T. "Priere de Nabonide," *Revue Biblique*, 63 (1956).

Mitchell, H. G. *A Critical and Exegetical Commentary on Haggai, Zechariah, Malachi and Jonah*. International Critical Commentary. Edinburgh, 1912.

Model, Ed. *The Kikuchi Diary: The Tanforan Journals of Charles Kikuchi: Chronicle from an American Concentration Camp*. Chicago, 1973.

Mol, H. *Churches and Immigrants: A Sociological Study of the Mutual Effect of Religion and Immigrant Adjustment*. 1961.

———. *Identity and the Sacred*. Oxford, 1976.

———. *Identity and Religion*. Studies in International Sociology, no. 16. London, Beverly Hills, 1978.

Moorey, P.R.S. "Iranian Troops at Deve Huyuk in Syria in the Earlier Fifth Century B.C.," *Levant*, 7 (1975).

Morgenstern, J. "A Chapter in the History of the High-Priesthood," *American Journal of Semitic Language and Literatures*, 60 (1938).

Mowinckel, S. *He that Cometh*. Oxford, 1956.

———. *Studien zu dem Buche Ezra-Nehemia*. 3 vols. Oslo, 1964.

Murphy, H.B.M. "The Camps," *Flight and Resettlement*. Geneva, 1955.

Myer, D. *Uprooted Americans: The Japanese Americans and War Relocation Authority during World War Two*. Tucson, 1971.

Myers, J. "Some Considerations Bearing on the Date of Joel," *Zeitschrift für die Alttestamentliche Wissenschaft* (Berlin), 74 (1962).

———. *Ezra and Nehemiah*. New York, 1965.

———. "Edom and Judah in the 6th–5th Centuries B.C.," *Near Eastern Studies in Honor of W. F. Albright*. Goedicke, ed. Baltimore, 1971.

Nagata, Judith. "In Defense of Ethnic Boundaries: The Changing Myths and Charters of the Malay Identity," in Charles Keyes, ed. *Ethnic Adaptation and Identity*. New York, 1979.

Neusner, J. "Messianic Themes in Formative Judaism," *Journal of the American Academy of Religion*, 52 (1984).

Nicholson, E. W. "The Centralization of the Cult in Deuteronomy," *Vetus Testamentum*, 13 (1963).

———. "The Meaning of the Expression, 'Am Ha'Aretz' in the Old Testament," *Journal of Semitic Studies* (Manchester), 10 (1965).

———. *Preaching to the Exiles: A Study of the Prose Tradition in the Book of Jeremiah.* Oxford, 1970.

———. *The Book of the Prophet Jeremiah, Ch. 26–52.* Cambridge, 1975.

Niditch, Susan, and Robert Doran. "The Success Story of the Wise Courtier: A Formal Approach," *Journal of Biblical Literature*, 92 (1977).

Nikel, J. *Die Wiederherstellung des judischen Gemeinwesens nach dem babylonischen Exil.* Freiburg, 1900.

North, Christopher Richard. *The Suffering Servant in Deutero-Isaiah: An Historical and Critical Study.* London, 1948.

North, Robert Grady. *Sociology of the Biblical Jubilee.* Analecta Biblica 4. Rome, 1954.

Noth, M. "Zur Komposition des Buches Daniel," *Theologische Studien und Kritiken*, 98/99 (1926).

———. *The History of Israel.* 2nd ed. London, 1960.

———. *Leviticus: A Commentary.* London, 1965.

———. *A History of Pentateuchal Traditions.* New York, 1972.

Oates, J. *Babylon.* London, 1979.

Oded, B. "Observations on Methods of Assyrian Rule in Transjordania After the Palestinian Campaign of Tiglath-Pileser III," *Journal of Near Eastern Studies*, 29 (1970).

———. *Mass Deportations and Deportees in the Neo-Assyrian Empire.* Wiesbaden, 1979.

Oelsner, J. "Continuity and Change in Babylon," *KLIO*, 40 (1978).

Okihiro, G. "Japanese Resistance in America's Concentration Camps: A Re-Evaluation," *Amerasia Journal*, 2 (1973). Special thanks to Prof. Peter Suzuki, Univ. of Nebraska, Omaha, for materials by Okihiro and further references.

Olshan, M. "Modernity, the Folk Society, and the Old Order Amish: An Alternative Interpretation," *Rural Sociology*, 46 (1981).

Opler, Marvin. "Japanese Folk Beliefs and Practices, Tule Lake, California," *Journal of American Folklore*, 63 (1950).

———, and F. Obayashi. "Senryu Poetry as Folk and Community Expression," *Journal of American Folklore*, 58 (1945).

Oppenheim, A. L. "A New Look at the Structure of Mesopotamian Society," *Journal of Economic and Social History of the Orient* (Leiden), 10 (1967).

Overholt, Thomas. "Jeremiah 27–29: The Question of False Prophecy," *Journal of the American Academy of Religion* (1970).

Pardee, D. *A Handbook of Ancient Hebrew Letters.* Chico, Calif., 1982.

Patterson, Orlando. *Slavery and Social Death: A Comparative Study.* Cambridge, Mass., 1982.

Paul, Shalom. "Literary and Ideological Echoes of Jeremiah in Deutero-Isaiah," *Fifth World Congress of Jewish Studies.* Peli, ed. Jerusalem, 1969.

Pedersen, J. L. *Israel: Its Life and Culture.* 4 vols. Oxford, 1940.

Petersen, David L. "Zerubbabel and Jerusalem Temple Reconstruction," *Catholic Biblical Quarterly*, 36 (1974).

──────. "Max Weber and the Sociological Study of Ancient Israel," *Sociological Inquiry*, 49 (1979).

Peterson, William. "A General Typology of Migration," *American Sociological Review*, 23 (1958).

Phillips, A. "Double for all Sins," *Zeitschrift für die Alttestamentliche Wissenschaft* (Berlin), 94 (1982).

Pierre, R. "Caribbean Religion: The Voodoo Case," *Sociological Analysis,* 38, (1977).

Porten, B. *Archives from Elephantine: The Life of an Ancient Jewish Military Colony.* Berkeley, 1968.

Pritchard, J. B., ed. *Ancient Near Eastern Texts.* Princeton, 1969.

Raboteau, A. J. *Slave Religion: The Invisible Insitution in the Antebellum South.* Oxford, 1978.

Rad, G. von. *Die Priesterschrift im Hexateuch.* BWANT. Stuttgart-Berlin, 1934.

Rahmani, L. Y. "Silver Coins of the Fourth Century," *Israel Exploration Journal,* 21 (1971).

Reade, J. E. "The Neo-Assyrian Court and Army: Evidence from the Sculptures," *Iraq,* 34 (1972).

Redford, D. *A Study of the Biblical Story of Joseph (Gen 37–50).* Leiden, 1970.

Rendsburg, G. "Late Biblical Hebrew and the Date of 'P,'" *The Journal of the Ancient Near Eastern Society of Columbia University,* 12 (1980).

Rendtorff, R. "Esra und das 'Gesetz,'" *Zeitschrift für die Alttestamentliche Wissenschaft* (Berlin), 96 (1984).

──────. *Die Gesetz in der Priesterschrift.* Göttingen, 1963.

Renger, J. "Wrongdoing and Its Sanctions: On 'Criminal' and 'Civil' Law in the Old Babylonian Period," *Journal of Economic and Social History of the Orient* (Leiden), 20 (1977).

Reventlow, Henning G. "Das Heiligkeitsgesetz formgeschichtlich untersucht," in Bornkamm and von Rad, eds. *Wissenschaftliche Monographien zum Alten und Neuen Testament.* Berlin, 1961.

Reviv, H. "On Urban Representative Institutions and Self-Government in Syra-Palestine in the Second Half of the Second Millennium B.C.," *Journal of Economic and Social History of the Orient* (Leiden), 12 (1969).

──────. "Elders and Saviours," *Oriens Antiquus,* 16 (1977).

Ringgren, H. *The Messiah in the Old Testament.* London, 1956.

Robinson, H. Wheeler. "The Hebrew Conception of Corporate Personality," in Volz, Stummer and Hempel, eds. *Werden und Wesen des Alten Testaments.* Berlin, 1936.

Rogerson, John. *Anthropology and the Old Testament.* Oxford, 1978.

Root, M. C. *The King and Kingship in Achaemenid Art: Essays on an Iconography of Empire.* Leiden, 1979.

Rosenthal, L. A. "Die Josephsgeschichte mit den Büchern Ester und Daniel verglichen," *Zeitschrift für die Alttestamentliche Wissenschaft* (Berlin), 15 (1895).

Rost, L. *Vorstufen zur Kirche und Synagoge im Alten Testament.* BWANT. Stuttgart, 1938.

Rowley, H. H. "The Unity of the Book of Daniel," in *The Servant of the Lord and other Essays on the Old Testament.* London, 1954.

———. "Nehemiah's Mission and Its Background," *Bulletin of the John Rylands Library,* 37 (1955).

Rowton, M. B. "Jeremiah and the Death of Josiah," *Journal of Near Eastern Studies,* 10 (1951).

Rubinger, N. "Jeremiah's Epistle to the Exiles and the Field on Anathoth," *Judaism,* 26 (1977).

Rudolph, W. *Jeremia Handbuch zum Alten Testament,* 12. Tübingen, 1947.

———. *Esra und Nehemia Handbuch zum Alten Testament.* Tübingen, 1949.

———. *Haggai — Sacharja 1–8 — Sacharja 9–14 — Maleachi.* Göttingen, 1976.

Sabloff, J. A., and Lamberg-Karlovsky. *Ancient Civilization and Trade.* Albuquerque, 1975.

Sanders, J. A. *Torah and Canon.* Philadelphia, 1972.

San Nicolo, M. "Eine Kleine Gefängnismeuterei in Eanna zur Zeit des Kambyses," *Münchener Beiträge zur Papyrusforschung und Antiken Rechtsgeschichte,* 2 (1945).

Sauer, G. "Serubbabel in der Sicht Haggais und Sacharjas," in *Das ferne und Nahe Wort.* Beihefte zur Zeitschrift für die Alttestamentliche Wissenschaft, 105. Berlin, 1967.

Sayigh, R. "Sources of Palestinian Nationalism: A Study of a Palestinian Camp in Lebanon," *Journal of Palestine Studies,* 6 (1977).

Schaeder, H. H. "Ezra der Schreiber," *Beiträge zur Historischen Theologie,* 5. Tübingen, 1930.

Scharbert, J. "Beyt 'Ab als soziologische Grösse im Alten Testament," in Delsman, Nelis, Peters, and Romer, eds. *Von Kanaan bis Kerala.* Berlin, 1982.

Schmid, H. H. *Der sogenannte Jahwist.* Zürich, 1976.

Scholem, G. *The Messianic Idea in Judaism.* New York, 1971.

Schultz, Carl. "The Political Tensions Reflected in Ezra-Nehemiah," in Hallo, Evans, and White, eds. *Scripture in Context.* Pittsburgh, 1980.

Scollon, R., and Suzanne Scollon. *Narrative, Literacy and Face in Inter-Ethnic Communication.* Norwood, N.J., 1981.

Seidl, Theodor. *Texte und Einheiten in Jeremia 27–29.* Arbeiten zu Text und Sprache im Alten Testament, 2. Munich, 1977.

———. *Formen und Formeln in Jeremia 27–29.* Arbeiten zu Text und Sprache im Alten Testament, 5. Munich, 1978.

Sellin, E. *Serubbabel: Ein Beitrag zur Geschichte der Messianischen Erwartung und der Entstehung des Judentums.* Leipzig, 1898.

Sharot, Stephen. "Minority Situation and Religious Acculturation: A Comparative Analysis of Jewish Communities," *Comparative Studies in Society and History,* 16 (1974).

Shibutani, Tamotsu, and Kian Kwan. *Ethnic Stratification: A Comparative Approach.* New York, 1965.

Siegal, B. "Some Methodological Considerations for a Comparative Study of Slavery," *American Anthropologist,* 47 (1945).

————. "Defense Structuring and Environmental Stress," *AJS*, 76 (1971).

Simons, J. *The Geographical and Topographical Texts of the Old Testament*. Leiden, 1959.

Skocpal, T., and M. Somers. "The Uses of Comparative History in Macro-Social Inquiry," *Comparative Studies in Society and History*, 22 (1980).

Smith, Anthony. *The Ethnic Revival in the Modern World*. Cambridge, 1981.

Smith, G. A. *Jeremiah*. London, 1939.

Smith, Morton. *Palestinian Parties and Politics That Shaped the Old Testament*. New York, 1971.

Smith, S. *Babylonian Historical Texts Relating to the Capture and Downfall of Babylon*. London, 1924.

————. "The Threshing Floor at the City Gate," *Palestine Exploration Quarterly*, 1946.

Smitten, W. T. "Historische Probleme zum Kyrosedikt und zum Jerusalemer Tempelbau von 515," *Persica*, 6 (1972–74).

Soggin, J. A. *Introduction to the Old Testament*. London, 1980.

South African Council of Churches. *Relocations: The Churches Report on Forced Removals in South Africa*, 1984.

Speiser, E. "'Coming' and 'Going' at the 'City Gate,'" in *Oriental and Biblical Studies*. Philadelphia, 1967.

————. "Leviticus and the Critics," in *Oriental and Biblical Studies*. Philadelphia, 1967.

Spicer, E., ed. *Perspectives in American Indian Culture Change*. Chicago, 1961.

————, and M. Opler. *Impounded People: Japanese-Americans in the Relocation Centers*. Tucson, 1969.

Spieckermann, H. *Juda unter Assur in der Sargonidenzeit*. Göttingen, 1982.

Stager, Lawrence. "The Archaeology of the Family in Ancient Israel," *BASOR*, 260 (1985).

Stern, Ephraim. *Material Culture of the Land of the Bible in the Persian Period 538–332 B.C.* Jerusalem, 1982 (Hebrew ed., 1973).

————. "Israel at the Close of the Period of the Monarchy: An Archaeological Survey," *Biblical Archaeologist*, 38 (1975).

Stern, M., ed. *Greek and Latin Authors on Jews and Judaism*. Jerusalem, 1974.

Stevenson, R. "Classes, Colonialism and Acculturation," *Studies in Comparative International Development*, 1 (1965).

Steward, J. *Irrigation Civilizations: A Comparative Study*. The Hague, 1955.

Sundklar, Bengt. *Bantu Prophets in South Africa*. Oxford, 1964.

Suzuki, P. "The Ethnolinguistics of Japanese Americans in the Wartime Camps." *Anthropological Linguistics* 18 (1976).

Swartz, M. *Local Level Politics: Social and Cultural Perspective*. Chicago, 1968.

Szwed, J. "The Politics of Afro-American Culture," in Dell Hymes, ed., *Reinventing Anthropology*. New York, 1974.

Tabori, P. *The Anatomy of Exile*. London, 1972.

Tadmor, H. "'The People' and the Kingship in Ancient Israel: The Role of Political Institutions in the Biblical Period," *Journal of World History*, 1968.

————. "Assyria and the West: The Ninth Century and Its Aftermath," in Goedicke and Roberts, eds. *Unity and Diversity: Essays in the History, Literature and Religion of the Ancient Near East.* Baltimore, 1975.

————. "History and Ideology in the Assyrian Royal Inscriptions," *Orientis Antiqui Collectio,* 17. Rome, 1981.

Tavuchis, N. *Pastors and Immigrants: The Role of a Religious Elite in the Absorption of Norwegian Immigrants.* The Hague, 1963.

Telcs, George. "Jeremiah and Nebuchadnezzar; King of Justice," *Canadian Journal of Theology,* 15 (1969).

Tessler, Mark A. "Ethnic Change and Non-Assimilating Minority Status: Jews in Tunisia and Morocco and Arabs in Israel," in Charles Keyes, ed. *Ethnic Adaptation and Identity.* New York, 1979.

Thomas, D. W. *"The Prophet" in the Lachish Ostraca.* London, 1946.

————. "The Age of Jeremiah in the Light of Recent Archaeological Discovery," *Palestine Exploration Quarterly* (London), 1950–51.

————. *Documents from Old Testament Times.* London, 1958.

————. "The Sixth Century B.C.: A Creative Epoch in the History of Israel," *Journal of Semitic Studies* (Manchester), 6 (1961).

Thomas, Dorothy Swain, and Richard Nishimoto. *The Spoilage: Japanese-American Evacuation and Resettlement During World War Two.* Los Angeles, 1969.

Thompson, T. *The Historicity of the Patriarchal Narratives.* Berlin, New York, 1974.

Thurlings, J.M.G. "Identity and Pluralism," in Mol, ed. *Identity and Religion.* Studies in International Sociology, no. 16. London, Beverly Hills, 1978.

Turner, V. *The Ritual Process.* Chicago, 1969.

Turner, J., and E. Bonanich. "Towards a Composite Theory of Middleman Minorities," *Ethnicity,* 7 (1980).

Ulmen, G. L., ed. *Society and History: Essays in Honor of Karl Wittfogel.* Paris, The Hague, New York, 1978.

Van den Berghe, P. L. *The Ethnic Phenomenon.* New York, 1981.

Van Seters, J. "Confessional Reformulation in the Exilic Period," *Vetus Testamentum,* 22 (1972).

————. *Abraham in History and Tradition.* New Haven and London, 1975.

————. "Recent Studies on the Pentateuch: A Crisis in Method," *Journal of the American Oriental Society* (New Haven), 99 (1979).

————. "The Place of the Yahwist in the History of Passover and Massot," *Zeitschrift für die Alttestamentliche Wissenschaft* (Berlin), 95 (1983).

Vaux, R. de. *Ancient Israel: Its Life and Institutions.* London, 1961.

Vermes, G. *The Dead Sea Scrolls in English.* London, 1975.

Vink, J. G. "The Date and Origin of the Priestly Code in the Old Testament," *Oudtestamentische Studien,* 15 (1969).

Voget, F. "The American Indian in Transition: Reformation and Accommodation," *American Anthropologist,* 58 (1956).

Vogt, H.C.M. *Studie Zur Nachexilischen Gemeinde in Esra-Nehemia.* Werl, 1966.

Volz, P. D. *Der Prophet Jeremia.* Kommentar zum Alten Testament. Erlangen, 1922.

von Soden, W. "Eine babylonische Volksüberlieferung von Nabonid in den Danielerzählungen," in *Zeitschrift für die Alttestamentliche Wissenschaft* (Berlin), 12 (1935).

Wagner, V. "Zur Existenz des sogenannten 'Heiligkeitsgesetzes,'" *Zeitschrift für die Alttestamentliche Wissenschaft* (Berlin), 86 (1974).

Walker, L., and Chester Hunt. *Ethnic Dynamics: Patterns of Intergroup Relations in Various Societies.* New York, 1974.

Wallace, Anthony. "Revitalization Movements," *American Anthropologist,* 58 (1956).

Wang, Martin C.C. "Jeremiah's Message of Hope in Prophetic Symbolic Action," *Southeast Asian Journal of Theology,* 14 (1972).

Wanke, G. *Untersuchungen zur sogenannten Baruchschrift.* Beihefte zur Zeitschrift für die Alttestamentliche Wissenschaft, 122. Berlin, 1971.

Waterman, L. "The Camouflaged Purge of Three Messianic Conspirators," *Journal of Near Eastern Studies,* 13 (1954).

Weber, Max. *Ancient Judaism.* New York, 1967.

Weglyn, M. *Years of Infamy (Japanese-American Internment).* New York, 1976.

Weidner, E. F. "Jojachin, Konig von Juda, In Babylonischen Keilschrifttexten," *Melanges Syriens Offerts à Monsieur René Dussaud.* Paris, 1939.

Weinberg, J. "Demographische Notizen zur Geschichte der nachexilischen Gemeinde in Juda," *KLIO,* 54 (1972).

———. "Die Agrarverhältnisse in der Bürger-Temple-Gemeinde der Achamenidenzeit," *Acta Antiqua,* 22 (1974).

———. "Der 'am ha'ares des 6–4 Jh. v.u.z.," *KLIO,* 56 (1974).

———. "'Netinim' und 'Sohne der Sklaven Salomos' im Jh. v.u.z.," *Zeitschrift für die Alttestamentliche Wissenschaft* (Berlin), 87 (1975).

———. "Bemerkungen zum Problem 'Der Vorhellenismus in Vorderen Orient,'" *KLIO,* 59 (1977).

———. "'Zentral- und Particular-gewalt im achaemenidischen Reich," *KLIO,* 59 (1977).

Weinberg, Saul S. "Post-Exilic Palestine," *Proceedings of the Israel Academy of Sciences and Humanities,* 4 (1971).

Weinfeld, M. "Elders," in *Encyclopedia Judaica.* Jerusalem, 1971.

———. "Jeremiah and the Spiritual Metamorphosis of Israel," *Zeitschrift für die Alttestamentliche Wissenschaft* (Berlin), 88 (1976).

Weisberg, D. L. *Guild Structure and Political Allegiance in Early Achaeminid Mesopotamia.* New Haven, 1967.

Weiser, A. *Das Buche des Propheten Jeremia.* 4th ed. Alte Testament Deutsch. Göttingen, 1960.

———. *Introduction to the Old Testament.* London, 1961.

Welch, A. "Jeremiah's Letter to the Exiles in Babylon," *The Expositor,* 131 (1921).

———. *Post-Exilic Judaism.* Edinburgh, 1935.

Wellhausen, J. "Die Rückkehr der Juden aus dem babylonischen Exil," *Nachrichten von der Königlichen Gesellschaft der Wissenschaften zu Göttingen*, 2 (1896).

——. *Prolegomena to the History of Ancient Israel*. New York, 1957

Westermann, Klaus. *Basic Forms of Prophetic Speech*. London, 1967.

White, J. L., ed. *Studies in Ancient Letter Writing*, Semeia 22. Chico, Calif., 1982.

Whitehouse, O. C. *Isaiah 40–66*. The Century Bible. Edinburgh, 1908.

Whitley, C. F. "Carchemish and Jeremiah," *Zeitschrift für die Alttestamentliche Wissenschaft* (Berlin), 80 (1968).

Wilkie, J. M. "Nabonidus and the Later Jewish Exiles," *Journal of Theological Studies* (Oxford, London), 2 (1951).

Wilson, B. "Sociological Methods in the Study of History," *Transactions of the Royal Historical Society*, 21 (1971).

——. *Magic and the Millennium*. London, 1975.

Wilson, R. *Prophecy and Society in Ancient Israel*. Philadelphia, 1980.

Wirth, Louis. *The Ghetto*. Chicago, 1928 (1956).

Wiseman, D. J. *Chronicles of Chaldean Kings (626–556) in the British Museum*. London, 1956.

Wittfogel, K. *Oriental Despotism*. New Haven, 1957.

Wolf, C. U. "Traces of Primitive Democracy in Ancient Israel," *Journal of Near Eastern Studies*, 6 (1947).

Wong, P. "The Social Psychology of Refugees in an Alien Social Milieu," *International Migration Review*, 5 (1967).

Wurthwein, E. "Der Am Ha'aretz im Alten Testament," *BWANT*, no. 17 (1936).

Wurz, H. "Die Wegführung der Juden durch König Nebukadnezzar II." Unpublished doctoral dissertation. Vienna, 1958.

Yoder, John H. "Exodus and Exile: The Two Faces of Liberation," *Cross Currents*, 23 (1973).

Zadok, R. *On West Semites in Babylonia During the Chaldean and Achaemenian Periods*. Jerusalem, 1977.

Zeitlin, S. "The Titles High Priest and the Nasi of the Sanhedrin," *Jewish Quarterly Review* (Leiden), 48 (1957).

Ziegler, J., ed. *Ieremias*. LXX Critical Edition, 15. Göttingen, 1957.

Zucker, H. *Studien zur Judischen Selbstverwaltung im Altertum*. Berlin, 1936.

Index of Scriptural References

Index of Authors

The same spirit that stealeth away the true simplicity, raiseth up and stealeth in a false image thereof; which there is no perceiving at present, unless the soul lie very low, and be kept open and clear in the pure light.

And here is the beginning of Babylon in the heart; here are the inward riches and treasures thereof. What can Zion pretend to, which Babylon hath not in resemblance?...Is there light in Zion? And is there not also light in Babylon?...

Therefore, wait for the raising of the true seed of life, in the true simplicity, whereby ye may serve God acceptably here, and be saved hereafter.

ISAAC PENINGTON
d. 1679